D1214013

Typo-Graphic Design Promotion

FOREWORD BY KIT HINRICHS

DESIGN BY DAVID BRIER

This book is printed in four-color process. A few of the designs reproduced here may appear to be slightly different than in their original reproduction.

ISBN 0-942604-25-3

. . . .

PRODUCTION CREDITS

Designer: David Brier

Design Associate: Denise M. Anderson

Editorial Associate: Marlene Hamerling

Administrative Associates:
Joelle Pastor
Chris Fuller
Hope Wenzel

Computer Typography:
Bonnie Cohen   Chris Fuller

Black & White Photography:
Stan Schnier

Cover & Divider Page Typography and Handlettering:
David Brier   Chris Fuller

The text in this volume is set in Adobe Garamond Italic & Futura Extra Bold

Library of Congress Catalog Card Number 92-060-790

Distriputors to the trade in the United States and Canada:
Van Nostrand Reinhold
115 Fifth Avenue
New York, NY 10003

Distributed throughout the rest of the world by:
Hearst Books International
1350 Avenue of the Americas
New York, NY 10019

Publisher:
Madison Square Press
10 East 23rd Street
New York, NY 10010

Printed in Hong Kong

ACKNOWLEDGMENTS

The following are acknowledged for their selfless assistance and persistence, which made this project possible:

Bonnie Cohen
Marlene Hamerling
Scott Harvin
Harvey Hirsch
Jerry McConnell
Joelle Pastor
Paul Pullara
Fox River Paper

My deepest thanks also go to the many other individuals who provided support along the way and, without whom, this volume would not exist.

DEDICATION

This second book in the series is dedicated to the late, great Herb Lubalin, who provided me my first inspiration as to what could possibly be achieved with design and typography.

David Brier
1993

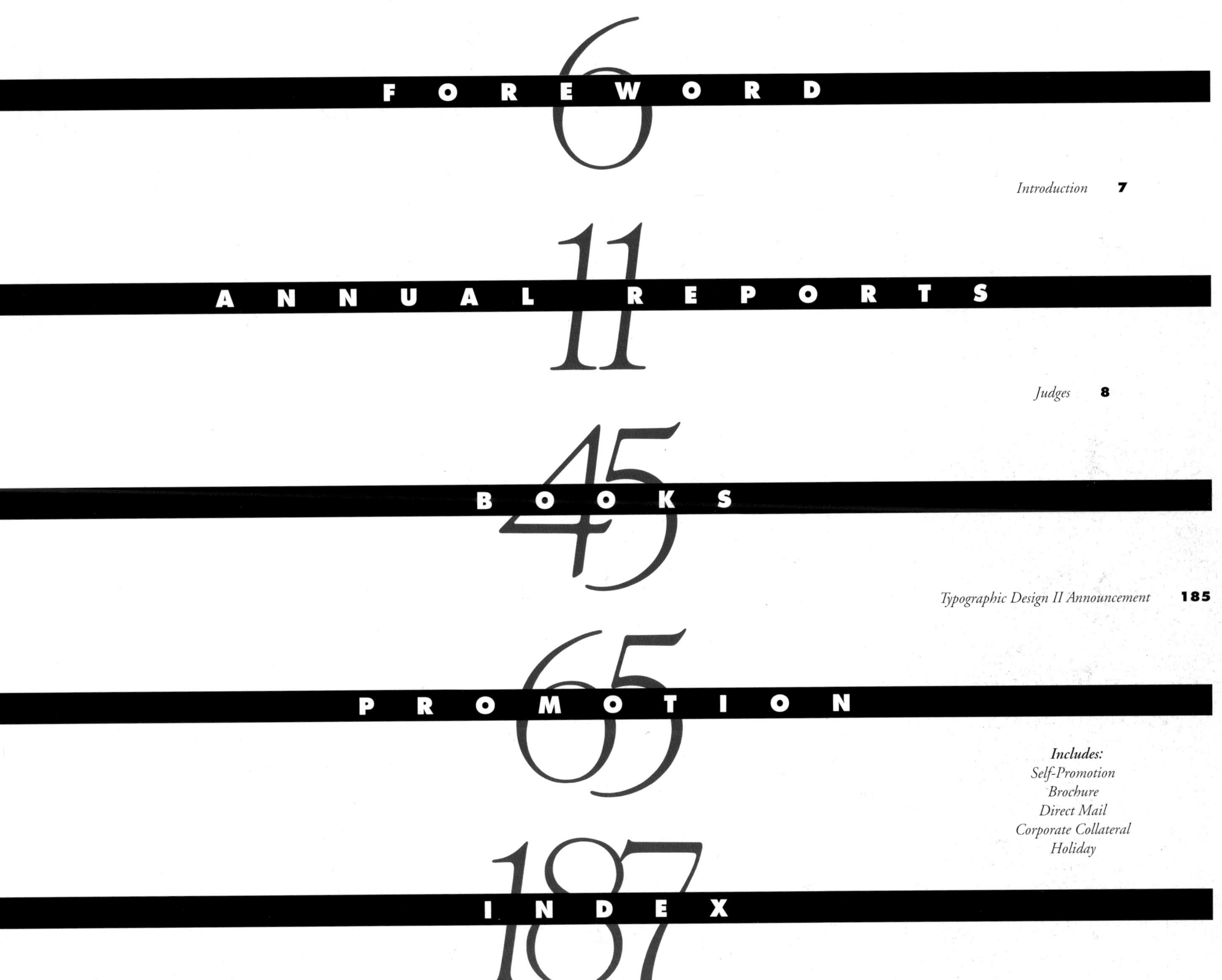

FOREWORD

Typography, appropriately used, is one of the most effective means of communicating ideas with mood, style, and emotion. Although ubiquitous in nearly every scrap of printed communications and electronic messages, typography continues to be a challenge to the master and novice alike.

Rapid technological changes over the past 10 years have had a profound effect on the character of typography within our profession. The "coming of age" of the computer has created on one hand, a reinvestigation of traditional hand-set type, while on the other, a complete abandonment of typographic standards, leading to grotesque distortion of classic typographic forms, from minor aberration to the grotesque.

Typographic Design may be the single document to chronicle, in detail, the typographic revolution of the editorial, promotional, corporate, and advertising design of the '80s.

KIT HINRICHS
Partner
Pentagram

This second book in the series of Typographic Design is dedicated to promotional design. This volume includes Annual Reports, Book Designs, and the broad category of Promotion itself. Typographic Design is the result of 14 months of orchestrating, administering, and designing this international collection of what we feel are the best promotional designs done from 1980 through 1990— selected from more than 7,000 entries.

The judges with whom I was honored to share the panel were Kit Hinrichs, Partner in Pentagram; Richard Wilde, Chairman of the School of Visual Arts Design and Advertising Department; and Fred Woodward, Art Director of Rolling Stone.

The work is presented in chronological order within each section. Because the book covers a decade, you may note trends that, while not "today's look" are, nonetheless, completely valid and classically timeless. Enjoy these as we did, then and now.

DAVID BRIER
Chairperson of Typographic Design
President & Creative Director
DBD International, Ltd.

DAVID BRIER
KIT HINRICHS

RICHARD WILDE
FRED WOODWARD

ANNUAL REPORTS

1

1

DESIGN FIRM: *Gunn Associates*
DESIGNER: *Robert Cipriani*
HEADLINE TYPEFACE: *ITC Garamond Bold Condensed*
TEXT TYPEFACE: *ITC Garamond Condensed*
CLIENT: *Charles Stark Draper Lab*

2

The gap between science and engineering is bridged by many mediums. By improving that bridging operation, we can make important gains in our delivery of useful products to end users.

There is a chasm between the scientific-educational community and the corporate community. A means of bridging this gap is the mission-oriented, not-for-profit, IR&D laboratory.

2
DESIGN FIRM: *Cipriani Kremer Design*
DESIGNER: *Robert Cipriani*
HEADLINE TYPEFACE: *Palatino Bold*
TEXT TYPEFACE: *Palatino*
CLIENT: *Charles Stark Draper Lab*

3
DESIGN FIRM: *Pentagram Design*
DESIGNER: *Kit Hinrichs and Barbara Vick*
HEADLINE TYPEFACE: *Times Roman Italic*
TEXT TYPEFACE: *Times Roman*
CLIENT: *Potlatch Corp.*

4
DESIGN FIRM: *Pentagram Design*
DESIGNER: *Kit Hinrichs and Nancy Koc*
HEADLINE TYPEFACE: *Times Roman Italic*
TEXT TYPEFACE: *Times Roman*
CLIENT: *Potlatch Corp.*

3

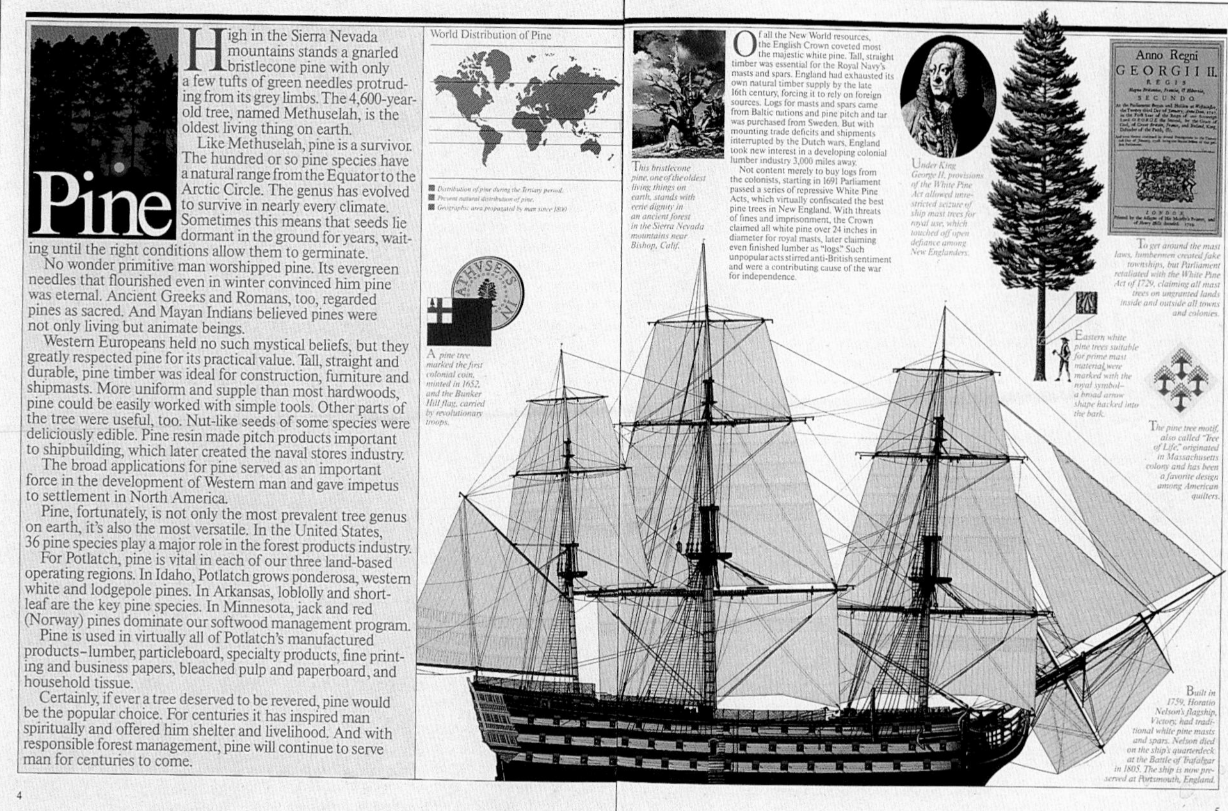

Pine

High in the Sierra Nevada mountains stands a gnarled bristlecone pine with only a few tufts of green needles protruding from its grey limbs. The 4,600-year-old tree, named Methuselah, is the oldest living thing on earth.

Like Methuselah, pine is a survivor. The hundred or so pine species have a natural range from the Equator to the Arctic Circle. The genus has evolved to survive in nearly every climate. Sometimes this means that seeds lie dormant in the ground for years, waiting until the right conditions allow them to germinate.

No wonder primitive man worshipped pine. Its evergreen needles that flourished even in winter convinced him pine was eternal. Ancient Greeks and Romans, too, regarded pines as sacred. And Mayan Indians believed pines were not only living but animate beings.

Western Europeans held no such mystical beliefs, but they greatly respected pine for its practical value. Tall, straight and durable, pine timber was ideal for construction, furniture and shipmasts. More uniform and supple than most hardwoods, pine could be easily worked with simple tools. Other parts of the tree were useful, too. Nut-like seeds of some species were deliciously edible. Pine resin made pitch products important to shipbuilding, which later created the naval stores industry.

The broad applications for pine served as an important force in the development of Western man and gave impetus to settlement in North America.

Pine, fortunately, is not only the most prevalent tree genus on earth, it's also the most versatile. In the United States, 36 pine species play a major role in the forest products industry.

For Potlatch, pine is vital in each of our three land-based operating regions. In Idaho, Potlatch grows ponderosa, western white and lodgepole pines. In Arkansas, loblolly and shortleaf are the key pine species. In Minnesota, jack and red (Norway) pines dominate our softwood management program.

Pine is used in virtually all of Potlatch's manufactured products–lumber, particleboard, specialty products, fine printing and business papers, bleached pulp and paperboard, and household tissue.

Certainly, if ever a tree deserved to be revered, pine would be the popular choice. For centuries it has inspired man spiritually and offered him shelter and livelihood. And with responsible forest management, pine will continue to serve man for centuries to come.

World Distribution of Pine

A pine tree marked the first colonial coin, minted in 1652, and the Bunker Hill flag, carried by revolutionary troops.

This bristlecone pine, one of the oldest living things on earth, stands with eerie dignity in an ancient forest in the Sierra Nevada mountains near Bishop, Calif.

Of all the New World resources, the English Crown coveted most the majestic white pine. Tall, straight timber was essential for the Royal Navy's masts and spars. England had exhausted its own natural timber supply by the late 16th century, forcing it to rely on foreign sources. Logs for masts and spars came from Baltic nations and pine pitch and tar was purchased from Sweden. But with mounting trade deficits and shipments interrupted by the Dutch wars, England took new interest in a developing colonial lumber industry 3,000 miles away.

Not content merely to buy logs from the colonists, starting in 1691 Parliament passed a series of repressive White Pine Acts, which virtually confiscated the best pine trees in New England. With threats of fines and imprisonment, the Crown claimed all white pine over 24 inches in diameter for royal masts, later claiming even finished lumber as "logs." Such unpopular acts stirred anti-British sentiment and were a contributing cause of the war for independence.

Under King George II, provisions of the White Pine Act allowed unrestricted seizure of ship mast trees for royal use, which touched off open defiance among New Englanders.

To get around the mast laws, lumbermen created fake townships, but Parliament retaliated with the White Pine Act of 1729, claiming all mast trees on ungranted lands inside and outside all towns and colonies.

Eastern white pine trees suitable for prime mast material were marked with the royal symbol–a broad arrow shape hacked into the bark.

The pine tree motif, also called "Tree of Life," originated in Massachusetts colony and has been a favorite design among American quilters.

Built in 1759, Horatio Nelson's flagship, Victory, had traditional white pine masts and spars. Nelson died on the ship's quarterdeck at the Battle of Trafalgar in 1805. The ship is now preserved at Portsmouth, England.

4 5

4

The Logger

Chainsaws and maneuverable skidding equipment have relieved loggers of much back-breaking labor. And, highways and four-wheel drive vehicles now allow them to commute to work from nearby communities.

While a logger's life is physically easier than a few decades ago, in many ways his skill is more critical. In centuries past, loggers concentrated on taking the best logs at the least cost and leaving the rest behind. Today most parts of the tree have value. Loggers must cut with the end uses in mind, while remaining sensitive to environmental concerns and the forest management plan.

Jon Biehl, an independent contractor for Potlatch in Minnesota, is among a new breed of loggers. A century ago the profession attracted many adventurers. Today loggers are often well-educated businessmen who look upon timber harvesting as a silvicultural science.

Logger Titles:
More Color than Pomp

Bull-of-the-Woods On-site boss of a logging operation. Now called "bullbuck."	***Sky Pilot*** A religious logger.
Chokersetter Person who attaches short cables, called chokers, to logs for skidding. Also known as a "hooker."	***Swivelhips*** A fast rigging man.
Donkey Puncher Yarding equipment operator. In the old days, portable steam engines were called "donkeys."	***Tally Whacker*** Person who recorded log measurements called by the scaler.
Hook Tender Boss of the rigging crew.	***Timber beast*** Any logger. Also called "brush ape."
Road Monkey Road maintenance man. Also called "swamper."	***Whistle Punk*** Person who passed signals from the rigging slinger or chokersetter to the donkey puncher when yarding logs.
	Woodpecker A poor hand with an ax.

5

History

The invention of paper in China in 105 A.D. created a force that transformed the world. In every culture it reached, paper provided a convenient means of disseminating knowledge and accelerated the development of civilization.

Before paper was introduced to the West in 1150, the written language was largely reserved for priests, scholars and aristocrats. The common man could neither read nor write. Writing materials were rare and expensive, and the task of writing itself was laborious. Parchment to make a single Gutenberg bible, for example, required the skins of 300 sheep.

At hand-made paper mills, the vatman dipped a sieve-like mould into a tub of watery pulp, then lifted the slurry of fibers and rocked it on the screen to form an even mat.

The coucher placed the mould at an angle to allow the barely solidified wet sheet to drain, then removed the sheet and stacked it flat and unwrinkled onto a felt cloth.

After pressing the sheets to wring out the water, the layman gently lifted the damp papers from the layers of felt and stacked them in piles and pressed them again.

In "spurs" of four or five sheets, paper was carried to the mill loft and hung on beeswax-coated rope lines to dry. Each paper-making team produced about 750 sheets a day.

6

Thales of Miletus, one of the fathers of Greek philosophy, founded his school of thought on the premise: "All things are water." Twenty-five hundred years later, nothing has changed in the world to diminish the place and importance of water. It is at the heart of all industries and essential to Potlatch.

Throughout Potlatch's 82-year history, water and the company's successful growth have been inextricably interwoven. In our forests, photosynthesis, the activity that ultimately makes life in the forest and elsewhere possible, would be extremely difficult without the key role played by water.

Rushing rivers in Idaho and Minnesota, and the log drives they sustained for decades, epitomized one of the most colorful and exciting chapters in Potlatch history. Since then, man-made changes in waterways near our operations have helped create major gateways to world markets for Potlatch products.

Water

Water is the common denominator of every living thing on earth. Reverently described by some as "Adam's ale," the world's appreciation for this precious resource is boundless. This is our story of how we use and respect water's many qualities in all of our activities.

Many Potlatch plants were built on rivers or lakes that provided low-cost power, log storage and transportation of supplies and finished goods. Lewiston at the confluence of the Snake and Clearwater, major tributaries of the Columbia; Brainerd on the Mississippi and Cloquet on the St. Louis rivers in northern Minnesota; and Cypress Bend several hundred miles farther south on the Mississippi River in Arkansas, are examples of major Potlatch mill sites that owe their existence to water.

In early Potlatch mills, steam was used to power lumber saws and waterwheels ran stone pulpwood grinders. Today, huge quantities of water are essential to Potlatch operations throughout the country.

The proper management of this resource in our forests, for transportation, manufacturing or power, and in the environment, remains vitally important to the company's future growth.

Minnesota boasts the largest area of water among Potlatch states. Its 12,000-plus lakes and 25,000 miles of rivers cover six percent of the entire state.

Northern Idaho's Lake Coeur d'Alene performs an important dual role as a transportation link for Potlatch raw materials and as a log storage facility for the Rutledge unit sawmill.

From its beginning in New England, the river drive was repeated across the U.S. for more than 200 years. Furious white-water was a constant danger. Potlatch ran the last major log drive in the nation on Idaho's Clearwater river in 1971. Charles "Red" McCollister, now retired in Orofino, supervised Clearwater log drives for 15 years.

5
DESIGN FIRM: *Pentagram Design*
DESIGNER: *Kit Hinrichs and Lenore Bartz*
HEADLINE TYPEFACE: *Times Roman Italic*
TEXT TYPEFACE: *Times Roman*
CLIENT: *Potlatch Corp.*

6
DESIGN FIRM: *Pentagram Design*
DESIGNER: *Kit Hinrichs and Lenore Bartz*
HEADLINE TYPEFACE: *Times Roman Italic*
TEXT TYPEFACE: *Times Roman*
CLIENT: *Potlatch Corp.*

7

8

9

7
DESIGN FIRM: *Richard Hess*
DESIGNER: *Richard Hess*
CLIENT: *Champion International Corp.*

8/9
DESIGN FIRM: *Samata Associates*
DESIGNER: *Pat Samata and Greg Samata*
HEADLINE TYPEFACE: *Bodoni Italic*
TEXT TYPEFACE: *Bodoni Italic*
CLIENT: *Leaf, Inc.*

10

11

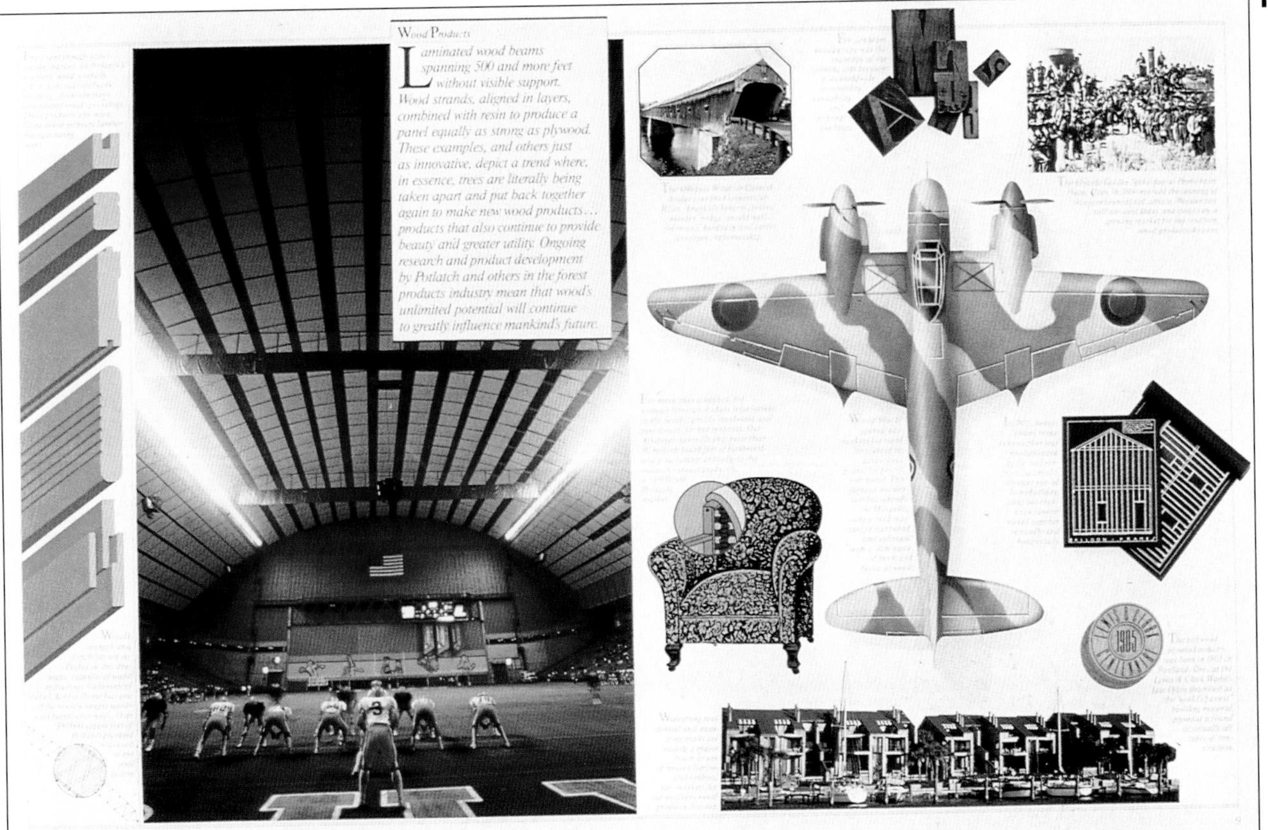

10
DESIGN FIRM: *RBMM/The Richards Group*
DESIGNER: *Stephen Miller*
HEADLINE TYPEFACE: *Garamond*
TEXT TYPEFACE: *Garamond and Garamond Italic*
CLIENT: *Lomas & Nettleton Mortgage Investors*

11
DESIGN FIRM: *Pentagram Design*
DESIGNER: *Kit Hinrichs and Lenore Bartz*
HEADLINE TYPEFACE: *Times Roman*
TEXT TYPEFACE: *Times Roman*
CLIENT: *Potlatch Corp.*

12

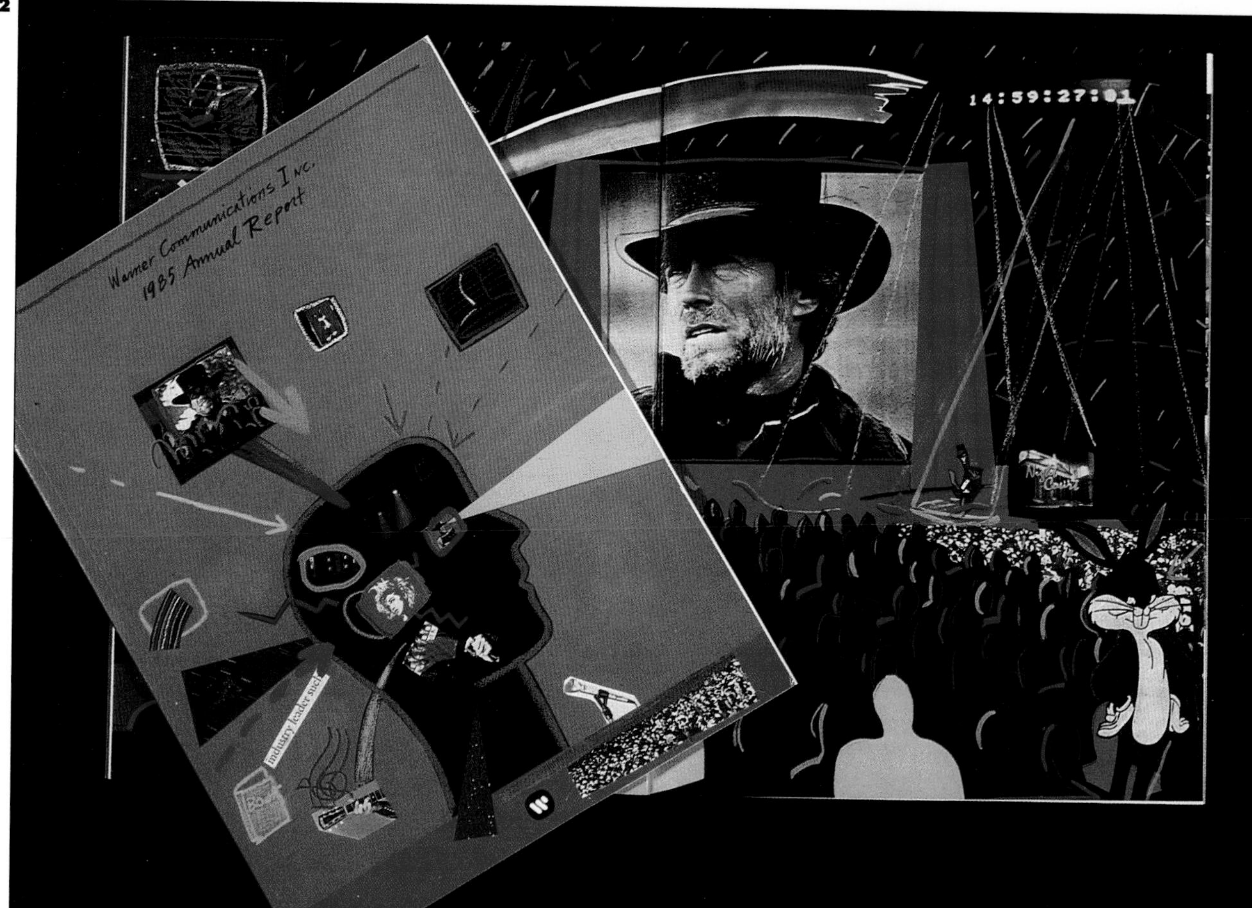

13

12/13
DESIGN FIRM: *Pentagram Design*
DESIGNER: *Peter Harrison and Susan Hochbaum*
LETTERER: *Donna Muir and Su Huntley*
HEADLINE TYPEFACE: *Copperplate Gothic*
TEXT TYPEFACE: *Garamond*
CLIENT: *Warner Communications*

14

15

16

LEAF SPECIAL BRANDS

Leaf, Inc.'s second U.S. domestic marketing group, Leaf Special Brands, markets all Leaf candy and gum products targeted at children. These include Jolly Rancher® hard candies and candy canes, Now & Later® taffy and several major brands of bubble gum, including Rain-Blo® and Super Bubble.®

Leaf Special Brands, which formerly was known as the Leaf Jolly Rancher group, was renamed in late 1987 to reflect the addition of several existing Leaf products into its line. With Leaf General Brands now handling products for the teen to adult market, Leaf Special Brands focuses more intently on products targeted to a younger audience.

Jolly Rancher, one of the top-selling branded hard candies in the United States, continued its longtime use of sports marketing to gain exposure and sales. Consistent with this image, Jolly Rancher is a featured brand in Leaf's Major League Baseball sponsorship.

To promote the sponsorship and other brand promotions, Leaf is more than doubling its advertising budget in 1988. Specific plans for Jolly Rancher candy include advertising on television game shows and in children's publications.

Rain-Blo was particularly active in 1987. To stimulate sales and interest from the trade, the brand received new packaging, new sizes and a cherry cola flavor. To reach its target market directly, Rain-Blo bubble gum samples were packed into 200 million cereal boxes.

Super Bubble bubble gum also introduced a cherry cola flavor and, in 1988, will unveil the Super Bubble cartoon character in all packaging and advertising.

Building representation in predominant candy price points plays an integral part in Leaf Special Brand's marketing strategy. Leaf can therefore gain wider distribution, particularly in supermarket outlets, and compete aggressively with similarly-priced items.

During the year, Leaf introduced 40-cent size Now & Later and Jolly Rancher bars, as well as a 35-cent Super Bubble pack. Leaf led the industry by testing Now & Later bars and Jolly Rancher stix at 25 cents. Both are emerging as popular in convenience stores as consumers trade up from the 10-cent level.

Leaf, the largest gum ball manufacturer in the United States, increased capacity at its Memphis plant.

Other brands marketed by Special Brands are Slo Poke® and Black Cow® caramel suckers, Sixlets® candy-coated chocolatey pieces, and Hot Dog® and Bub's Daddy® bubble gums.

JOLLY RANCHER
Assorted Fruit CANDY KISSES
1/2 lb.
Super Bubble
NOW & LATER

14
DESIGN FIRM: *Samata Associates*
DESIGNER: *Greg Samata*
HEADLINE TYPEFACE: *Garamond*
TEXT TYPEFACE: *Kunstler*
CLIENT: *Kemper Reinsurance Co.*

15/16
DESIGN FIRM: *Samata Associates*
DESIGNER: *Greg Samata*
HEADLINE TYPEFACE: *Univers 83*
TEXT TYPEFACE: *Bodoni Book*
CLIENT: *Leaf, Inc.*

17

18

17
DESIGN FIRM: *The Duffy Design Group*
DESIGNER: *Sharon Werner and Haley Johnson*
HEADLINE TYPEFACE: *Cheltenham Old Style*
CLIENT: *US West*

18/19
DESIGN FIRM: *RBMM/The Richards Group*
DESIGNER: *Brian Boyd*
LETTERER: *Brian Boyd*
HEADLINE TYPEFACE: *Handlettering*
TEXT TYPEFACE: *Caslon 540*
CLIENT: *Chili's, Inc.*

19

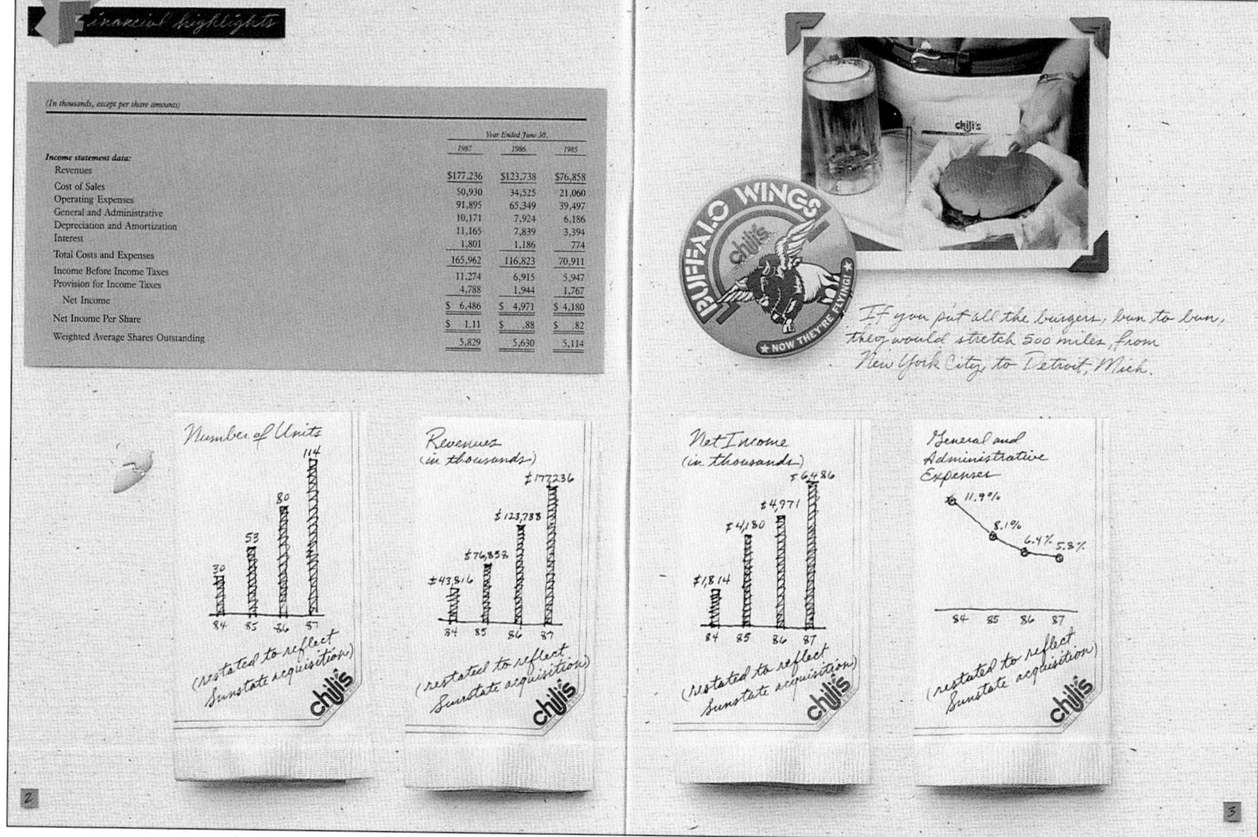
Financial highlights

(In thousands, except per share amounts)

	Year Ended June 30,		
	1987	1986	1985
Income statement data:			
Revenues	$177,236	$123,738	$76,858
Cost of Sales	50,930	34,525	21,060
Operating Expenses	91,895	65,349	39,497
General and Administrative	10,171	7,924	6,186
Depreciation and Amortization	11,165	7,839	3,394
Interest	1,801	1,186	774
Total Costs and Expenses	165,962	116,823	70,911
Income Before Income Taxes	11,274	6,915	5,947
Provision for Income Taxes	4,788	1,944	1,767
Net Income	$ 6,486	$ 4,971	$ 4,180
Net Income Per Share	$ 1.11	$ .88	$ .82
Weighted Average Shares Outstanding	5,829	5,630	5,114

20

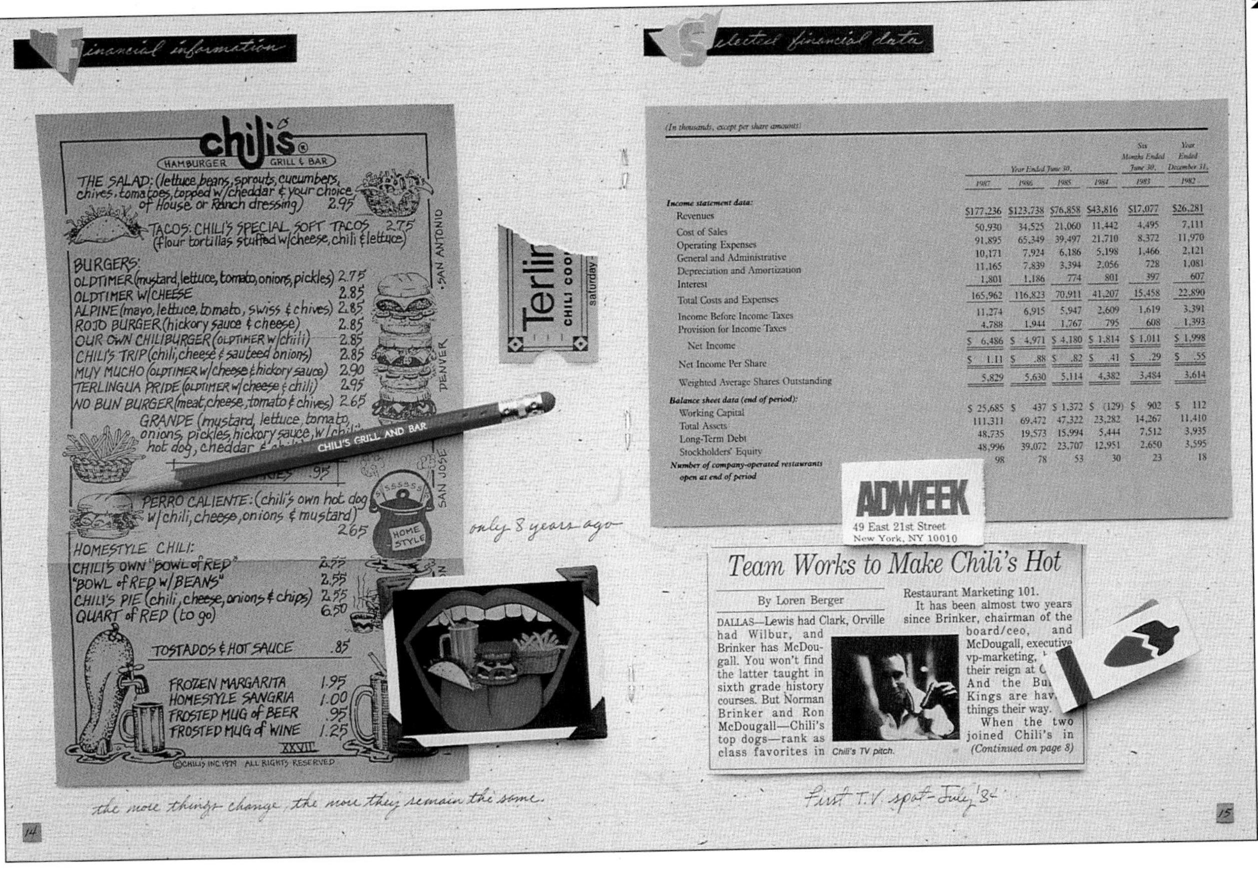

(In thousands, except per share amounts)

	Year Ended June 30, 1987	1986	1985	1984	Six Months Ended June 30, 1983	Year Ended December 31, 1982
Income statement data:						
Revenues	$177,236	$123,738	$76,858	$43,816	$17,077	$26,281
Cost of Sales	50,930	34,525	21,060	11,442	4,495	7,111
Operating Expenses	91,895	65,349	39,497	21,710	8,372	11,970
General and Administrative	10,171	7,924	6,186	5,198	1,466	2,121
Depreciation and Amortization	11,165	7,839	3,394	2,056	728	1,081
Interest	1,801	1,186	774	801	397	607
Total Costs and Expenses	165,962	116,823	70,911	41,207	15,458	22,890
Income Before Income Taxes	11,274	6,915	5,947	2,609	1,619	3,391
Provision for Income Taxes	4,788	1,944	1,767	795	608	1,393
Net Income	$ 6,486	$ 4,971	$ 4,180	$ 1,814	$ 1,011	$ 1,998
Net Income Per Share	$ 1.11	$ .88	$ .82	$ .41	$ .29	$ .55
Weighted Average Shares Outstanding	5,829	5,630	5,114	4,382	3,484	3,614
Balance sheet data (end of period):						
Working Capital	$ 25,685	$ 437	$ 1,372	$ (129)	$ 902	$ 112
Total Assets	111,311	69,472	47,322	23,282	14,267	11,410
Long-Term Debt	48,735	19,573	15,994	5,444	7,512	3,935
Stockholders' Equity	48,996	39,072	23,707	12,951	2,650	3,595
Number of company-operated restaurants open at end of period	98	78	53	30	23	18

21

mental in creating the Bennigan's® concept. His experience also includes senior management positions with Burger King Corporation, The Pillsbury Company, Sara Lee and Proctor and Gamble.

Jim Parish is Executive Vice President and Chief Financial Officer for Chili's and has been with the Company since 1983. Jim's experience includes nine years of food and food service experience prior to his four years with Chili's. He held positions of steadily increasing responsibility with Hunt International Resources, a diversified company with major food processing, restaurant and oil and gas interests.

Creed Ford III joined the Company in 1976 and is Executive Vice President – Operations. With 14 years experience in full-service restaurant operations, Creed has directed operations for Chili's since 1978.

Needless to say, it is a strong, professional management team with a proven business philosophy in place. It's a sound organization that performs exceptionally well, but it is also poised to take advantage of new opportunities for improvement. This team has proven Chili's can travel and adapt as the needs of our customers change.

20/21
DESIGN FIRM: *RBMM/The Richards Group*
DESIGNER: *Brian Boyd*
LETTERER: *Brian Boyd*
HEADLINE TYPEFACE: *Handlettering*
TEXT TYPEFACE: *Caslon 540*
CLIENT: *Chili's, Inc.*

22
DESIGN FIRM: *Pentagram Design*
DESIGNER: *Colin Forbes and Michael Gericke*
HEADLINE TYPEFACE: *Franklin Gothic*
TEXT TYPEFACE: *Bembo*
CLIENT: *Drexel Burnham Lambert*

23
DESIGN FIRM: *Pentagram Design*
DESIGNER: *Kit Hinrichs and Lenore Bartz*
HEADLINE TYPEFACE: *Times Roman*
TEXT TYPEFACE: *Times Roman*
CLIENT: *Potlatch Corp.*

24

Immunex Manufacturing Corporation owns and operates a 10,000 square foot fermentation and pharmaceutical finishing facility located in the Seattle headquarters of Immunex Corporation. The plant was completed in April of 1988. It is large and flexible enough to manufacture clinical, and some commercial, quantities of each of the therapeutic products currently under development by Immunex and its collaborators. Planning is now underway for engineering and construction of a second, full-scale, plant to be ready for production in 1991.

IN ITS FIRST SIX MONTHS OF OPERATION, THE PILOT PLANT PRODUCED INITIAL RUNS OF FIVE DIFFERENT LYMPHOKINE PRODUCTS; ALREADY IN 1989, MANUFACTURING HAS ORDERS FROM COLLABORATORS FOR CLINICAL TRIAL QUANTITIES OF GM-CSF, IL-3, IL-4, G-CSF, AND IL-1. IMMUNEX WILL ALSO USE IL-1 IN ITS OWN TRIALS.

IMMUNEX 1988 ANNUAL REPORT

25

24
DESIGN FIRM: *Pentagram Design*
DESIGNER: *Kit Hinrichs and Belle How*
TEXT TYPEFACE: *Bembo*
CLIENT: *Immunex Corp.*

25
DESIGN FIRM: *Pentagram Design*
DESIGNER: *Kit Hinrichs and Belle How*
TEXT TYPEFACE: *Janson*
CLIENT: *Immunex Corp.*

26
DESIGN FIRM: *The Duffy Design Group*
DESIGNER: *Sharon Werner*
HEADLINE TYPEFACE: *Sabon*
CLIENT: *US West*

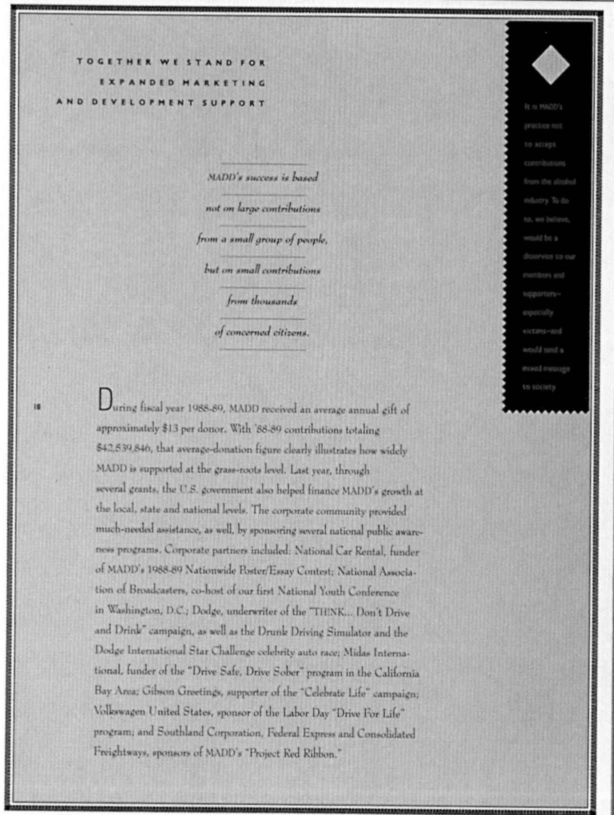

TOGETHER WE STAND FOR EXPANDED MARKETING AND DEVELOPMENT SUPPORT

MADD's success is based not on large contributions from a small group of people, but on small contributions from thousands of concerned citizens.

It is MADD's practice not to accept contributions from the alcohol industry. To do so, we believe, would be a disservice to our members and supporters—especially victims—and would send a mixed message to society.

18

During fiscal year 1988-89, MADD received an average annual gift of approximately $13 per donor. With '88-89 contributions totaling $42,539,846, that average-donation figure clearly illustrates how widely MADD is supported at the grass-roots level. Last year, through several grants, the U.S. government also helped finance MADD's growth at the local, state and national levels. The corporate community provided much-needed assistance, as well, by sponsoring several national public awareness programs. Corporate partners included: National Car Rental, funder of MADD's 1988-89 Nationwide Poster/Essay Contest; National Association of Broadcasters, co-host of our first National Youth Conference in Washington, D.C.; Dodge, underwriter of the "THINK... Don't Drive and Drink" campaign, as well as the Drunk Driving Simulator and the Dodge International Star Challenge celebrity auto race; Midas International, funder of the "Drive Safe, Drive Sober" program in the California Bay Area; Gibson Greetings, supporter of the "Celebrate Life" campaign; Volkswagen United States, sponsor of the Labor Day "Drive For Life" program; and Southland Corporation, Federal Express and Consolidated Freightways, sponsors of MADD's "Project Red Ribbon."

27/28
DESIGN FIRM: *Peterson & Company*
DESIGNER: *Bryan L. Peterson*
HEADLINE TYPEFACE: *Handlettering*
TEXT TYPEFACE: *Cloister*
CLIENT: *Mothers Against Drunk Driving*

29

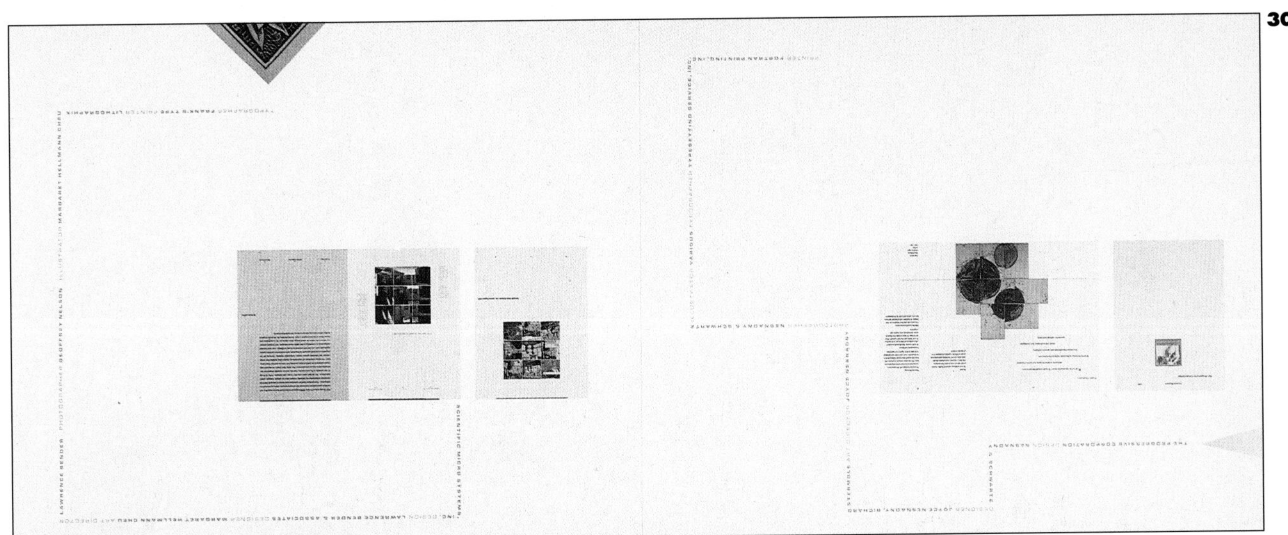
30

29/30
DESIGN FIRM: *Samata Associates*
DESIGNER: *Pat Samata*
HEADLINE TYPEFACE: *Eurostyle*
TEXT TYPEFACE: *Eurostyle*
CLIENT: *Mead Paper*

31

PUBLISHING AND RELATED DISTRIBUTION

WCI's Publishing division consists of Warner Books, DC Comics, Mad magazine and Warner Publisher Services. In 1987, revenues declined marginally to $130.3 million, while the division's operating income increased to $11.6 million from $11.3 million the year before.

WARNER BOOKS *The division's bestselling paperback was Sidney Sheldon's* Windmills of the Gods, *with more than four million copies in print.* Windmills, *Sheldon's eighth bestselling novel for Warner Books, was adapted into a four-hour mini-series for CBS. In hardcover,* The Discovery of the Titanic *by Robert G. Ballard was the biggest non-fiction title.* ❖ *Other successful titles included two books by celebrated author Andrew M. Greeley,* Rite of Spring *and* Patience of a Saint, *and also,* Fit For Life *by Harvey and Marilyn Diamond.* ❖ *In 1988, Warner Books' release schedule will include paperback reprints of national bestsellers* Presumed Innocent *by Scott Turow,* Bandits *by Elmore Leonard and* The Art of the Deal *by Donald Trump and Tony Schwartz. In addition, several hardcovers with broad-base appeal will be published:* Keeping Secrets *by Suzanne Sommers,* Angel Fire *by Andrew M. Greeley, and* The Charm School *by Nelson DeMille.*

MAD MAGAZINE *The world's most popular satirical magazine,* Mad *magazine reported operating gains due to new growth in newsstand sales, subscriptions and foreign royalties. In 1988,* Mad *expects to enhance its performance through licensed product merchandising.*

DC COMICS *The nation's oldest publisher of comic books, DC Comics continued to show excellent growth in its publishing operations due in part to the expansion of comic specialty stores and the growing consumer demand for DC Comics specialty products. Included among DC's properties are such world famous characters as Superman, Batman, Wonder Woman, and the Teen Titans. In 1987,* Superman *continued to benefit from its modernization and relaunch. The bestselling* Batman: Son of the Demon *became DC's first original*

32

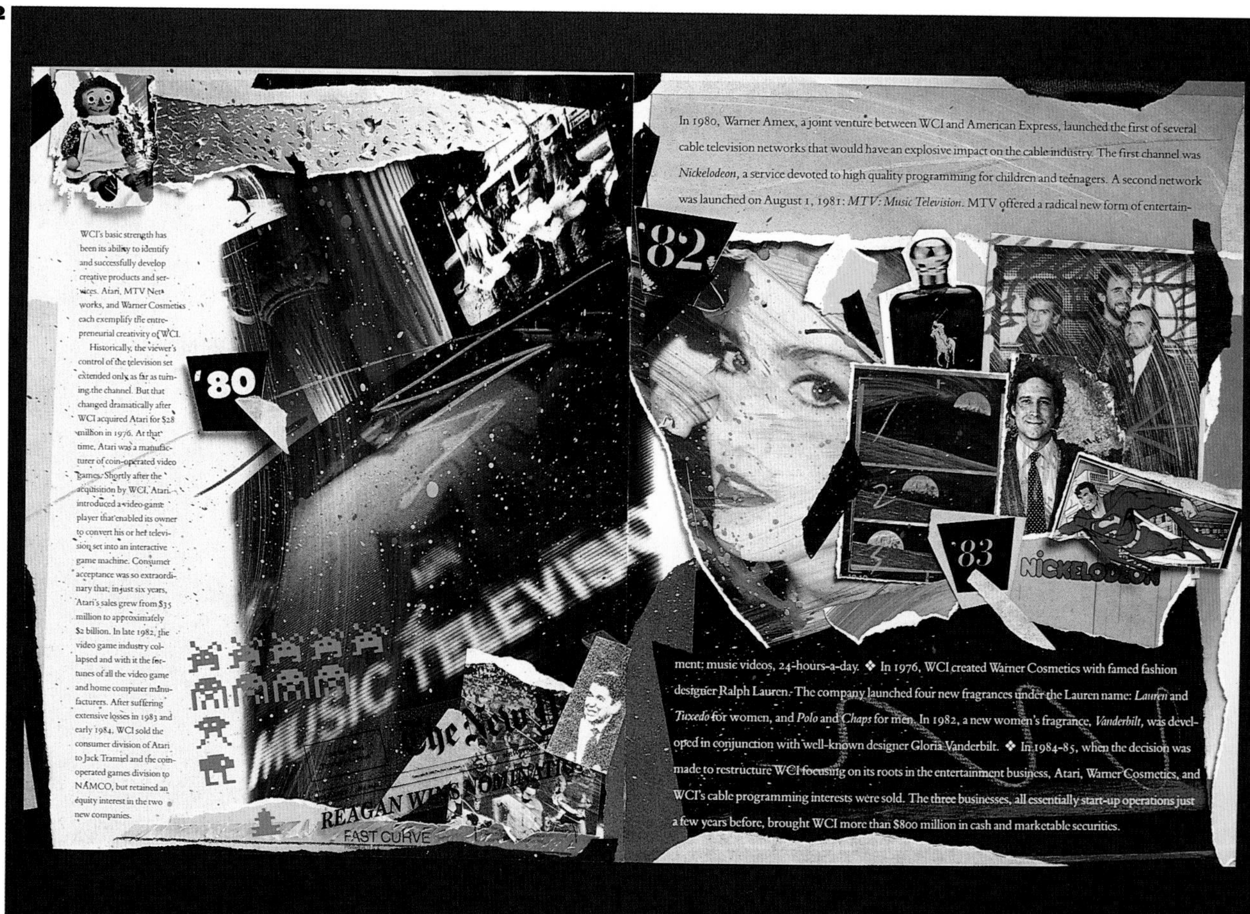

WCI's basic strength has been its ability to identify and successfully develop creative products and services. Atari, MTV Networks, and Warner Cosmetics each exemplify the entrepreneurial creativity of WCI.

Historically, the viewer's control of the television set extended only as far as turning the channel. But that changed dramatically after WCI acquired Atari for $28 million in 1976. At that time, Atari was a manufacturer of coin-operated video games. Shortly after the acquisition by WCI, Atari introduced a video-game player that enabled its owner to convert his or her television set into an interactive game machine. Consumer acceptance was so extraordinary that, in just six years, Atari's sales grew from $35 million to approximately $2 billion. In late 1982, the video game industry collapsed and with it the fortunes of all the video game and home computer manufacturers. After suffering extensive losses in 1983 and early 1984, WCI sold the consumer division of Atari to Jack Tramiel and the coin-operated games division to NAMCO, but retained an equity interest in the two new companies.

In 1980, Warner Amex, a joint venture between WCI and American Express, launched the first of several cable television networks that would have an explosive impact on the cable industry. The first channel was *Nickelodeon*, a service devoted to high quality programming for children and teenagers. A second network was launched on August 1, 1981: *MTV: Music Television*. MTV offered a radical new form of entertainment: music videos, 24-hours-a-day. ❖ In 1976, WCI created Warner Cosmetics with famed fashion designer Ralph Lauren. The company launched four new fragrances under the Lauren name: *Lauren* and *Tuxedo* for women, and *Polo* and *Chaps* for men. In 1982, a new women's fragrance, *Vanderbilt*, was developed in conjunction with well-known designer Gloria Vanderbilt. ❖ In 1984-85, when the decision was made to restructure WCI focusing on its roots in the entertainment business, Atari, Warner Cosmetics, and WCI's cable programming interests were sold. The three businesses, all essentially start-up operations just a few years before, brought WCI more than $800 million in cash and marketable securities.

31/32
DESIGN FIRM: *Pentagram Design*
DESIGNER: *Harold Burch and Peter Harrison*
HEADLINE TYPEFACE: *Bembo*
TEXT TYPEFACE: *Bembo Roman Italic*
CLIENT: *Warner Communications*

33

34

33
DESIGN FIRM: *Pentagram Design*
DESIGNER: *Kit Hinrichs and Lenore Bartz*
HEADLINE TYPEFACE: *News Gothic Extra Condensed Oblique*
TEXT TYPEFACE: *Bodoni Book*
CLIENT: *Cooper-Hewitt Museum*

34
DESIGN FIRM: *Concrete Design Communications*
DESIGNER: *Diti Katona*
HEADLINE TYPEFACE: *Corvinus*
TEXT TYPEFACE: *Centaur*
CLIENT: *First Mercantile Currency Fund*

35

WESTERN REDCEDAR

Thuja plicata

Durable, straight-grained, free of pitch, and resistant to shrinkage, decay and insect damage, western redcedar has served multiple uses for centuries. Pacific Northwest Indians carved totem poles and ocean-worthy canoes from western redcedar, using the stringy cinnamon-red bark from young trees for fishing lines and in weaving baskets and blankets. As settlers moved west of the Rockies, western redcedar was logged to make fences, telegraph poles and split-cedar shingles. The inner, fibrous bark was used to stuff upholstery.

In Idaho, western redcedar is still a high-value commercial species. Redcedar stands comprise about 20 percent of Potlatch's Idaho forest holdings. Potlatch converts this wood into a variety of lumber products, including boards, interior paneling, exterior siding and fencing materials. Redcedar also is used in bleached pulp and paper products.

Western redcedar grows to magnificent proportions. Idaho's largest known tree is a western redcedar that is more than 16-1/2 feet in diameter and believed to be over 1,000 years old. Old-growth redcedar on Potlatch land can tower over 150 feet in height.

Some of the beauties of this species are indicated by its Latin name, *Thuja plicata*: A tree with sweet-smelling, colorful wood whose leaves are folded and interlaced.

Redcedar's tiny, scalelike leaves form flat, lacy sprays. When bruised, the leaves release a pleasing fragrance.

A variety of lumber products are made from western redcedar.

12

36

35
DESIGN FIRM: *Pentagram Design*
DESIGNER: *Kit Hinrichs and Terri Driscoll*
HEADLINE TYPEFACE: *Aldus*
TEXT TYPEFACE: *Aldus*
CLIENT: *Potlatch Corp.*

36
DESIGN FIRM: *SBG Partners*
DESIGNER: *Barbara Vick*
HEADLINE TYPEFACE: *Bank Gothic and Stuyvesant*
TEXT TYPEFACE: *Bembo*
CLIENT: *Capital Guaranty*

37
DESIGN FIRM: *Morla Design*
DESIGNER: *Jennifer Morla*
HEADLINE TYPEFACE: *Copperplate Gothic*
TEXT TYPEFACE: *Futura Bold, Janson, and Italic*
CLIENT: *San Francisco Airports Commission*

38

38
DESIGN FIRM: *Concrete Design Communications*
DESIGNER: *Diti Katona*
HEADLINE TYPEFACE: *Maraine and Garamond*
TEXT TYPEFACE: *Garamond*
CLIENT: *Noranda, Inc.*

E N V I R O N M E N T

aste—some offices are taking steps to recycle the rated every year. Office paper recycling programs are ywhere, including Noranda Inc.'s corporate office in ht months of a recycling program there, organizers col- ewer than five tons of paper.

, Noranda Inc. communications officer Denis Leclerc ffice paper recycling program, following suggestions from rned to Pat McVeigh, manager, facilities management at Services. McVeigh offered advice based on his office's paper recycling. Other offices within the Noranda group ing operations in place as well, including the Calgary cen- cen. Using McVeigh's advice, Leclerc worked closely with mail room clerk Colin Tattrie to develop the program.

To institute it, Leclerc first had to find a contractor who would pick up the mounds of waste paper every two weeks and deliver them to a plant that recycles office waste paper. Because Noranda does not currently recycle office waste paper, Leclerc stipulated that the plant chosen not be a direct competitor with Noranda paper mills. Then, he and Tattrie installed huge blue plastic bar- rels at strategic locations around Noranda's Toronto Commerce Court West offices: next to computer printers and photocopiers.

The next step was to publicize and educate office staff via flyers and bulletin board announcements. After a few months they refined the program by placing blue waste paper baskets in all the offices on the floor. Now everyone has a per- sonal blue basket.

Leclerc says that despite the initial organizing and publicity, the program is remarkably simple to run. Shortly after it started, the designers ensured its proper execution by visiting individual employees to encourage and educate them on what to put in their blue baskets—and what not to. One of the biggest difficulties with recycling programs is the contamination of useful material with materials that cannot be recycled. The corporate offices can recycle most white paper except envelopes, which often have unusable sticky labels attached to them, as well as fax paper, coloured stock, and waxed and glossy papers. The used Noranda paper is made into useful products such as facial tissues, toilet paper and paper towels.

Eventually, the corporate office program may actually form a resource loop. Noranda may have its waste paper shipped to its recycled fine paper mill at Thorold, Ont. when the mill will be equipped to process it. Already, the office is using Noranda Forest Recycled Papers' fine paper for its photocopiers.

Leclerc and Tattrie are rightly proud of this small but meaningful step at curbing waste. "At our office we don't make paper and don't work in a mine," Leclerc says. "But we can do our share to protect the environment. It's only the first step, and we're trying to find other programs to increase our involvement in protecting the environment."

N CO FINDS A NEW ANGLE

The Great Sand Hills of western Saskatchewan are different from most places on the Canadian prairies. Here, instead of flat or gently rolling fields of grain the Sand Hills are a wild place, a semi-arid steppe of short and tall grasses, shrubs, and clusters of trees known on the Canadian prairies as bluffs. Just beneath this fragile mat of vegetation are the sand hills, which threaten to burst out into life-choking dunes if the surface is disturbed. Located near the Alberta border 150 kms west of Swift Current, the Sand Hills have long been leased by the govern- ment to ranchers and as community pastures. When North Canadian Oils Limited (NCO) began planning a drilling program to tap the area's shallow gas fields, it developed a special environmental plan that minimized impact in an area classified by the provincial government as sensitive terrain. Obtaining regu- latory approval for NCO's 66-well program in the Sand Hills wasn't easy. In late 1988, NCO and Western Oil Field Environmental Services, a consulting com- pany, began developing a complex plan, pinpointing the best well pad locations and their access routes. The sites were chosen on the basis of proximity to the gas reservoir, but also to minimize environmental disturbance. The access routes were carefully chosen to avoid wildlife habitats such as large trees. Animal dens and burrows were avoided, and an inventory of the natural vegeta- tion was made so that it could be replanted during site reclamation. In another bid to limit the disruption to the surface, NCO reduced the number of drilling pads markedly through an ingenious combination of conventional vertical and diagonal drilling. Of the 66 wells in the program, 44 were inclined, slanting downward from common pads. Although inclined wells cost 40 per cent more to drill, NCO figures on substantial savings in the future, because site reclama- tion costs will be less with fewer drilling pads and access routes. NCO has taken other steps to protect the Sand Hills as well. Drilling fluids are contained in special tanks. The "drilling mud", which lubricates the drill bit as it bores through the earth also received special treatment. Drilling mud is a slurry of clay, water and addi- tives, including potassium chloride, a salty substance which, in large concentra- tions, can harm vegetation. NCO's drilling contractors substituted ammonium sulphate fertilizer to minimize the harm. The drillers recycled and reused as much of the mud as possible to reduce the volumes that would have to be dis- posed of, some of which farmers eventually took to fertilize their fields.

Before drilling began on May 15, 1989, NCO officials met with govern-

9

39

KEMPER REINSURANCE COMPANY

ANNUAL REPORT 1989

40

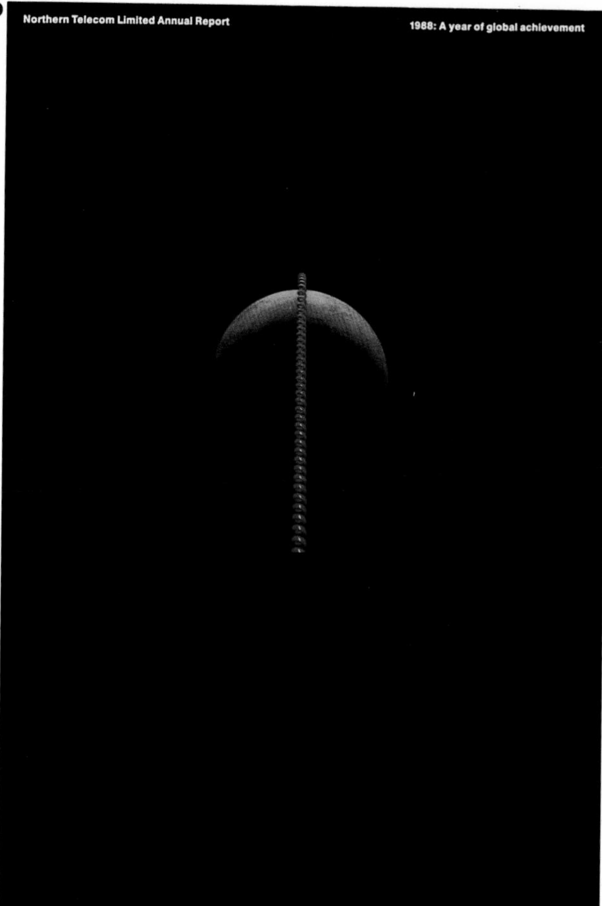

41

1988: A year of global achievement

“ The corporation is uniquely positioned through its world network of subsidiary operations, strategic alliances, joint ventures and licensee relationships ”

Communications systems for Chinese industry

Important sales and joint ventures in 1988 enhanced Northern Telecom's presence in key global markets. In the Pacific, the corporation scored a strategic advantage in April when President David G. Vice signed an agreement to form a joint venture with China Tong Guang Electronics to manufacture Meridian SL-1 systems in Guangdong

30,000 lines of Meridian SL-1 for France

province. In France, the newly created NT Meridian subsidiary won contracts by yearend for 30,000 lines of Meridian SL-1. Last spring, Northern Telecom and Nippon Telegraph and Telephone (NTT) installed a DMS-10, the first non-Japanese switch in the NTT network. The current contract calls for the delivery of more than 700 switches by 1993. Elsewhere, 1988 saw DMS Family sales and contracts in the Bahamas, Jamaica,

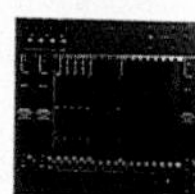

Spanning continents with data packet networks

Morocco, Puerto Rico, and Australia. Northern Telecom's DPN-100 Family of data packet switching equipment continued its global success in 1988 with sales to public or private networks in Australia, Hong Kong, Norway, and Sweden. The corporation also agreed to supply the European Academic Research Network with a DPN-100 packet switching system, to link universities and academic research centers throughout Europe.

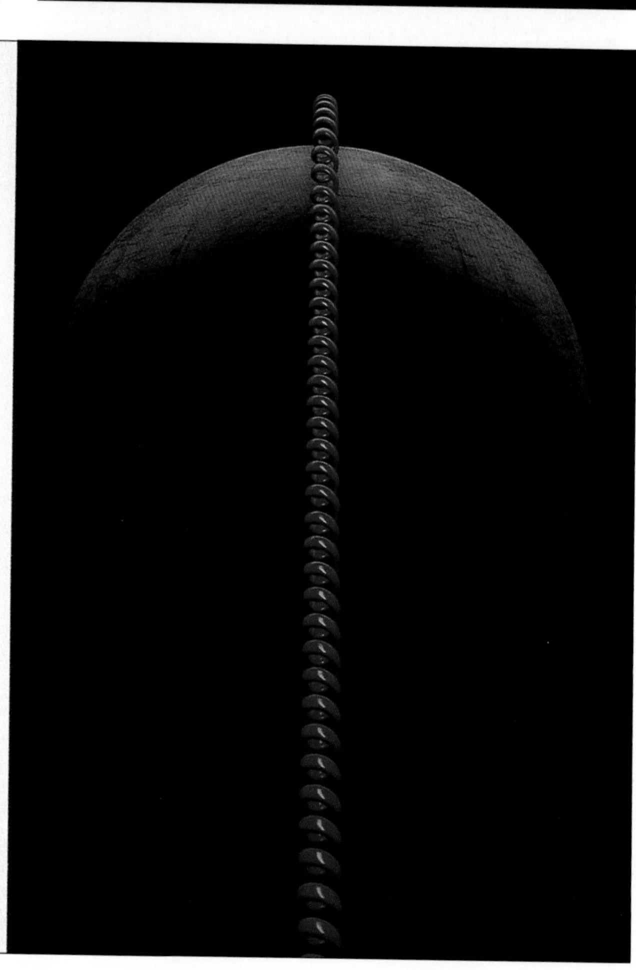

39
DESIGN FIRM: *Samata Associates*
DESIGNER: *Greg Samata*
HEADLINE TYPEFACE: *Engravers Roman*
TEXT TYPEFACE: *Sabon*
CLIENT: *Samata Associates*

40/41
DESIGN FIRM: *Pentagram Design*
DESIGNER: *Woody Pirtle and Leigh Brownsword*
HEADLINE TYPEFACE: *Helvetica Bold*
TEXT TYPEFACE: *Garamond #3*
CLIENT: *Northern Telecom Ltd.*

42

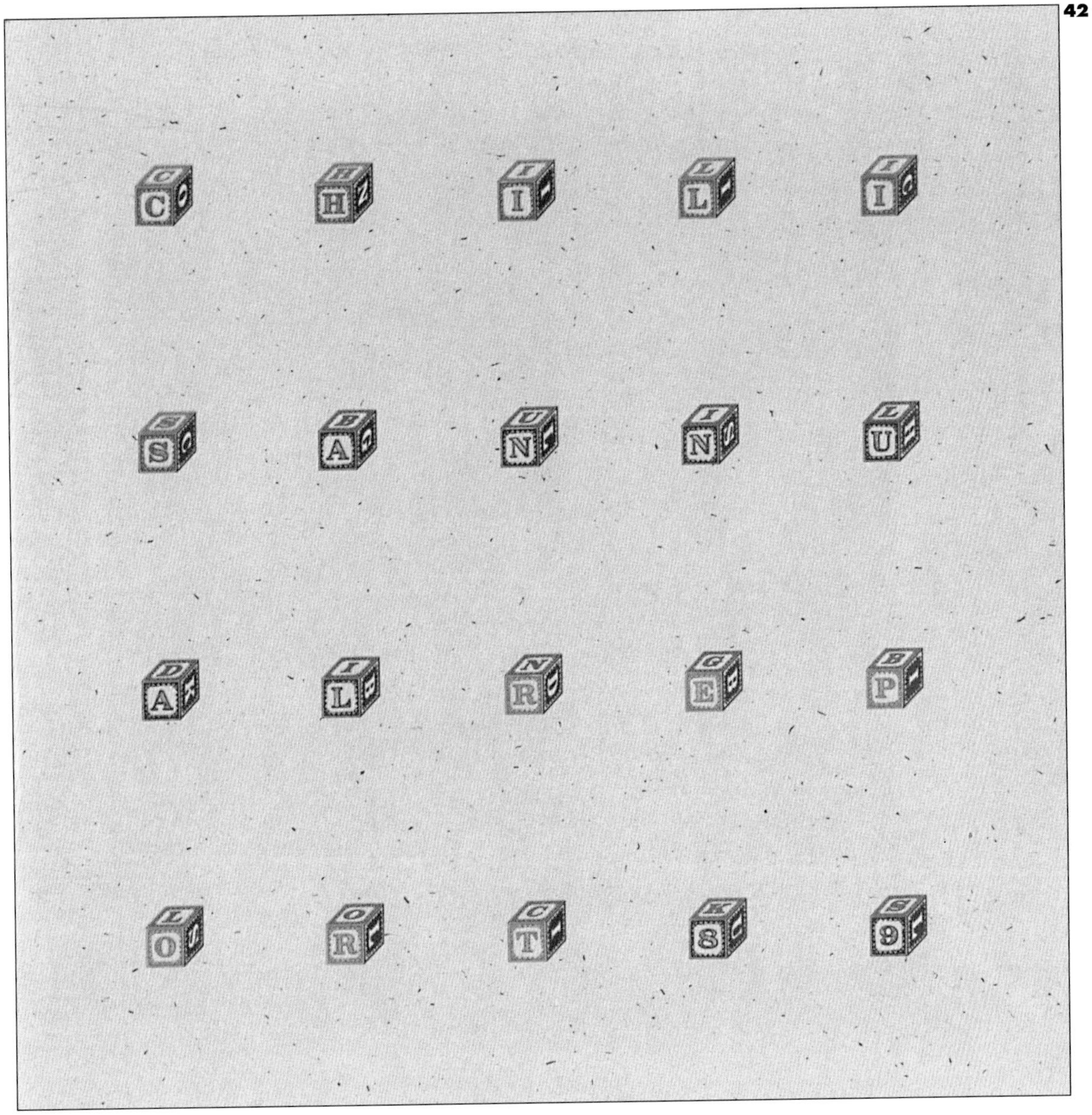

43

42/43
DESIGN FIRM: *RBMM/The Richards Group*
DESIGNER: *Brian Boyd*
HEADLINE TYPEFACE: *Clarendon Bold*
TEXT TYPEFACE: *Goudy Oldstyle*
CLIENT: *Chili's, Inc.*

44/45/46
DESIGN FIRM: *Van Dyke Company*
DESIGNER: *John Van Dyke*
HEADLINE TYPEFACE: *Garamond #3 Italic*
TEXT TYPEFACE: *Futura Black*
CLIENT: *Expeditors International*

44

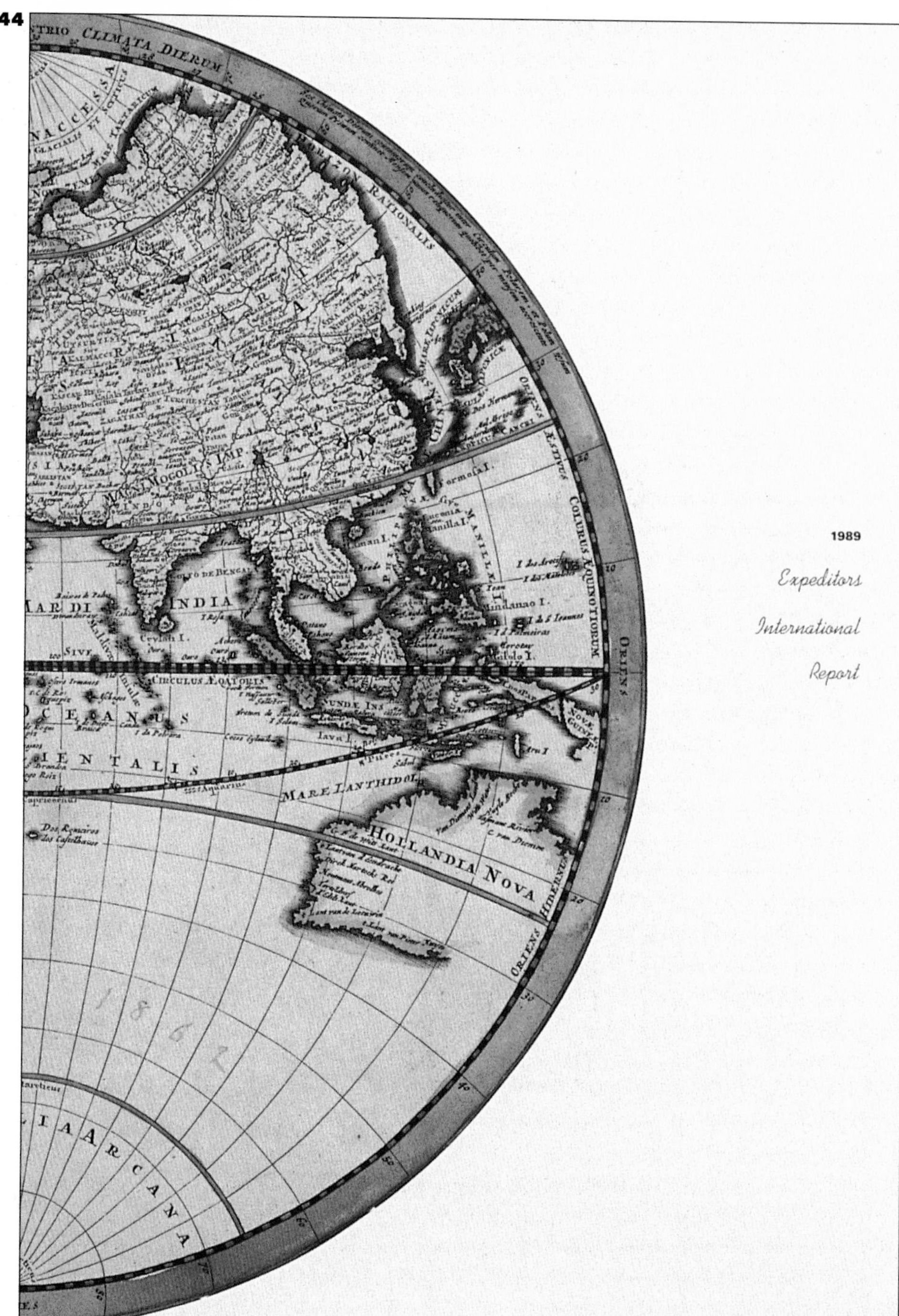

45

46

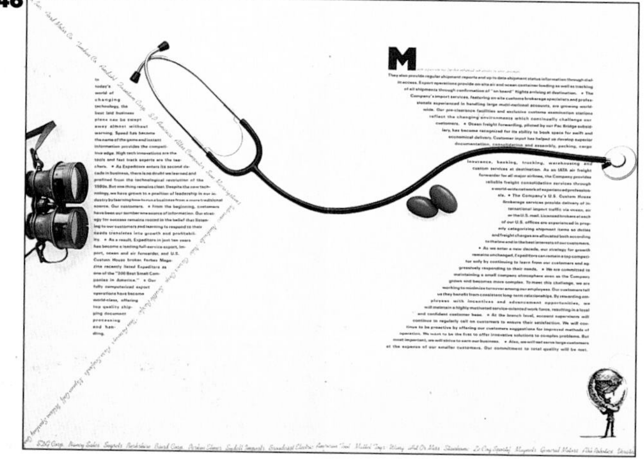

47

WARNER COMMUNICATIONS INC. 1988 ANNUAL REPORT

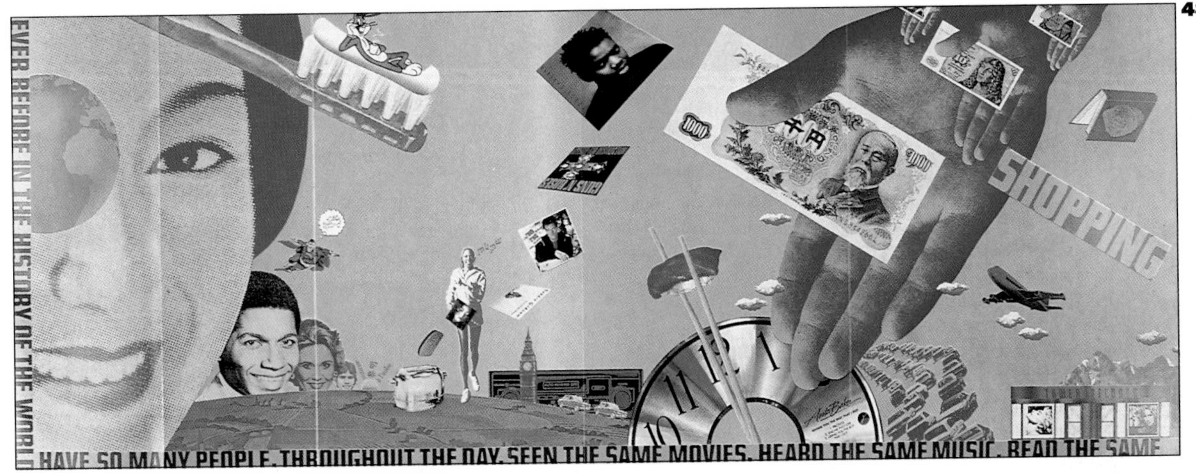

48

47/48
DESIGN FIRM: *Pentagram Design*
DESIGNER: *Peter Harrison and Harold Burch*
HEADLINE TYPEFACE: *Univers*
TEXT TYPEFACE: *Stempel Garamond*
CLIENT: *Warner Communications*

49

49
DESIGN FIRM: *Peterson & Company*
DESIGNER: *Scott Ray*
TEXT TYPEFACE: *ITC Fenice*
CLIENT: *Dallas Zoological Society*

50

The Zoo's animal collection currently contains approximately 1,400 animals, representing over 300 species of birds, mammals, reptiles, and amphibians. Included in this population are a significant number of endangered and threatened species. ❧ The Zoo has an impressive record of breeding rare, endangered, and threatened animals. It is only one of five U.S. zoos to successfully breed okapi; there have been 16 born at the Zoo. Approximately 66 okapi are in zoos and wildlife parks world-wide; eight reside at the Zoo. ❧ The Zoo has been successful at breeding all three species of Great Ape — gorillas, orangutans, and chimpanzees; all of these apes are endangered. In 1989, a female black rhino was born at the Zoo. The rhino giving birth was one of ten brought to the U.S. from Zimbabwe through a joint effort of several zoos and a Ft. Worth wildlife organization. A male and a female were brought to the Dallas Zoo. Black rhinos are seriously endangered in their native habitats, mainly due to poaching. ❧ Also in 1989, two male Grevy's zebras were born at the Zoo. Grevy's are one of the 50 species managed under the Species Survival Plan of the AAZPA. In April, 1989, a male and female Nile lechwe were born. Other endangered mammals born include a Speke's gazelle, a dusky leaf monkey, a mona monkey, and a white-handed gibbon.

The Zoo's bird collection includes the endangered Bali mynah, Andean condor, Kori bustard, and Congo peafowl. In 1989, the Zoo became the third U.S. zoo to successfully hatch a sunbird species, and the first to hatch a collared sunbird. Also in '89, two buff-crested bustards were hatched. The Zoo is the first U.S. zoo to successfully parent-raise buff-crested bustards.

Throughout 1989, the Bird Department continued to participate in the Condor Recovery Program. The Zoo has been assisting in efforts to save the California condor from extinction since 1981, when the Zoo sent an Andean condor egg to the Bronx Zoo. (The Bronx Zoo was a pioneer in using Andean condors in research programs to save the California birds.) In 1989, the Zoo sent another Andean egg to Los Angeles to be hatched by researchers who hope to release Andean condors into the California condors' territory as part of a pre-release study for the California species.

Endangered reptiles at the Zoo include the Aruba Island rattlesnake, the Radiated tortoise, the San Francisco garter snake, and the Dumeril's ground boa. In 1989, two clutches of the threatened bushmaster were hatched at the Zoo, as well as two each of Grant's New Caledonian gecko and leaf-tailed gecko.

The Aquarium staff successfully spawned the fountain darter, a species native to Central Texas. Fountain darters are endangered due to a limited habitat and the overpumping of the springs in which they are found.

The Zoo actively pursues breeding programs with all the animals in its collection. In 1989, over 200 animals were born at the Zoo.

51

Research has been an integral part of the Zoo's agenda for many years. In 1989, the Zoo curators and staff continued to pursue aggressively their research goals, guided by the Research Master Plan. The Plan was established to coordinate both new and on-going research at the Zoo. ❧ Zoo curators and staff regularly publish papers in scientific journals of record, such as the *International Zoo Yearbook* and the *Bulletin of Psychonomics*; they also routinely present papers and monographs at scientific conferences and seminars, such as the American Society of Ichthyology meeting, the AAZPA conference, and meetings of the Texas Parks and Wildlife Department. ❧ In 1989, the Zoo hosted a seminar, "Applying Behavioral Research to Animal Management," for the second consecutive year. Thirty-two scientists and zoologists representing 24 zoos from across the United States and as far away as Australia spent eight days at the Zoo attending lectures and conducting research. The purpose of the workshop was to offer participants an opportunity to study methods of research on animal behavior in zoos and to encourage the study of captive animal behavior. ❧ The opening of the Wilds of Africa has allowed the Zoo unprecedented opportunities to study animals in two different environments. Many of the Zoo's mammals were moved to unfenced, open habitats in the Wilds from more confining enclosures in ZooNorth. The Zoo staff used this once-in-a-lifetime opportunity to do pre- and post-occupancy studies of the gorillas, the mandrill baboons, and the okapi. A mother/infant study is being carried out on the okapi, as well as on the Speke's gazelle, the slender-horned oryx, and the dik-dik. ❧ Mammal research in 1989 included the Gorilla Ethology Study, an examination of the Zoo's four lowland gorillas which will provide a descriptive catalogue of many of their behaviors. ❧ In 1989, telemetry studies with the red (lesser) panda continued, as did the Zoo's participation in Chimpanzoo. The Chimpanzoo project collects data on captive chimps in various zoos and compares this data with information on wild chimps; it was created by Jane Goodall and her research teams in Africa and the United States. ❧ In 1989, the Bird Department conducted a study on the space utilization of a breeding pair of Goliath herons, to use as a pre-model for designing exhibit space in the Wilds of Africa. Bird Department staff continued field research on the black-capped vireo habitats in Texas. ❧ The Reptile Department continued studies on feeding and behavior of the bushmaster, as well as studying predatory behavior in this snake. The department also collected data on perch selection of the green tree python and conducted a study of Texas rat snakes.

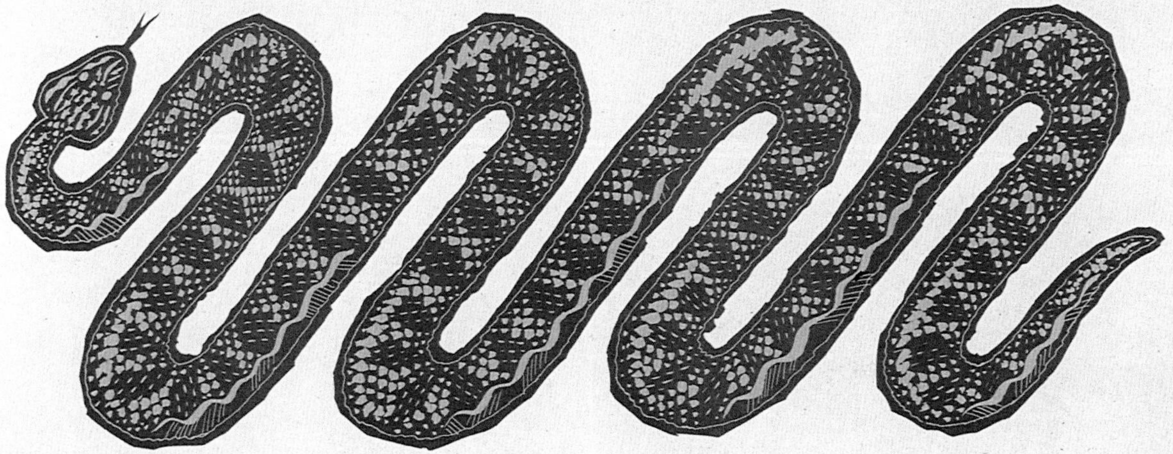

50/51
DESIGN FIRM: *Peterson & Company*
DESIGNER: *Scott Ray*
TEXT TYPEFACE: *ITC Fenice*
CLIENT: *Dallas Zoological Society*

52

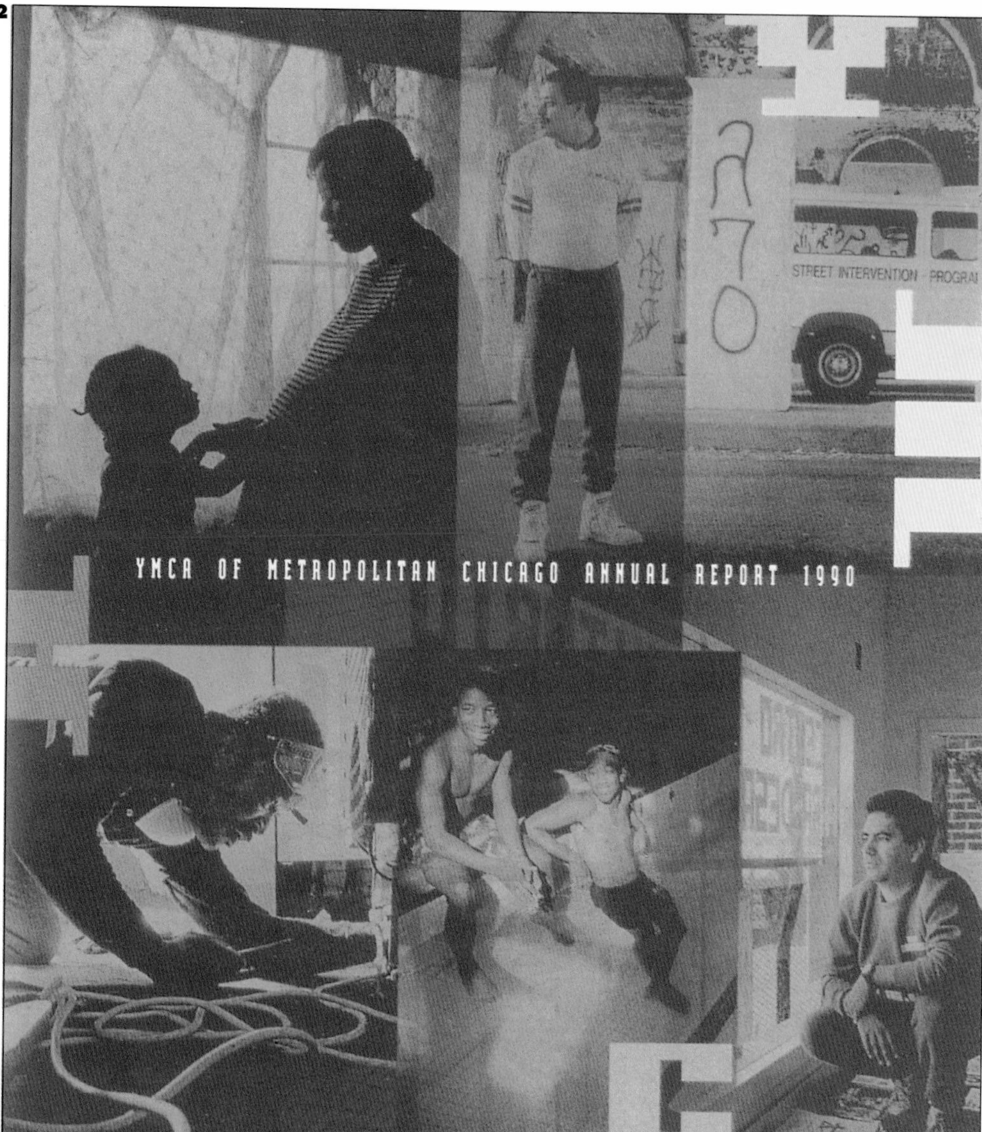

53

52/53
DESIGN FIRM: *Samata Associates*
DESIGNER: *Pat Samata and Greg Samata*
HEADLINE TYPEFACE: *Park Avenue*
TEXT TYPEFACE: *Modula*
CLIENT: *YMCA of Metropolitan Chicago*

54
DESIGN FIRM: *Pentagram Design*
DESIGNER: *Woody Pirtle and Jennifer Long*
HEADLINE TYPEFACE: *Helvetica Bold*
TEXT TYPEFACE: *Garamond #3*
CLIENT: *Northern Telecom Ltd.*

55
DESIGN FIRM: *Peterson & Company*
DESIGNER: *Bryan L. Peterson*
HEADLINE TYPEFACE: *Moderna Condensed*
TEXT TYPEFACE: *Perpetua*
CLIENT: *Centex Corp.*

55

56

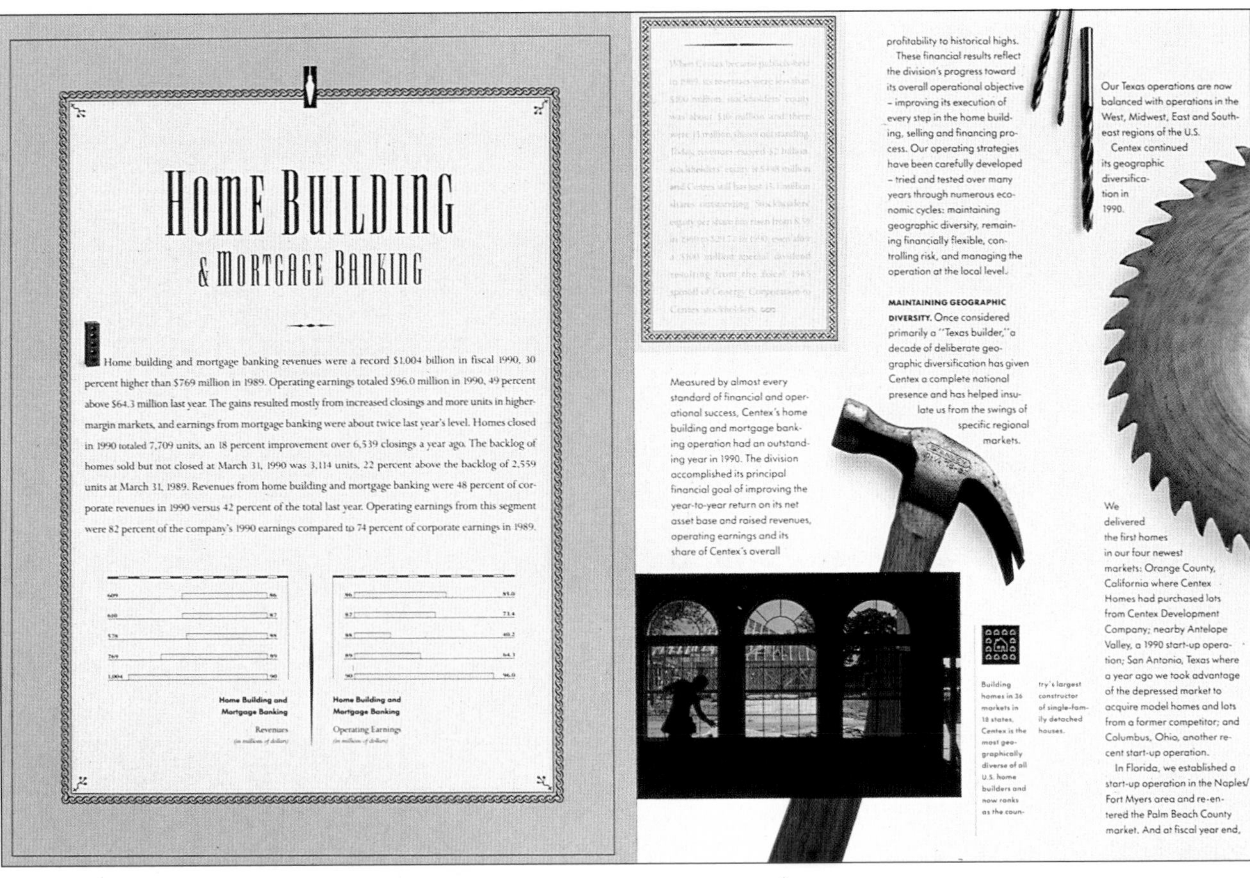

HOME BUILDING
& MORTGAGE BANKING

Home building and mortgage banking revenues were a record $1.004 billion in fiscal 1990, 30 percent higher than $769 million in 1989. Operating earnings totaled $96.0 million in 1990, 49 percent above $64.3 million last year. The gains resulted mostly from increased closings and more units in higher-margin markets, and earnings from mortgage banking were about twice last year's level. Homes closed in 1990 totaled 7,709 units, an 18 percent improvement over 6,539 closings a year ago. The backlog of homes sold but not closed at March 31, 1990 was 3,114 units, 22 percent above the backlog of 2,559 units at March 31, 1989. Revenues from home building and mortgage banking were 48 percent of corporate revenues in 1990 versus 42 percent of the total last year. Operating earnings from this segment were 82 percent of the company's 1990 earnings compared to 74 percent of corporate earnings in 1989.

Home Building and Mortgage Banking
Revenues

Home Building and Mortgage Banking
Operating Earnings

Measured by almost every standard of financial and operational success, Centex's home building and mortgage banking operation had an outstanding year in 1990. The division accomplished its principal financial goal of improving the year-to-year return on its net asset base and raised revenues, operating earnings and its share of Centex's overall profitability to historical highs.

These financial results reflect the division's progress toward its overall operational objective – improving its execution of every step in the home building, selling and financing process. Our operating strategies have been carefully developed – tried and tested over many years through numerous economic cycles: maintaining geographic diversity, remaining financially flexible, controlling risk, and managing the operation at the local level.

MAINTAINING GEOGRAPHIC DIVERSITY. Once considered primarily a "Texas builder," a decade of deliberate geographic diversification has given Centex a complete national presence and has helped insulate us from the swings of specific regional markets.

Our Texas operations are now balanced with operations in the West, Midwest, East and Southeast regions of the U.S.

Centex continued its geographic diversification in 1990.

We delivered the first homes in our four newest markets: Orange County, California where Centex Homes had purchased lots from Centex Development Company; nearby Antelope Valley, a 1990 start-up operation; San Antonio, Texas where a year ago we took advantage of the depressed market to acquire model homes and lots from a former competitor; and Columbus, Ohio, another recent start-up operation.

In Florida, we established a start-up operation in the Naples/Fort Myers area and re-entered the Palm Beach County market. And at fiscal year end,

Building homes in 36 markets in 18 states, Centex is the most geographically diverse of all U.S. home builders and now ranks as the country's largest constructor of single-family detached houses.

57

56
DESIGN FIRM: *Peterson & Company*
DESIGNER: *Bryan L. Peterson*
HEADLINE TYPEFACE: *Moderna Condensed*
TEXT TYPEFACE: *Perpetua*
CLIENT: *Centex Corp.*

57
DESIGN FIRM: *SBG Partners*
DESIGNER: *Barbara Vick*
HEADLINE TYPEFACE: *Castellar*
TEXT TYPEFACE: *Gill San Light and Centaur*
CLIENT: *Capital Guaranty*

58/59
DESIGN FIRM: *Pentagram Design*
DESIGNER: *Woody Pirtle, Peter Harrison, and Nancy Hoefig*
HEADLINE TYPEFACE: *Torino Roman and Helvetica Bold*
TEXT TYPEFACE: *Century Condensed*
CLIENT: *MCI Communications Corp.*

60

61

Q. Please comment on Hasbro's financial condition. A. John T. O'Neill – Chief Financial Officer: Financially, we are very sound. Our balance sheet is stronger than ever before, reflecting a total liabilities-to-equity ratio of 0.55. To a great extent, this strength resulted from more aggressive management of assets and a series of concrete steps taken to accelerate our cash flow. At the same time, we continued to improve our ability to monitor market demand and adjust production accordingly. *Q. What kind of year was 1989 for Milton Bradley?* A. George R. Ditomassi, Jr. – President, Milton Bradley: In spite of a difficult environment, 1989 was Milton Bradley's fifth consecutive year of revenue growth.

Two new entries – Shark Attack™ for preschoolers and Scattergories® in the adult market – achieved volume in the million-unit range. In December, Milton Bradley experienced some of the strongest consumer demand ever in a single month. In a year when the video category completely dominated the boys' market, Marble Madness,™ introduced during the second quarter, finished 1989 as one of the year's top-selling Nintendo® cartridges. One-on-One Basketball,™ featuring NBA stars Michael Jordan and Larry Bird, also made a very strong showing. *Q. What's the outlook in games and puzzles for 1990?* A. Ditomassi: Overall, we are optimistic. It's clear that the video segment

Scattergories®

already has begun to stabilize, which suggests that sales of games and puzzles should remain on solid footing. For 1990, Milton Bradley is introducing two strong follow-ups to Scattergories in the all-family category – TABOO™ and READY! SET! SPAGHETTI!™ SABADO GIGANTE,™ based on the popular TV show, is the first Spanish-language board game marketed by a major manufacturer and aimed at America's fast-growing Hispanic market. Milton Bradley's solid record of consumer acceptance and dependable profitability for retailers remain our greatest strengths and ensure continued broad distribution. *Q. How does Hasbro plan to realize further growth, given the relatively flat volume of the past three years?* A. Barry J. Alperin – Co-Chief Operating Officer: It's important to understand that even though revenues have remained steady, our product mix constantly changes in response to our markets. For example, while promotional toy volume has declined overall, all the other parts of our business – games and puzzles, preschool and Europe – have continued to grow. And while we're always looking for promotional hits, you can't predict them and you can't stake your future on them. As a result, we're thinking longer-term and shifting our investment strategy to reflect this new thinking. For example, we've begun to aggressively approach the Asian market, where rising

Cabbage Patch Kids®

"Oh Wow!" "Adorable"

60/61
DESIGN FIRM: *Pentagram Design*
DESIGNER: *Harold Burch and Peter Harrison*
HEADLINE TYPEFACE: *Various*
TEXT TYPEFACE: *Goudy Oldstyle*
CLIENT: *Hasbro, Inc.*

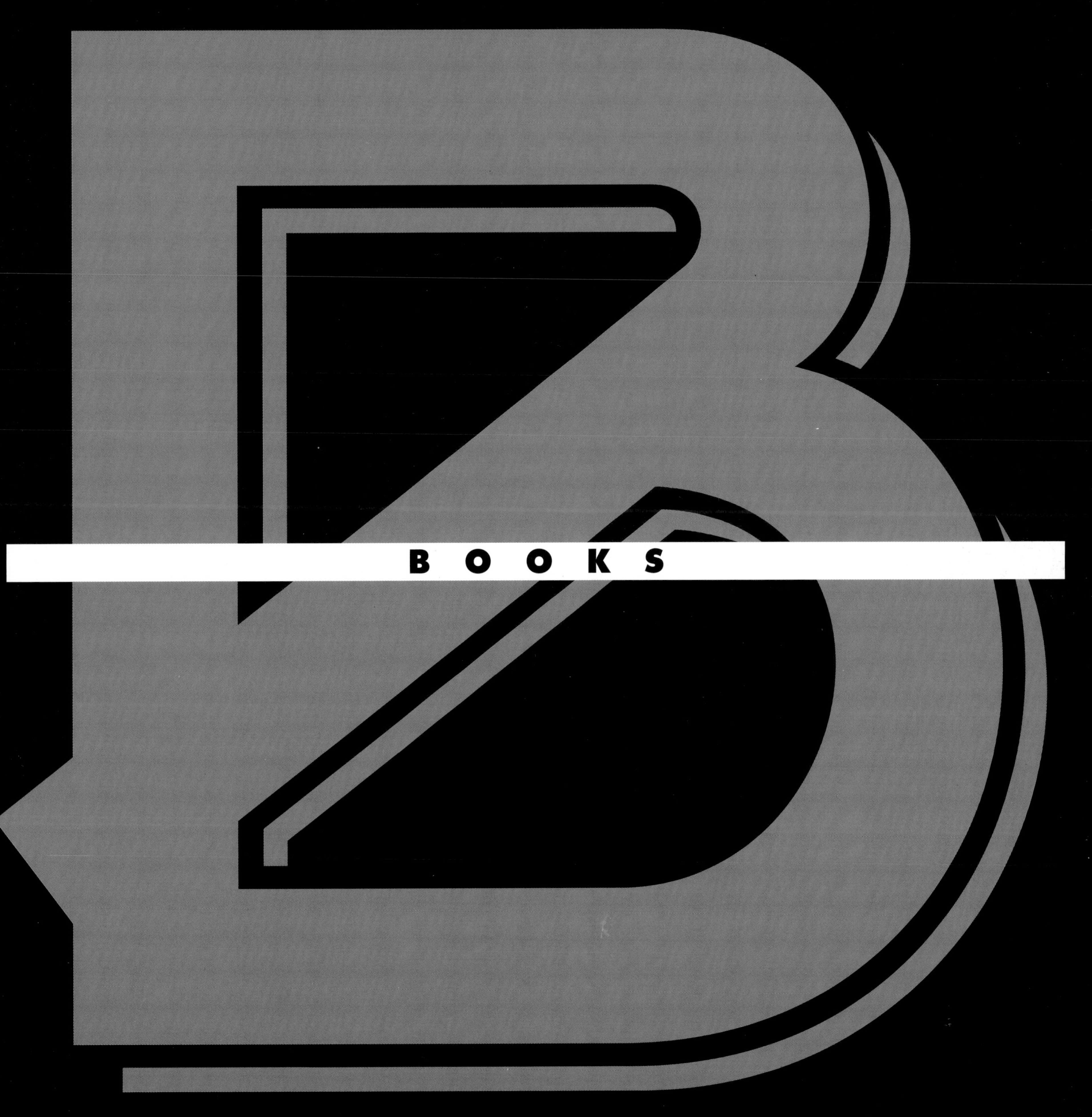
BOOKS

1

PANTHEON MODERN CLASSICS

Young Törless

ROBERT MUSIL

2

1
DESIGN FIRM: *Louise Fili, Ltd.*
DESIGNER: *Louise Fili*
LETTERER: *Louise Fili*
HEADLINE TYPEFACE: *Handlettering*
CLIENT: *Pentheon Books*

2
DESIGN FIRM: *Eric Baker Design Associates*
DESIGNER: *Michael Doret*
LETTERER: *Michael Doret*
HEADLINE TYPEFACE: *Huxley*
TEXT TYPEFACE: *Kabel*
CLIENT: *Chronicle Books*

3

4

3
DESIGN FIRM: *Gerard Huerta Design, Inc.*
DESIGNER: *Gerard Huerta*
LETTERER: *Gerard Huerta*
HEADLINE TYPEFACE: *Handlettering*
CLIENT: *Graphic Artists Guild*

4
DESIGN FIRM: *Eric Baker Design Associates*
DESIGNER: *Michael Doret*
LETTERER: *Michael Doret*
HEADLINE TYPEFACE: *Handlettering*
TEXT TYPEFACE: *Bodoni*
CLIENT: *Chronicle Books*

5

6

LOVE & **PLANTS**

July 29, 1981, was the day Prince Charles and Princess Diana were married. It was also the day a mysterious new flower bloomed at the Waimea Arboretum and Botanical Garden in Hawaii.♥

The white beauty turned out to be a hybrid of two different varieties of hibiscus from separate islands, and no one knows how they got together. The bloom was named "Royal Wedding." Cuttings were forwarded to the Royal Botanical Gardens in London.♥

As Scandinavian mythology has it, the good god of light was killed by the bad god with a mistletoe dart. It became a custom to kiss under the mistletoe to show that the plant was no longer a symbol of death, but of love. It's bad luck to say no to someone who wants to kiss you under the mistletoe.♥

Friendship is a plant of slow growth, and must undergo and withstand the shocks of adversity before it is entitled to the appellation.
—George Washington

♥4 UNUSUAL REQUESTS FOR WEDDING FLOWERS AND GREENERY FROM FLOWER FASHIONS, INC., BEVERLY HILLS

1. Karen Black's 1975 sunrise wedding-in-the-woods. The Flower Fashions crew was up most of the night at the Beverly Hills reservoir clearing land and tying ribbons and flower garlands onto trees.
2. A nudist wedding in which the bride carried a small nosegay. "I don't think the groom wore a boutonniere," says co-owner Fred Gibbons.
3. Fifth Dimension singer Florence LaRue's wedding in a hot air balloon festooned with flowers.
4. A winter-theme wedding in the heat of a Las Vegas summer for a casino owner's daughter. Flower Fashions flew in fresh evergreens and created frozen fountains and two ice skating rinks. The bridesmaids wore fur.

♥Nobody loves me. I'm going into the garden and eat worms.
—Anonymous

5/6
DESIGN FIRM: *Galarneau & Sinn, Ltd.*
DESIGNER: *Paul Sinn and Mark Galarneau*
HEADLINE TYPEFACE: *Goudy Oldstyle*
TEXT TYPEFACE: *Various*
CLIENT: *Simon & Schuster, Inc.*

7

8

9

10

7
DESIGN FIRM: *Delessert & Marshall*
DESIGNER: *Rita Marshall*
HEADLINE TYPEFACE: *Carlton*
TEXT TYPEFACE: *Futura Light and Berkeley Oldstyle*
CLIENT: *Clarkson Potter*

8
DESIGN FIRM: *Delessert & Marshall*
DESIGNER: *Rita Marshall*
HEADLINE TYPEFACE: *Futura Extra Bold*
TEXT TYPEFACE: *Berkeley Old Style*
CLIENT: *Redpath Press*

9
DESIGN FIRM: *Delessert & Marshall*
DESIGNER: *Rita Marshall*
HEADLINE TYPEFACE: *Futura Extra Bold*
TEXT TYPEFACE: *Berkeley Old Style*
CLIENT: *Redpath Press*

10
DESIGN FIRM: *Delessert & Marshall*
DESIGNER: *Rita Marshall*
HEADLINE TYPEFACE: *Futura Extra Bold*
TEXT TYPEFACE: *Berkeley Old Style*
CLIENT: *Redpath Press*

11

DESIGN FIRM: *David Lance Goines*

LETTERER: *David Lance Goines*

HEADLINE TYPEFACE: *Narrow Bembo (Fairbank)*

TEXT TYPEFACE: *Monotype Bembo*

CLIENT: *David R. Goine, Publisher*

12

DESIGN FIRM: *Delessert & Marshall*

DESIGNER: *Rita Marshall*

HEADLINE TYPEFACE: *Brighton Light*

TEXT TYPEFACE: *ITC Garamond Light*

CLIENT: *Stewart, Tabori, & Chang*

11

The Letter Q

Q Construct first a square ABCD. Bisect AC at E, BD at F, AB at G, and CD at H. Draw the straight lines EF and GH, thus establishing a point I at their intersection. From the center I, describe a circle JIK on EF, the diameter of which is one-ninth the distance AB. Using the same radius, describe circles from the centers J and K, thereby establishing the points L and M, the point L being at the inferior intersection of the circles I and K, and the point M being at the superior intersection of J and I. Draw now the straight line LIM, and produce it to intersect AG at N and HD at O. From the center I describe a circle tangential to the square ABCD, intersecting NM at P and LO at Q. From the center P, describe a circle the diameter of which is ML, thereby establishing on NP the point R and on PM the point S. Using that same radius, describe circles from the centers R and S. From the center I, describe a circle bisecting the intersection of the circles R and P, and a circle bisecting the intersection of the circles P and S, thus establishing a point X on RP, and a point Y on QO. From the center I, construct a line at right angles to NO. The intersection of this line with EC is the point T, and with BF the point U. Thus also have been established a point V on IU and a point W on TI, on the perimeter of the smallest circle I. From the center W, describe a circle intersecting the point P. Using that same radius, describe a circle from the point V. From the center L, describe a circle intersecting X, thus establishing a point Z on HD. From the center M, describe a circle intersecting Y, thus establishing a point *h* on HO. Describe from the center E a circle the diameter of which is ML, thus establishing a point *a* on ET. Draw the straight line *az*, and produce it to *b*. Produce IF its own length to *c*, and beyond *c* to *d*. From the center *c*, describe a circle the diameter of which is ML, thereby establishing a point *e* on *cd*. Describe a similar circle from the center *e*, thereby establishing a point *f* on *ed*. Draw the straight line *c*D, thereby establishing a point *g* on *c*D. From the center *f*, describe a circle tangential to *zb*, and, using the same radius, a circle from the center *g*. From the point *h*, draw a straight line tangential to the circle *g*.

Q.E.F.

[42]

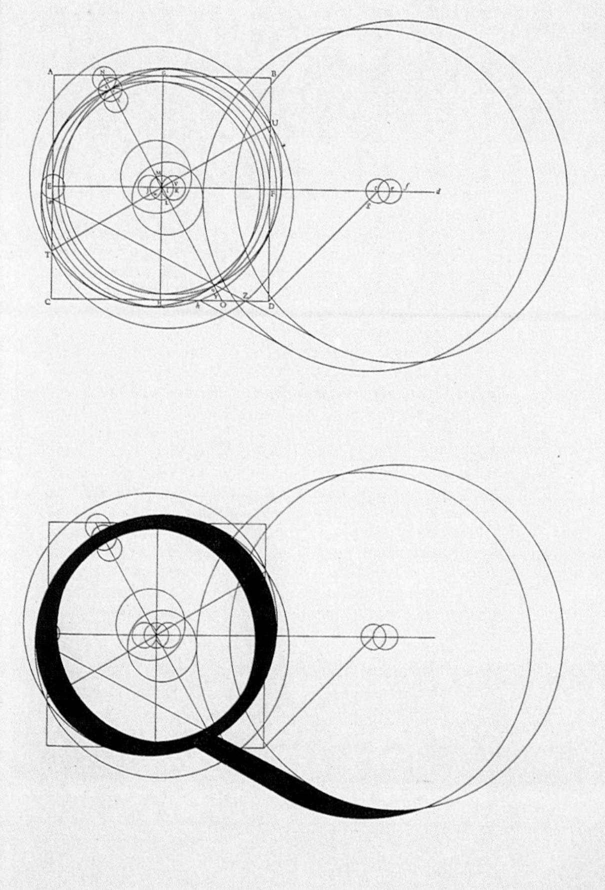

12

Maroon Bells, Colorado

JUNE

B I R T H D A Y S

13

14

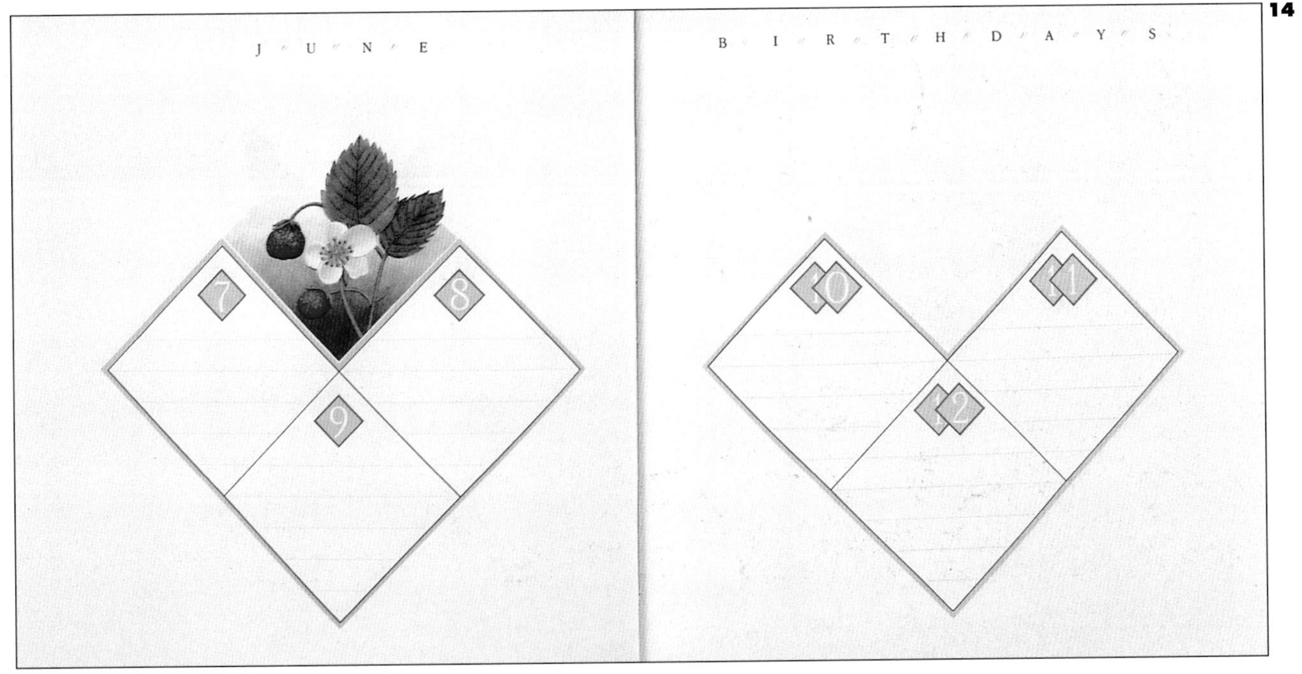

13/14
DESIGN FIRM: *Delessert & Marshall*
DESIGNER: *Rita Marshall*
HEADLINE TYPEFACE: *Brighton Light*
TEXT TYPEFACE: *ITC Garamond Light*
CLIENT: *Stewart, Tabori, & Chang*

15
DESIGN FIRM: *Pentagram*
DESIGNER: *Kit Hinrichs*
HEADLINE TYPEFACE: *Futura Extra Bold*
TEXT TYPEFACE: *Bodoni Book*
CLIENT: *Chronicle Book*

16
DESIGN FIRM: *Jessica Shatan*
DESIGNER: *Jessica Shatan*
HEADLINE TYPEFACE: *Parisian & Trompez*
TEXT TYPEFACE: *Bodoni Book*
CLIENT: *Random House, Inc.*

15

STARS&STRIPES

By Kit Hinrichs

A Celebration of the American Flag by 96 International Designers and Artists

16

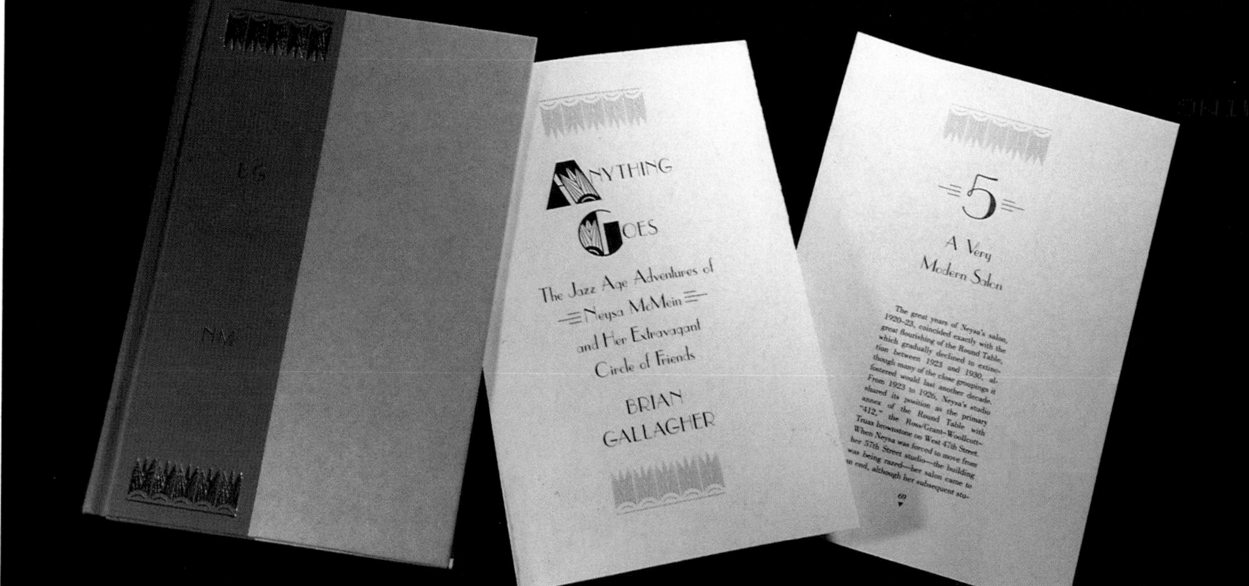

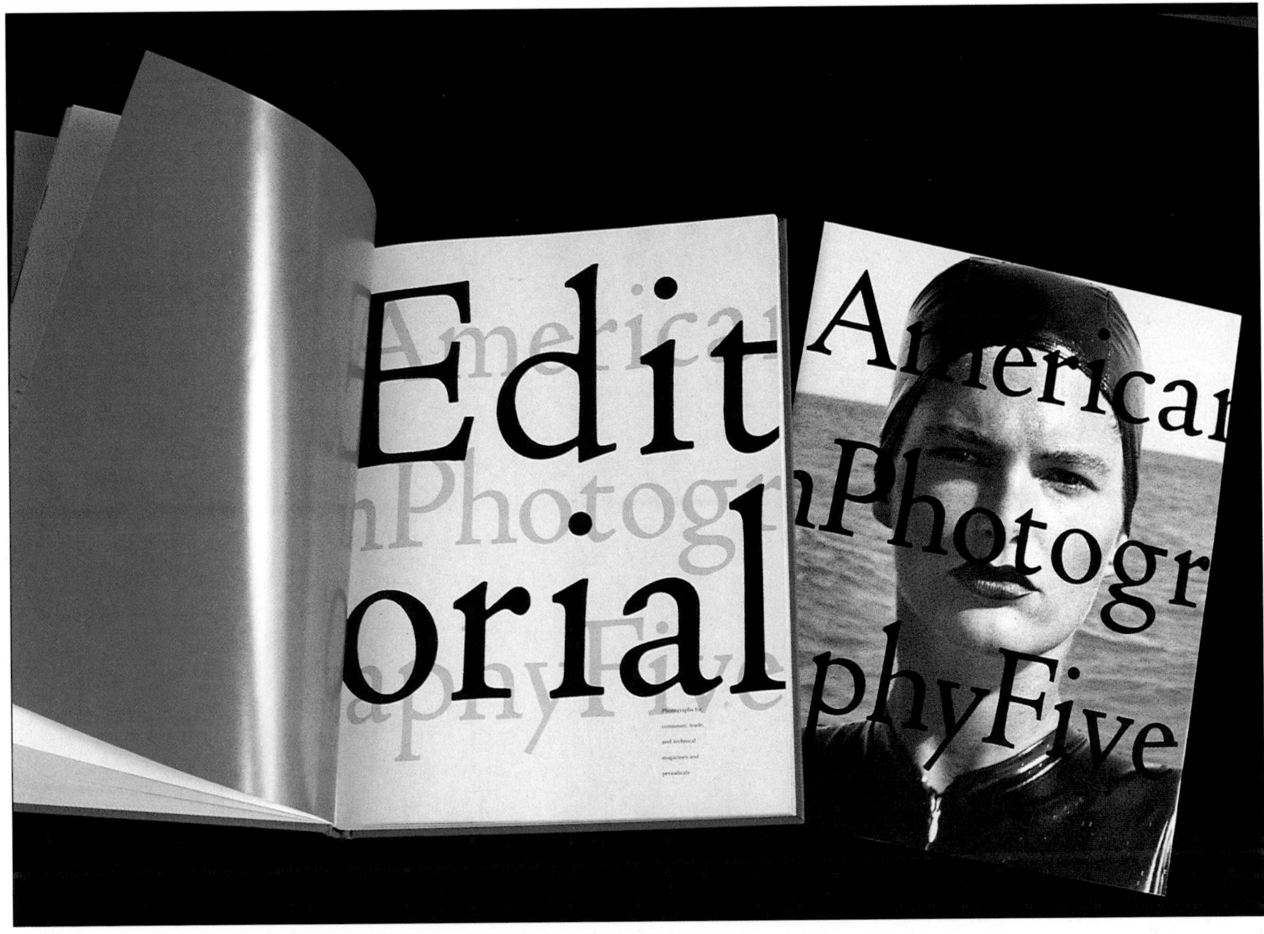

The first request Gulliver made after obtaining his liberty from the Lilliputians was for permission to visit the capital of their empire, the metropolis Mildendo, which lay a short distance – relatively speaking – from the beach where he had been tied. The sight of the city's towers in the not-too-distant distance, the puffs of smoke rising from ten thousand miniature chimneys aroused his curiosity. And, with passport in hand, Gulliver covered the distance between port and town in a couple of careful strides. ■ Sitting on a hillside overlooking Mildendo's walls, Man-Mountain surveys the scene: a model city whose architectural details are familiar in every respect, with the exception of their Lilliputian size. No doubt the view makes this onlooker feel as if he were somewhat out of sync and, no doubt, certain fears cloud his mind – for how will he fill his belly in a world where a farm is no bigger than a flower bed and cattle stand four and a half inches high? But concerns over dislocation fade as he considers the advantages that his unique vantage provides: nearly two centuries before man learns to fly, Gulliver sees an entire city from the sky. In an instant, he grasps the logic of its overall design. ■ BY DOUGLAS BLAU

Brobdingnag

37

17/18
DESIGN FIRM: *Drenttel Doyle Partners*
DESIGNER: *Steven Doyle*
HEADLINE TYPEFACE: *Cloister*
TEXT TYPEFACE: *New Baskerville*
CLIENT: *American Illustration*

19
DESIGN FIRM: *Kan Tai-keung Design & Associates Ltd.*
HEADLINE TYPEFACE: *Century Book*
TEXT TYPEFACE: *Century Book*
CLIENT: *Camera 22 Ltd.*

19

Leong Ka Tai on China: One to Twenty Four

是五年，六年，還是七年？
我的中國旅程始於黃河，下游至渤海，
上溯至源頭；然後走川藏；北京九十日；
「長征」；黃土高原。
在這五，六，或七年中，
難道我只拍了廿四張滿意的照片？
老實說。
經過這五，六，或七年，我的旅程還是剛開始呢。

梁家泰中國影像一至廿四

20

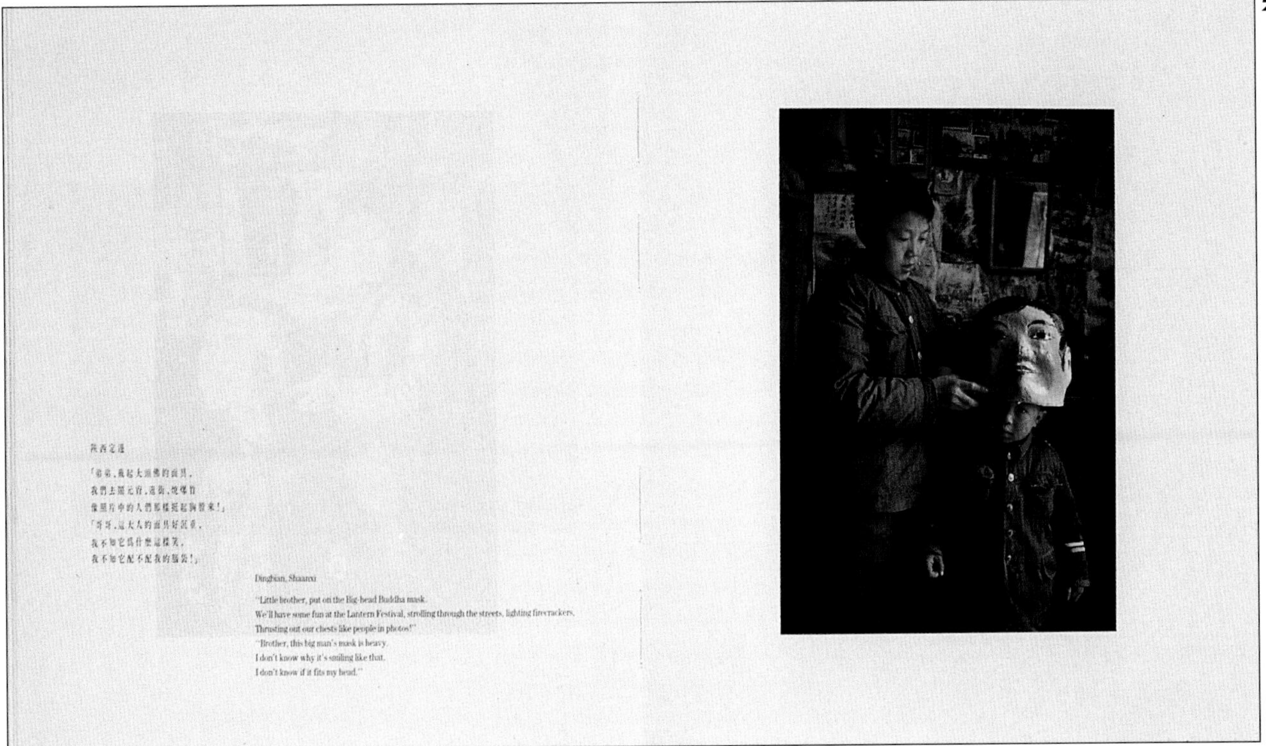

21

22

20
DESIGN FIRM: *Kan Tai-keung Design & Associates Ltd.*
HEADLINE TYPEFACE: *Century Book*
TEXT TYPEFACE: *Century Book*
CLIENT: *Camera 22 Ltd.*

21
DESIGNER FIRM: *Delessert & Marshall*
DESIGNER: *Rita Marshall*
HEADLINE TYPEFACE: *Antique Wood*
TEXT TYPEFACE: *Simonicni Garamond*
CLIENT: *Houghton Mifflin*

22
DESIGN FIRM: *Delessert & Marshall*
DESIGNER: *Rita Marshall*
HEADLINE TYPEFACE: *Antique Wood*
TEXT TYPEFACE: *Simoncini Garamond*
CLIENT: *Houghton Mifflin*

23

24

25

23
DESIGN FIRM: *Delessert & Marshall*
DESIGNER: *Rita Marshall*
HEADLINE TYPEFACE: *Antique Wood*
TEXT TYPEFACE: *Simoncini Garamond*
CLIENT: *Houghton Mifflin*

24/25
DESIGN FIRM: *Pentagram Design*
DESIGNER: *Peter Harrison and Susan Hochbaum*
HEADLINE TYPEFACE: *Garamond*
TEXT TYPEFACE: *Garamond*
CLIENT: *Fannie Mae*

26

THE

FILLYJONK

WHO

BELIEVED

IN

DISASTERS

TOVE

JANSSON

CREATIVE SHORT STORY

26
DESIGN FIRM: *Delessert & Marshall*
DESIGNER: *Rita Marshall*
HEADLINE TYPEFACE: *Bauer Text Initials*
TEXT TYPEFACE: *Simoncini Garamond*
CLIENT: *Creative Education*

27

THE
PARSLEY GARDEN
WILLIAM SAROYAN
CREATIVE SHORT STORY

28

29

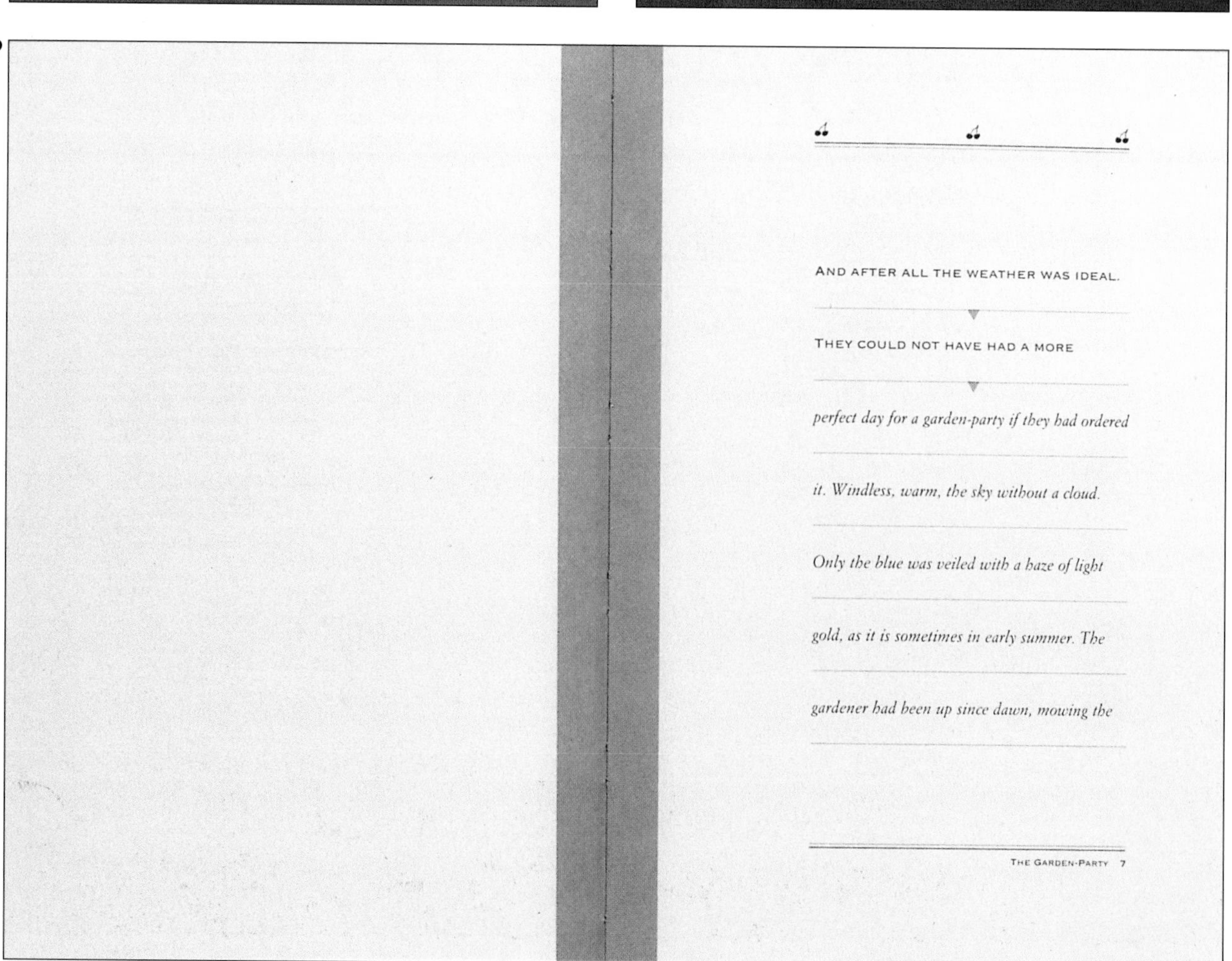

AND AFTER ALL THE WEATHER WAS IDEAL. THEY COULD NOT HAVE HAD A MORE *perfect day for a garden-party if they had ordered it. Windless, warm, the sky without a cloud. Only the blue was veiled with a haze of light gold, as it is sometimes in early summer. The gardener had been up since dawn, mowing the*

THE GARDEN-PARTY 7

27
DESIGN FIRM: *Delessert & Marshall*
DESIGNER: *Rita Marshall*
HEADLINE TYPEFACE: *Bauer Text Initials*
TEXT TYPEFACE: *Simoncini Garamond*
CLIENT: *Creative Education*

28/29
DESIGN FIRM: *Delessert & Marshall*
DESIGNER: *Rita Marshall*
HEADLINE TYPEFACE: *Bauer Text Initials*
TEXT TYPEFACE: *Simoncini Garamond*
CLIENT: *Creative Education*

30

EVELINE

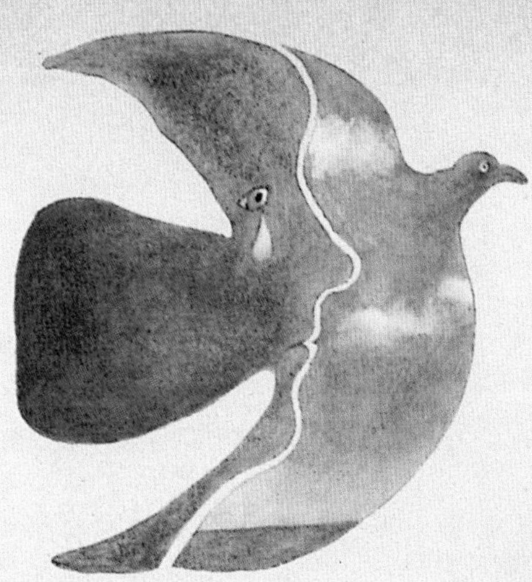

JAMES
JOYCE

CREATIVE
SHORT STORY

30
DESIGN FIRM: *Delessert & Marshall*
DESIGNER: *Rita Marshall*
HEADLINE TYPEFACE: *Bauer Text Initials*
TEXT TYPEFACE: *Simoncini Garamond*
CLIENT: *Creative Education*

31
DESIGNER: *Charles Spencer Anderson*
HEADLINE TYPEFACE: *Various*
TEXT TYPEFACE: *Various*
CLIENT: *Warner Books*

31

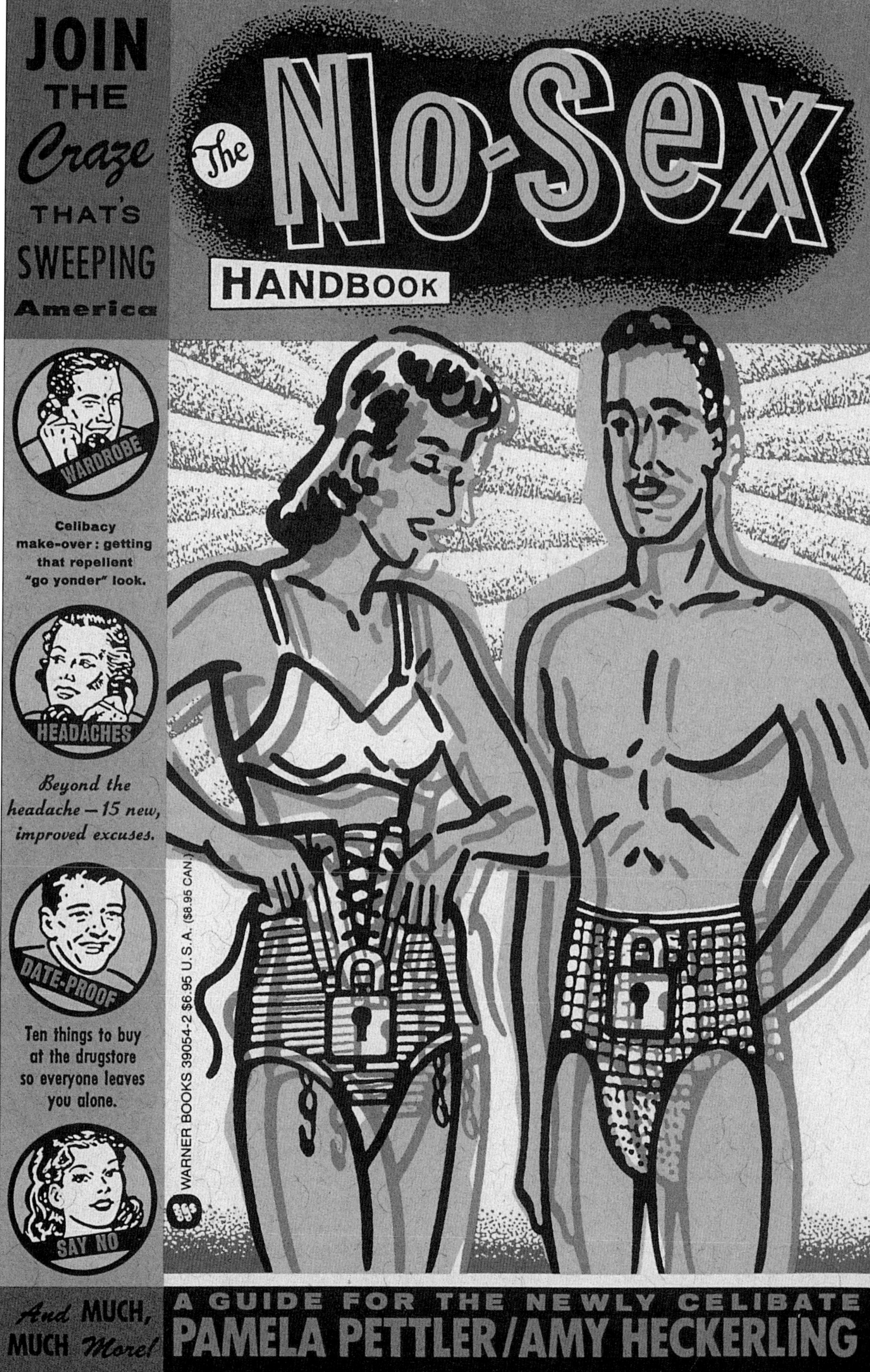

32

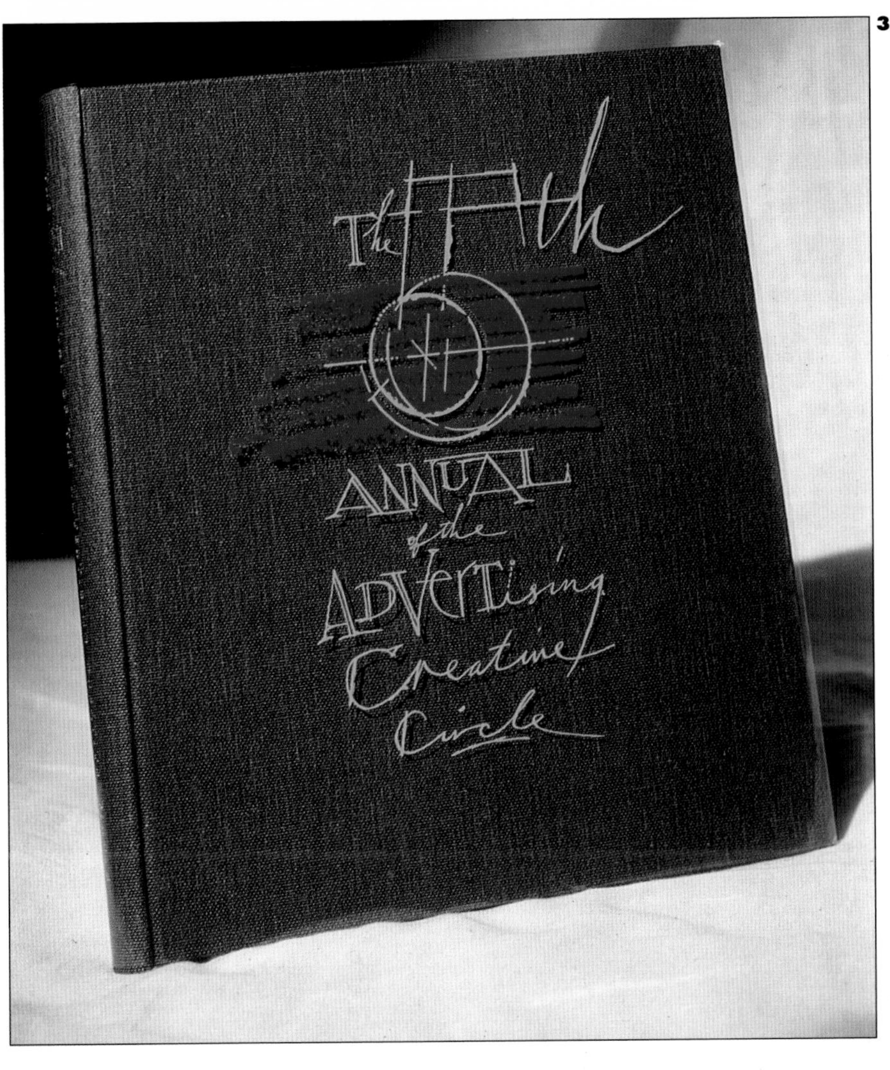

33

32
DESIGN FIRM: *The Consul*
DESIGNER: *Jim Williams and Eric Tilley*
LETTERER: *David Hughes*
TEXT TYPEFACE: *Helvetica and Joanna Italic*
CLIENT: *The Creative Circle*

33
DESIGN FIRM: *Grauerholz Design Inc.*
HEADLINE TYPEFACE: *Franklin Gothic Bold*
TEXT TYPEFACE: *Trade Gothic and Caslon*
CLIENT: *National Gallery of Canada*

34

35

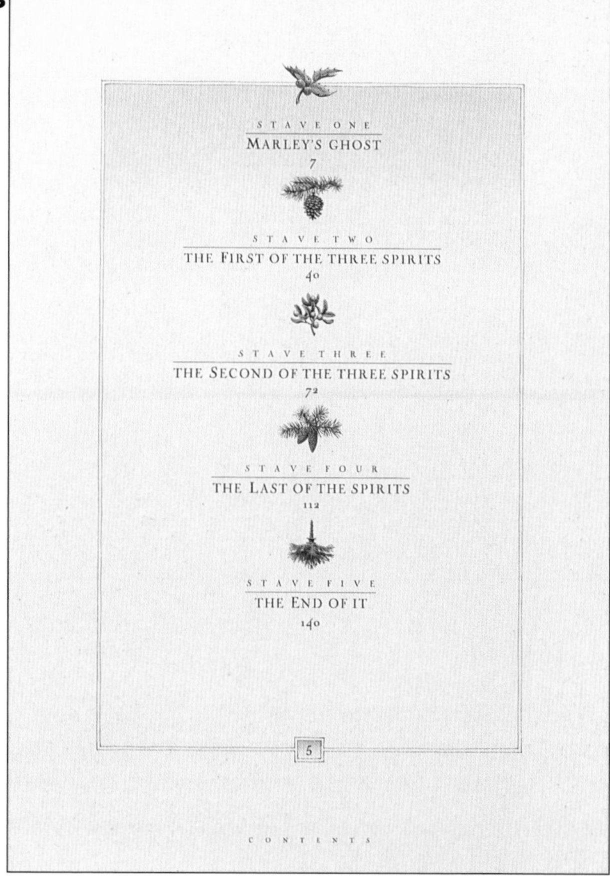

5
CONTENTS

34/35/36
DESIGN FIRM: *Delessert & Marshall*
DESIGNER: *Rita Marshall*
HEADLINE TYPEFACE: *Nicholas Cochin*
TEXT TYPEFACE: *Nicholas Cochin*
CLIENT: *Creative Education*

36

very day of the funeral, and solemnised it with an undoubted bargain.

The mention of Marley's funeral brings me back to the point I started from. There is no doubt that Marley was dead. This must be distinctly understood, or nothing wonderful can come of the story I am going to relate. If we were not perfectly convinced that Hamlet's Father died before the play began, there would be nothing more remarkable in his taking a stroll at night, in an easterly wind, upon his own ramparts, than there would be in any other middle-aged gentleman rashly turning out after dark in a breezy spot—say Saint Paul's Churchyard for instance—literally to astonish his son's weak mind.

Scrooge never painted out Old Marley's name. There it stood, years afterwards, above the warehouse door: Scrooge and Marley. The firm was known as Scrooge and Marley. Sometimes people new to the business called Scrooge Scrooge, and sometimes Marley, but he answered to both names. It was all the same to him.

Oh! But he was a tight-fisted hand at the grindstone, Scrooge! a squeezing, wrenching, grasping, scraping, clutching, covetous old sinner! Hard and sharp as flint, from which no steel had ever struck out generous fire; secret, and self-contained, and solitary as an oyster. The cold within him froze his old features, nipped his pointed nose, shrivelled his cheek, stiffened his gait;

8

MARLEY'S GHOST

37
DESIGN FIRM: *Delessert & Marshall*
DESIGNER: *Rita Marshall*
HEADLINE TYPEFACE: *Antique Wood*
TEXT TYPEFACE: *Simoncini Garamond*
CLIENT: *Creative Education*

PROMOTION

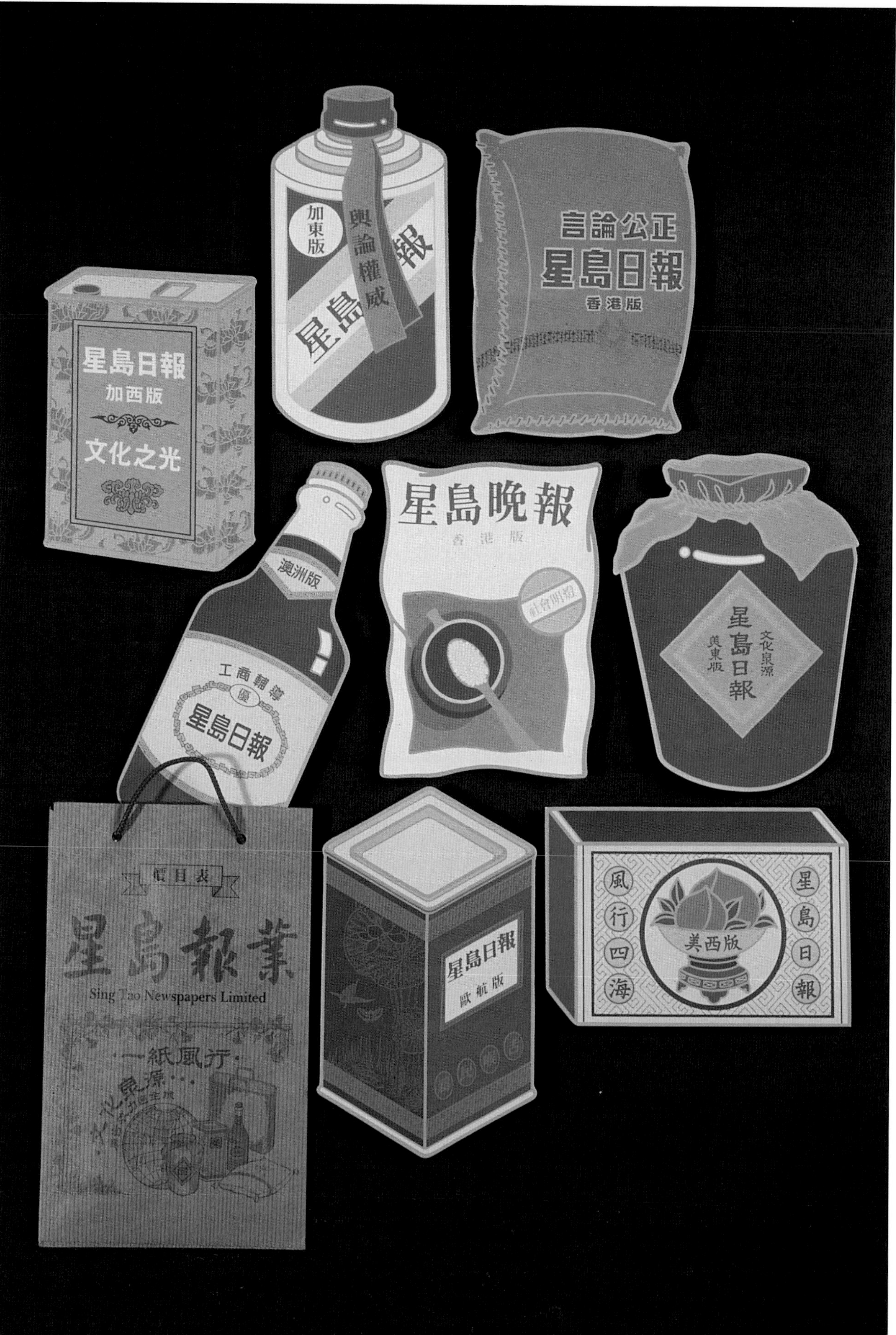

1
DESIGN FIRM: *Kan Tai-keung Design & Associates Ltd.*
DESIGNER: *Kan Tai-keung*
HEADLINE TYPEFACE: *Handlettering, Chinese Calligraphy, and Baskerville Bold*
CLIENT: *Sing Tao Newspapers Ltd.*

2

3

4

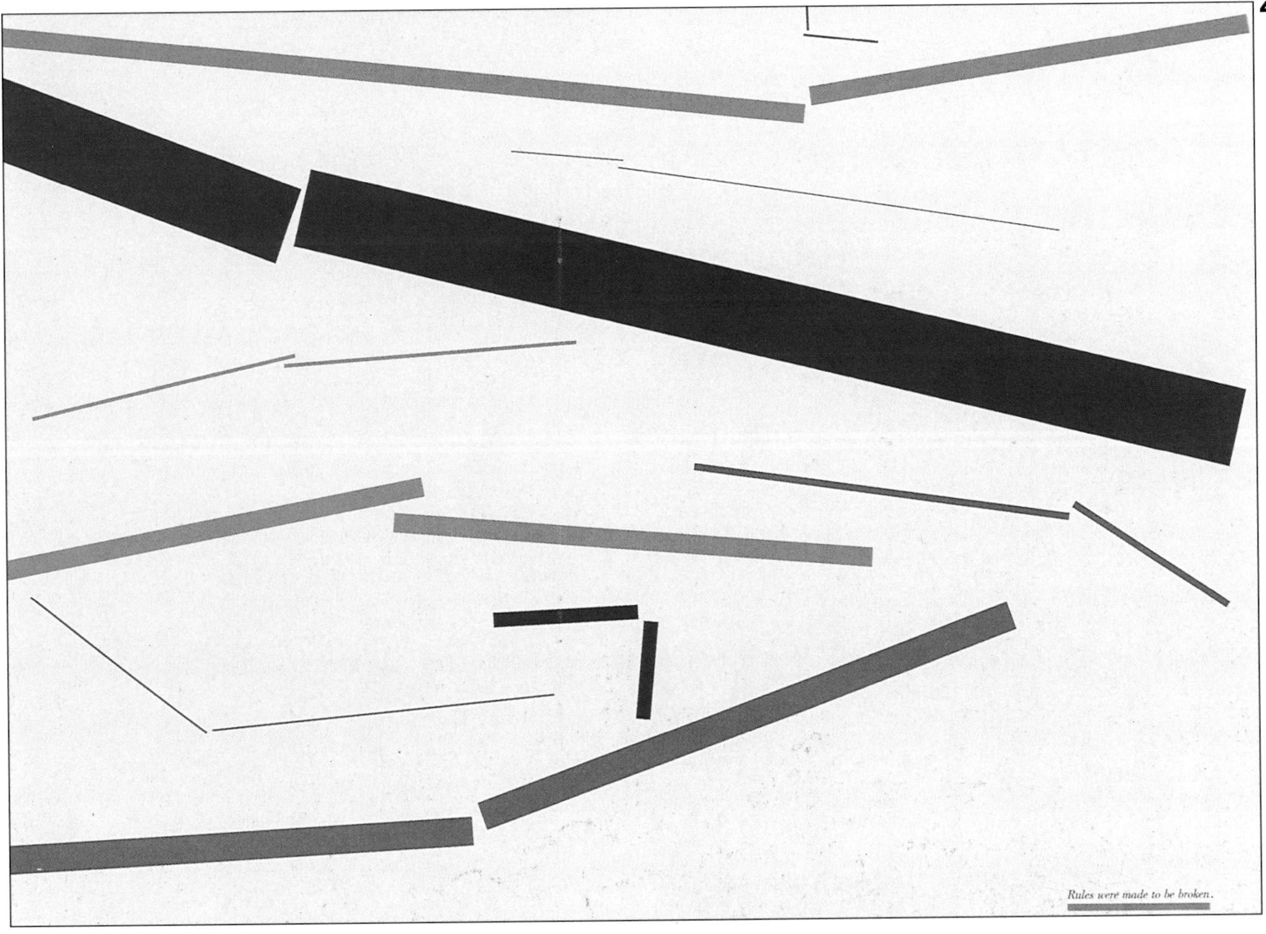

2
DESIGN FIRM: *Summerford Design, Inc.*
DESIGNER: *Jack Summerford*
LETTERER: *Jack Summerford*
CLIENT: *Dallas Society of Visual Communications*

3/4
DESIGN FIRM: *Summerford Design, Inc.*
DESIGNER: *Jack Summerford*
HEADLINE TYPEFACE: *Franklin Gothic Condensed*
TEXT TYPEFACE: *Bodoni*
CLIENT: *Typographers International Association*

5

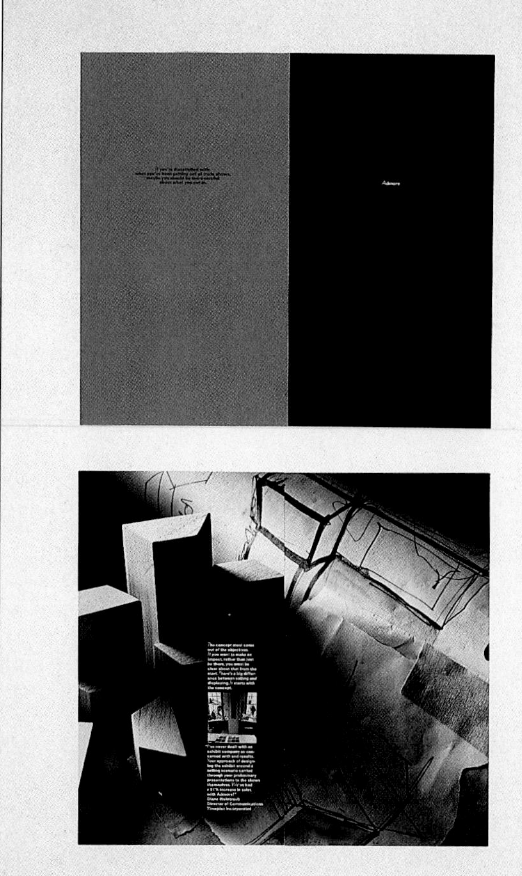

6

"**Design is an attitude.**"
L Moholy-Nagy

"Graphics need to reflect the nature and purpose of the proposition. Design is not merely a matter of 'taste,' it is an understanding of the problem. Does it fulfill the function? Will it capture attention? Can it sustain interest? If the solution doesn't incorporate these criteria then it probably doesn't work – it's really as simple as that. Although graphic design is not necessarily an art, it is even less a science. In the end there is only one universal test, 'Does it work?' and only one universal principle, 'Could it have been better?'" John McConnell

"**For modern advertising and for the modern exponent of the form, the individual element – the artist's 'own touch' – is of absolutely no consequence.**" **El Lissitzky**

"*It is a primary function of the designer to be an innovator: not to impose his fancies on a reluctant market, but to extend the horizons and enhance the lives of the users. It is palpably true that no innovation worthy of the name ever resulted from market research or indeed any other enquiries into people's needs and wants. The true innovator therefore is always the individual, answerable, in the first place at least, only to himself.*" Kenneth Grange

"A design is not to be confused with its end purpose. The end purpose of design is not necessarily aesthetically pleasing; it can be so, it often is so, but it need not be so.

A design is a plan to make something. If the plan works, then the product (not the design, but the product) is appropriate, or truthful, or functional or whatever. If the plan demands aesthetic standards, and it works, then the product is beautiful or elegant or whatever. If the purpose of the plan is to make something which was not there before, and it works, then the designer who is concerned with that process is creative. If the plan needs techniques and skills to succeed, and it succeeds, then the designer can also be complimented as a professional." Peter Gorb

"Design comes from a combination of intelligence and artistic ability. A designer is someone who should solve problems. He is a borrower, co-ordinator, assimilator, juggler, and collector of material, knowledge and thought from the past and present, from other designers, from technology and from himself. His style and individuality come from the consistency of his own attitudes and approach to the expression and communication of a problem. It is a devotion of the designer to the task of fully understanding the problem and then expressing those ideas which come from this search in its appropriate form that make him a professional.

There is a large body of designers, clients and consumers who don't really care very much about very much. The joy and pleasure of doing a good job for its own sake has not been discovered by enough people." Ivan Chermayeff

"As designers we are, as a group, measurably responsible for the visual form of our culture. We are the funnels through which the possibilities of technology and the requirements of trade are expressed in terms of experience of people. Perhaps one of our problems is to learn how to provide people with experiences that will open them to growth. I suppose it is important to make people feel something; not just dangle an image before their eyes, but open up a successful communication and if possible, transform somebody's attitude toward something." Saul Bass

"There is an old romantic idea that intuition and intellect do not mix. There is an equally erroneous belief that inspiration takes the place of industry. Fortified with such misconceptions, it is understandable that we tend to minimize the importance of learning the rules, the fundamentals, which are the raw material of the artist's craft.

In graphic design, as in all creative expression, art evolves from craft. In dancing, craft is mastering the basic steps; in music, it is learning the scales.

In typographic design, craft deals with points, lines, planes, picas, ciceros, leads, quads, serifs, letters, words, folios, pages, signatures, paper, ink, color, printing, and binding.

The vocabulary of form (art) includes, among others: space, proportion, scale, size, shape, rhythm, repetition, sequence, movement, balance, volume, contrast, harmony, order, and simplicity.

Just as there is no art without craft and no craft without rules, so too there is no art without fantasy, without ideas. A child's art is much fantasy but little craft. It is the fusion of the two that makes the difference." Paul Rand

"The thing that is so hard for us to do is look at problems from something other than the designer's point of view. We agonize over the difference between Caledonia and Fairfield. The people that we deal with can hardly tell the difference between typewriter type and Futura. It's hard to get away from limited perspectives that we have. If you are going to be any good as a designer, you have to have a tendency – and I think this is essential – to limit your view." Lou Danziger

"The printed page is not primarily a medium for self-expression. Design for print is not Art. At best it is a highly skilled craft. A sensitive, inventive, interpretive craft, if you will, but in no way related to painting.

The immature avant-garde designer seems bitter about the mainstream of American advertising. He hates the 'hard-sell' and avoids clients who interfere with his freedom. He believes that the role of business should be one of patron of the Arts, and insists that his craft is art.

I do not argue for the return to any form of traditionalism. I do argue for a sense of responsibility on the part of the designer, and a rational understanding of his function.

I think he should avoid designing for designers.

I suggest that the word 'design' be considered as a verb, in the sense that we design something to be communicated to someone." William Golden

"The use of words – their sounds, their meanings, and their collective letterforms – has been an intriguing aspect of design since the invention of the alphabet. Contemporary designers continue to use this play with words in their design concepts. A picture may be worth a thousand words, but as one wit pointed out: It takes words to say that." Allen Hurlburt

"For a number of reasons - good and bad - design is a confusing subject. Among the good reasons is the elusiveness of definition: a person who does a line of dresses for a couturier house and someone who draws a plan for a jet engine are both called designers. Each arrives at solutions within a context: money limitations, materials available, skills and tools at hand, existing state of the art, competition.

A design may be very beautiful, but it is not art; a design has to do something. The artist works to make a kind of visual statement that has, for him, some important connection with reality as he perceives it. The designer needs a client to present a problem, and a factory to make his design in quantity.

The scientist believes that problems can be solved with his intellectual equipment plus instruments. His answers are always quantifiable. The designer goes along with this to a great extent, but he also relies on the evidence of his senses and his intuition. So his work falls somewhere between art and science." George Nelson

"Type is a thing of constant interest . . . It is sometimes a serious and useful tool, employed to deliver a message, sell a specific article or give life to an idea.

At other times it is a plaything that affords personal amusement and recreation. It is fun to produce fresh designs and unexpected ideas with letters and numbers – by themselves, or together with other graphic objects. Type is a medium of philosophical enjoyment. It is interesting to discover typographic rules containing inconsistencies in logic, which are in use only because of tradition. It is also interesting to ponder the origin of these errors, the practical reasons for their perpetuation, and to suggest remedies.

An interest in Type provides a broader knowledge of history, including the appreciation of such related arts as painting, architecture and literature – and even business and politics. This affords opportunity for pleasant romantic indulgence. At the same time, it develops confidence in one's practical ability to specify appropriate type faces to accompany creative work of specific periods.

In short, Type can be a tool, a toy and a teacher; it can provide a means of livelihood, a hobby for relaxation, an intellectual stimulation – and a spiritual satisfaction.

I believe an avid interest in Type necessarily includes a zest for everyday life." Bradbury Thompson

"The designer should not be led in his work by his egotistic urge to offer something radically new, to flatter, to comfort the reader with a sphinx-like enigma, but rather common sense should be the foremost guide in his work. For what may be acceptable to us experts may not be good for the largely untrained readers." Max Caflisch

"Americans, unlike the Europeans, are a homogeneous group made up of many nationalities and ethnic backgrounds. Because of this, we possess the most colorful language in the world. The American language is humorously voluptuous. It is a creative language that thus defies rigid typographical principles and encourages the many means of conceptual typographic exploitation. Precise intellectual design is not our bag; ideation is." Herb Lubalin

7

The preceding spread is a small sampling of work designed and produced by Galarneau, Deaver and Sinn.

Usually in a self-promotional piece of this sort, one is supposed to cover the process of creative problem-solving, understanding the client's communication and marketing objectives, generating results through innovative design, and all of those wonderful things.

But we decided against that, for one simple reason:

We were stuck.

No matter how hard we tried, we just couldn't come up with anything that sounded right.

Which left us with three alternatives:

1. Stick with it. Keep trying until the problem is solved, which would mean holding up the production of this brochure, which in turn would be totally unacceptable because it was already two months overdue.

2. Scrap the whole thing. Admit defeat. Meaning we'd have to find something to fill these two pages. Or delete them altogether. But who ever heard of a 30-page plus cover?

3. Redefine the problem. Who knows, maybe there's an easier solution. Besides, we'd rather spend the time on the board anyway.

We decided to go with number three.

We'll simply state what we believe in, what we do, who we are, and how we do it.

The quotes on the front cover pretty much sum up our thoughts on design—so that takes care of that. We doubt very much anybody can say it better than those guys anyway.

The samples on the following twenty-four pages demonstrate our capabilities.

Which leaves us with only two more things:

Who we are and how we do it.

Now that's simple.

We are Mark Galarneau, Georgia Deaver and Paul Sinn—three designers with a very special interest in type and lettering.

How we do it?

Easy. We work. Hard.

And love every minute of it.

GALARNEAU ★ DEAVER & SINN ★

5

DESIGN FIRM: *Cipriani Kremer Design*
DESIGNER: *Bruce McIntosh and Robert Cipriani*
HEADLINE TYPEFACE: *Univers Black 75*
TEXT TYPEFACE: *Univers Black 75*
CLIENT: *Admore*

6/7

DESIGN FIRM: *Galarneau, Deaver & Sinn Promotions*
DESIGNER: *Mark Galarneau, Paul Sinn, and Georgia Deaver*
HEADLINE TYPEFACE: *Various*
TEXT TYPEFACE: *Century Oldstyle*
CLIENT: *Galarneau, Deaver & Sinn Promotions*

8

Some of the most beautiful horses in the world are raised on the Palouse prairie near Lewiston. The Palouse is home to the famous Appaloosa, the dappled horses bred by the Nez Perce Indians.

Harry Treloar, retired St. Maries safety coordinator, designed this pewter buckle for the St. Maries plywood and sawmill complex.

Proud warriors are a favorite theme on western buckles.

Todd Maddock, Idaho public affairs director, designed this log drive buckle for the Lewiston mill.

Lewiston takes pride in its cowboys and loggers. The town's largest employer, Potlatch manufactures a broad range of forest products including lumber, plywood, household tissue and paperboard at its Lewiston mill complex.

Buckle Art

Belt buckles have moved up a few notches from the days when they were seen as just a means of holding up one's pants. In Idaho forest country, where millworkers regularly wear denims and blue cotton shirts, belt buckles have become a functional art form—so much so, that in recent years, Potlatch issued its own safety award buckles for Lewiston and St. Maries employees. Like quilts, whittled toys, whimsical weather vanes, and other Americana before them, belt buckles carry forth the tradition of practicality combined with simple expressions of everyday life.

Cast from pewter, silver, brass, and sometimes even gold, buckle art frequently depicts themes westerners love most—nature and the land, forest animals, old west legends, cowboy lore and the romance of the forest industry. In fact, belt buckles can literally be a "walking" guide to Idaho.

Weighing as much as 500 pounds, grizzly bears sometimes feed along the Clearwater River.

Gangly but graceful, moose frequently roam on Potlatch forestland.

Logging and mining are key industries in Coeur d'Alene, where Potlatch makes softwood lumber products.

One of the nation's top rodeos, the Lewiston Round-up draws professional cowboys from around the world to the annual fall competition.

The chainsaw, the quintessential tool of every logger, easily earned its place in the buckle art world. This replica was cast in pewter.

Lovers of the great outdoors consider northern Idaho one of the most picturesque places in the world.

Chief Joseph of the Nez Perce tribe tried to keep his people out of the 1884–1887 Indian Wars.

Photography: Henrik Kam Illustration: Gerard Huerta

8 9

9

8
DESIGN FIRM: *Pentagram Design*
DESIGNER: *Kit Hinrichs and Lenore Bartz*
TEXT TYPEFACE: *Times Roman*
CLIENT: *Potlatch Corp.*

9
DESIGN FIRM: *Cipriani Kremer Design*
DESIGNER: *Robert Cipriani and Bruce McIntosh*
LETTERER: *Tony Di Spigna*
HEADLINE TYPEFACE: *Helvetica Regular*
TEXT TYPEFACE: *Helvetica Light and Various*
CLIENT: *Monadnock Paper Mills, Inc.*

10

DESIGN FIRM: *Kan Tai-keung Design & Associates*
DESIGNER: *Lau Siu-hong*
HEADLINE TYPEFACE: *Chinese Calligraphy*
CLIENT: *Yiu Kwai & Wai Ling Candiee*

11/12

DESIGN FIRM: *Summerford Design, Inc.*
DESIGNER: *Jack Summerford*
HEADLINE TYPEFACE: *Garamond #3*
TEXT TYPEFACE: *Garamond #3*
CLIENT: *Heritage Press*

10

11 12

13

13

DESIGN FIRM: *Summerford Design, Inc.*
DESIGNER: *Jack Summerford*
HEADLINE TYPEFACE: *Goudy Oldstyle*
CLIENT: *Weir Bros, Inc.*

14

GREAT
BEGINNINGS

THE
METAMORPHOSIS
1919

1

As Gregor Samsa awoke one morning from **uneasy** dreams he found himself transformed in his bed into a **gigantic** insect. He was lying on his hard, as it were **armor-plated**, back and when he lifted his head a little he could see his **dome-like** brown belly divided into stiff arched **segments** on top of which the bed **quilt** could hardly keep in position and was about to slide off completely. His numerous **legs**, which were pitifully thin compared to the rest of his bulk, waved **helplessly** before his **eyes**

FRANZ KAFKA

15

GREAT
BEGINNINGS

Faust
1832

You come back, wavering shapes,
out of the past
In which you first appeared to
clouded eyes.
Should I attempt this time to
hold you fast?
Does this old dream still thrill a
heart so wise?
You crowd? You press? Have, then,
your way at last.

As from the mist around me you arise;
My breast is stirred and feels
with youthful pain
The magic breath that hovers
round your train.

With you return pictures of
joyous days,
Shadows that I once loved again
draw near;
Like a primeval tale, half lost
in haze,
First love and friendship
also reappear;

14/15
DESIGN FIRM: *Koppel & Scher*
DESIGNER: *Paula Scher*
HEADLINE TYPEFACE: *Various*
TEXT TYPEFACE: *Various*
CLIENT: *Koppel & Scher*

16

GREAT BEGINNINGS

PART ONE

1

Early one evening, during an exceptional heat wave in the beginning of July, a young man walked out into the street from the closetlike room he rented on Stoliarny Place. Slowly, as though he could not make up his mind, he began to move in the direction of the Kokushkin Bridge.

He had managed to avoid meeting his landlady on the stairs. He lived practically under the roof of a five-floor house, in what was more a cupboard than a room. In an apartment one flight below lived his landlady, from whom he rented this garret, dinner and service thrown in. Every time he went out he had to pass her kitchen door, which almost always stood open facing the stairs.

FYODOR DOSTOYEVSKY

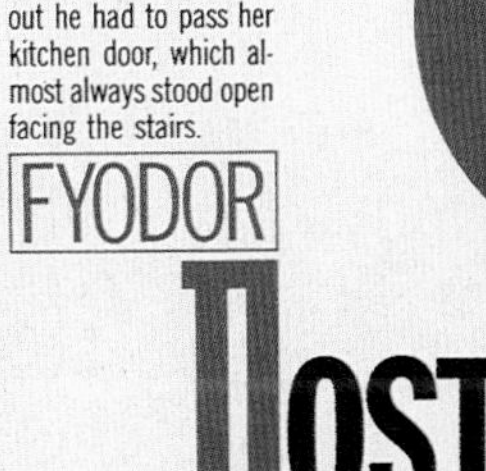

17

GREAT BEGINNINGS

THE MAGIC MOUNTAIN

1924

CHAPTER 1

ARRIVAL.

An unassuming young man was travelling, in midsummer, from his native city of Hamburg to Davos-Platz in the Canton of the Grisons, on a three weeks' visit.

From Hamburg to Davos is a long journey—too long, indeed, for so brief a stay. It crosses all sorts of country; goes up hill and down dale, descends from the plateau of Southern Germany to the shore of Lake Constance, over its bounding waves and on across marshes once thought to be bottomless.

THOMAS MANN

16/17
DESIGN FIRM: *Koppel & Scher*
DESIGNER: *Paula Scher*
HEADLINE TYPEFACE: *Various*
TEXT TYPEFACE: *Various*
CLIENT: *Koppel & Scher*

18

19

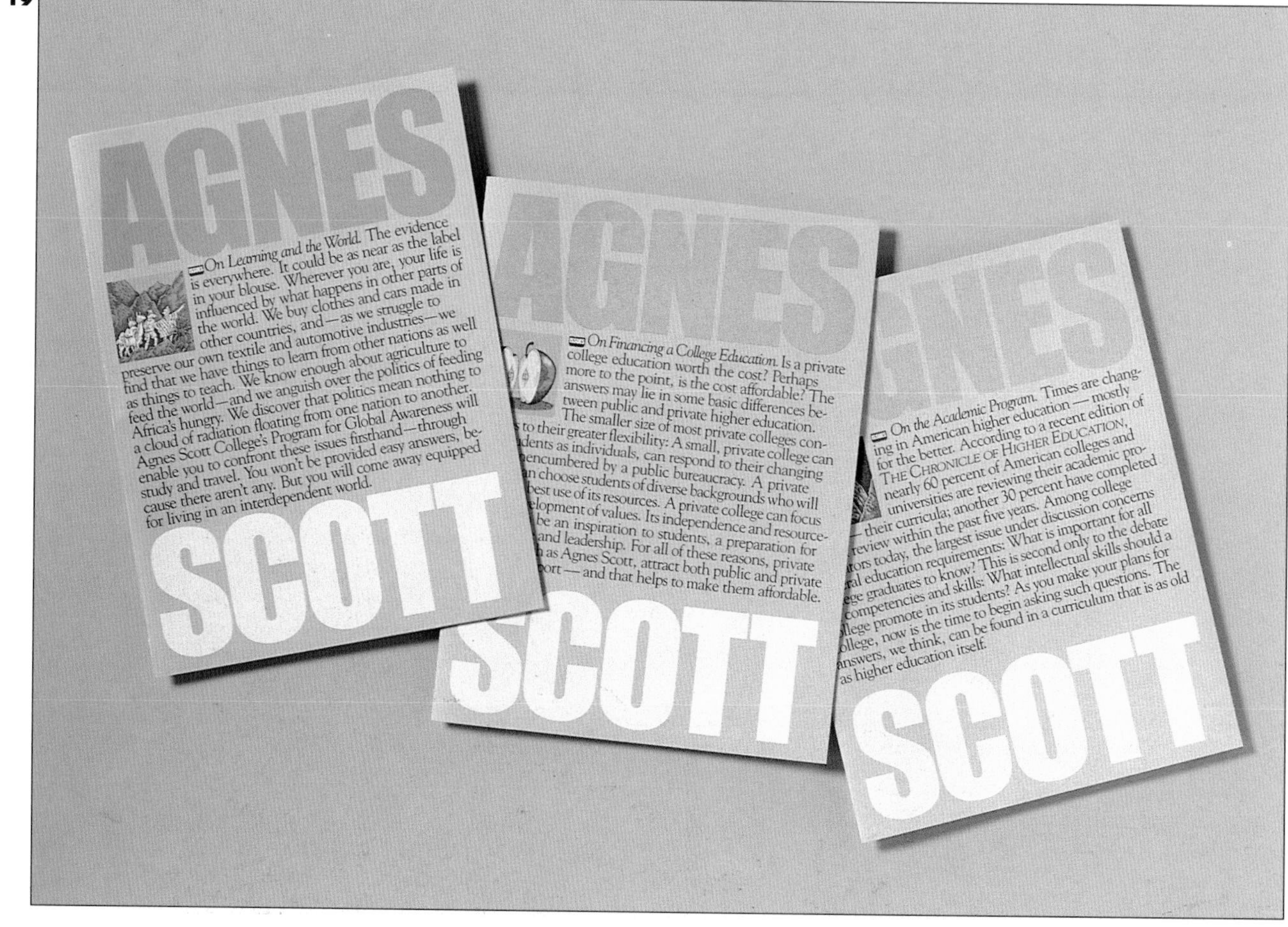

18
DESIGN FIRM: *Jonson, Pedersen, Hinrichs, & Shakery*
DESIGNER: *Adrian Pulfer*
TEXT TYPEFACE: *Futura Bold Condensed*
CLIENT: *Hopper Papers*

19
DESIGN FIRM: *The North Charles Street Design Organization*
CLIENT: *Agnes Scott College*

20

21

22

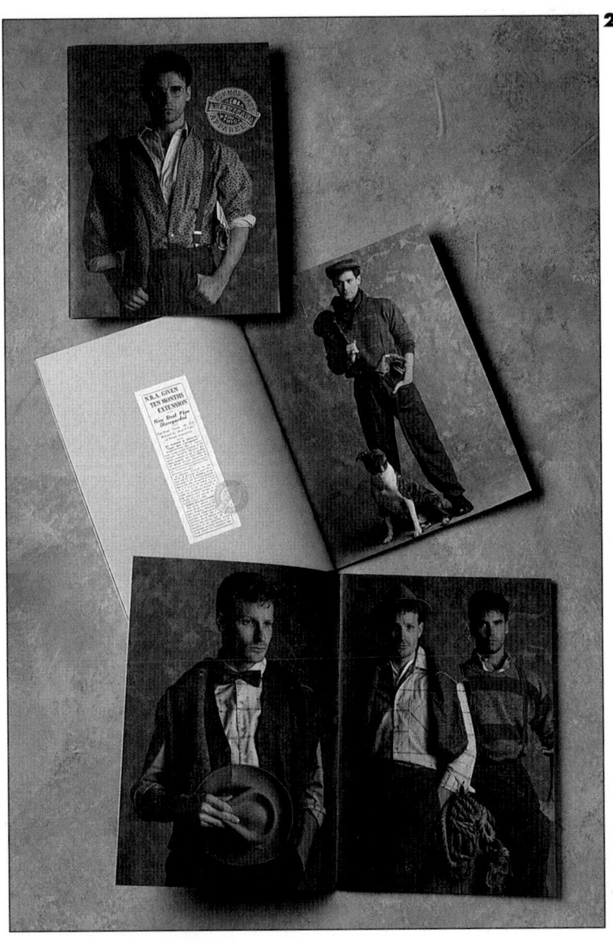

20/21
DESIGN FIRM: *Cipriani Kremer Design*
DESIGNER: *Bruce McIntosh and Robert Cipriani*
HEADLINE TYPEFACE: *Administer Bold*
TEXT TYPEFACE: *Administer*
CLIENT: *Monadnock Paper Mills, Inc.*

22
DESIGN FIRM: *Morla Design*
DESIGNER: *Jennifer Morla*
HEADLINE TYPEFACE: *Typewriter, Univers 49, 53, 47, and Garfield*
CLIENT: *Common Man's Apparel*

23

24

25

FIGHT NIGHT™

FROM ACCOLADE™

23
DESIGN FIRM: *Pentagram Design*
DESIGNER: *Kit Hinrichs and Franca Bator*
HEADLINE TYPEFACE: *Franklin Gothic Extra Condensed*
TEXT TYPEFACE: *Garamond*
CLIENT: *Simpson Paper Company*

24
DESIGN FIRM: *Morla Design*
DESIGNER: *Jennifer Morla*
HEADLINE TYPEFACE: *Univers 49*
TEXT TYPEFACE: *Futura Bold and Futura Extra Bold*
CLIENT: *Phil and Jean Makanna*

25
DESIGN FIRM: *Galarneau & Sinn Ltd.*
DESIGNER: *Mark Galarneau*
HEADLINE TYPEFACE: *ITC American Typewriter Medium*
TEXT TYPEFACE: *ITC American Typewriter Light Condensed*
CLIENT: *Accolade*

26

Sucker Punch. Just when you think you've got their number, watch out for their SUPER PUNCH—a sucker punch that will pulverize you into literal oblivion. These are street smart fighters who will do anything and everything necessary to win: Dip Stick gives new meaning to the word "low-blow;" British Bulldog has a rail roundhouse, 360 jump-spin punch that's deadly; Hu Him is not above throwing a surprise karate kick; Kid Kastro has perfected a double-fisted head punch and the Bronx Bomber has a hammer blow that pummels most men to a pulp. **Build Your Own Boxer.** The magic of Fight Night's boxing construction set is the thrill of creating and training that special fighter who you believe is invincible. Carefully choose his head, body, legs, trunks, gloves and name. Perhaps you'll opt for the thickly muscled torso of a power slugger, a slender but agile defender of a completely unpredictable fighter with great endurance.

27

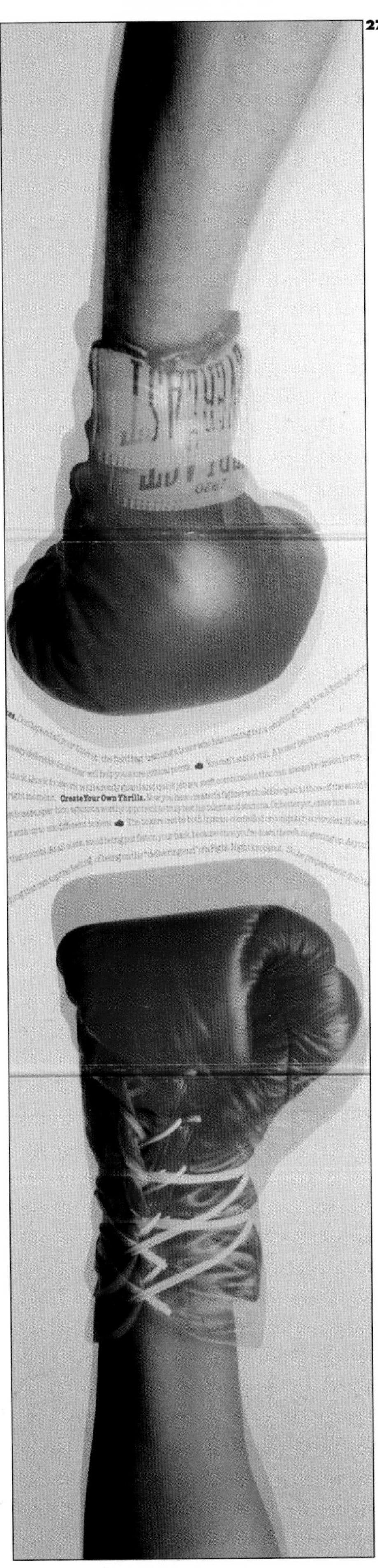

26/ 27
DESIGN FIRM: *Galarneau & Sinn Ltd.*
DESIGNER: *Mark Galarneau*
HEADLINE TYPEFACE: *ITC American Typewriter Medium*
TEXT TYPEFACE: *ITC American Typewriter Light Condensed*
CLIENT: *Accolade*

28

28
DESIGN FIRM: *Jonson, Pederson, Hinrichs, & Shakery*
DESIGNER: *Adrian Pulfer*
TEXT TYPEFACE: *Futura Bold Condensed*
CLIENT: *Hopper Papers*

29
DESIGN FIRM: *Pentagram Design*
DESIGNER: *Kit Hinrichs and Lenore Bartz*
HEADLINE TYPEFACE: *Times Roman*
TEXT TYPEFACE: *Times Roman*
CLIENT: *Potlatch Corp.*

29

Paper Forgeries

Forgery has threatened the integrity of historical records since ancient times. In fact, it has thrived since humans learned to scratch their thoughts on clay tablets in the bazaars of Mesopotamia over 5,000 years ago. But paper—the very medium that makes modern forgery possible—also presents the would-be forger with a variety of pitfalls.

As every mystery buff knows, paper often betrays the forger of phony wills and fraudulent deeds. It's one of the first clues an expert checks when trying to solve a suspected forgery.

The process of papermaking has changed in so many subtle ways over the centuries that an analysis of paper can reveal significant information, sometimes as specific as the approximate time and place the paper was made. There are a myriad of clues invisible to the novice. Manufacturers differ in their use of wood and rag fibers—aspen, for instance, didn't come into use until the 1950s. Coatings, inks and calendering processes also change regularly.

As a result, a successful forger must be intimately familiar with the history of papermaking. Especially when dealing with historical documents, a single oversight can prove fatal. For example, George Washington could not have written on wood-pulp paper, because wood pulp was unknown in his day.

Watermarks also can expose a forgery. These designs, produced by a wire-covered "dandy roll" on a paper machine and carefully cataloged by manufacturers, can be used to trace the origin of a paper sample, often to a particular mill during a specific time period.

One well-known example, Tennessee's Cloth-Garrett inheritance case of 1913, hinged on the authenticity of a will, dated 1898, which was written on a sheet of paper watermarked "W S & B REGENT BOND." All seemed to be in order until the paper's manufacturer, Southworth Paper Co., revealed that prior to the year 1900 that brand always had been marked "REGENT BOND W S & B."

Although only 17 years old, William Henry Ireland understood the importance of paper in a credible forgery. In the 18th century, young Ireland shocked England by "discovering" a secret stash of documents belonging to William Shakespeare. Seemingly authentic in every detail, they included everything from sales receipts signed by the poet himself to "Vortigern and Rowena," a previously "unknown" play.

Ireland became an instant celebrity. But he knew what everyone around him was too excited to notice—that the documents were mere forgeries, the products of his own youthful imagination and painstaking research.

Ireland's hoax began innocently enough. Prompted by his father's avid interest in Shakespeare's works, young Ireland decided to counterfeit the bard's signature and persuade the old man of its authenticity. "It occurred to me," he explained years later, "that if some old writing could be produced, and passed for Shakespeare's, it might occasion a little mirth, and shew (sic) how far credulity would go in the search for antiquities."

Even Ireland himself could not have guessed how far that was.

He decided to start by forging Shakespeare's signature to a land deed—a relatively simple task. After studying Shakespeare's handwriting, Ireland obtained a scrap of aging vellum and a recipe for a special ink which, mixed with a few drops of acid, could pass for that used in the days of the Spanish Armada. Armed with these unassuming weapons, he produced a document that looked for all the world like a relic from the Elizabethan age.

Ireland's painstaking study of the paper of Shakespeare's day paid off. Eighteenth-century England initially hailed his Shakespearean forgeries as "the find of the ages."

Ireland's father, a noted printer and engraver, was elated by his son's "discovery." But the game soon got out of hand. Word of the find spread quickly, along with rumors that the lad had access to an extensive cache of lost Shakespearean documents. Caught up in the excitement, and unable to explain the source of his discovery, Ireland was trapped by his own success.

For a time, he was able to stay a step or two ahead of his growing army of admirers. Switching from vellum to paper, he began churning out large numbers of letters, contracts, notes and receipts, all of them allegedly written or signed by the Bard of Avon. He even forged a love letter from Anne Hathaway to Shakespeare, adding a lock of hair to make it appear more genuine.

Unlike many older, more experienced forgers, this youngster did his homework, and his research paid off. Aware that paper samples can be dated by means of watermarks, Ireland frequented old bookstores in search of appropriate writing materials. He was rewarded by finding a supply of ledger books from Shakespeare's time whose blank flyleaves served his purposes well.

Later, learning that the jug symbol was a commonly used watermark during the Elizabethan era, Ireland watched for that sign on his secretive shopping expeditions. But, leery of attracting too much attention to the watermark itself, he carefully intermingled watermarked sheets with blank, unmarked leaves in his forged documents. The experts never noticed the deception.

The scam might have worked if Ireland had been content with mere forgeries. But success went to his head. He decided that a man who could copy Shakespeare's handwriting so convincingly could mimic his style, as well.

At first, Ireland's literary efforts were remarkably successful. His forgery of a "lost" version of "King Lear," com-

16 17

30

31

30
DESIGN FIRM: *Pentagram Design*
DESIGNER: *Kit Hinrichs, D. J. Hyde, and Lenore Bartz*
HEADLINE TYPEFACE: *Various*
TEXT TYPEFACE: *Various*
CLIENT: *Chronicle Books Publishing*

31
DESIGN FIRM: *Pentagram Design*
DESIGNER: *Linda Hinrichs and Natalie Kitamura*
HEADLINE TYPEFACE: *Bodoni Book*
TEXT TYPEFACE: *Bodoni Book*
CLIENT: *Logo Paris*

32

33

ACE OF ACES

ACCOLADE™

32
DESIGN FIRM: *Pentagram Design*
DESIGNER: *Kit Hinrichs*
HEADLINE TYPEFACE: *Onyx*
TEXT TYPEFACE: *Century Old Style*
CLIENT: *Pentagram Design*

33
DESIGN FIRM: *Galarneau & Sinn Ltd.*
DESIGNER: *Mark Galarneau*
HEADLINE TYPEFACE: *ITC Bookman*
TEXT TYPEFACE: *ITC Cheltenham*
CLIENT: *Accolade*

34/35
DESIGN FIRM: *Galarneau & Sinn Ltd.*
DESIGNER: *Mark Galarneau*
HEADLINE TYPEFACE: *ITC Bookman*
TEXT TYPEFACE: *ITC Cheltenham*
CLIENT: *Accolade*

36
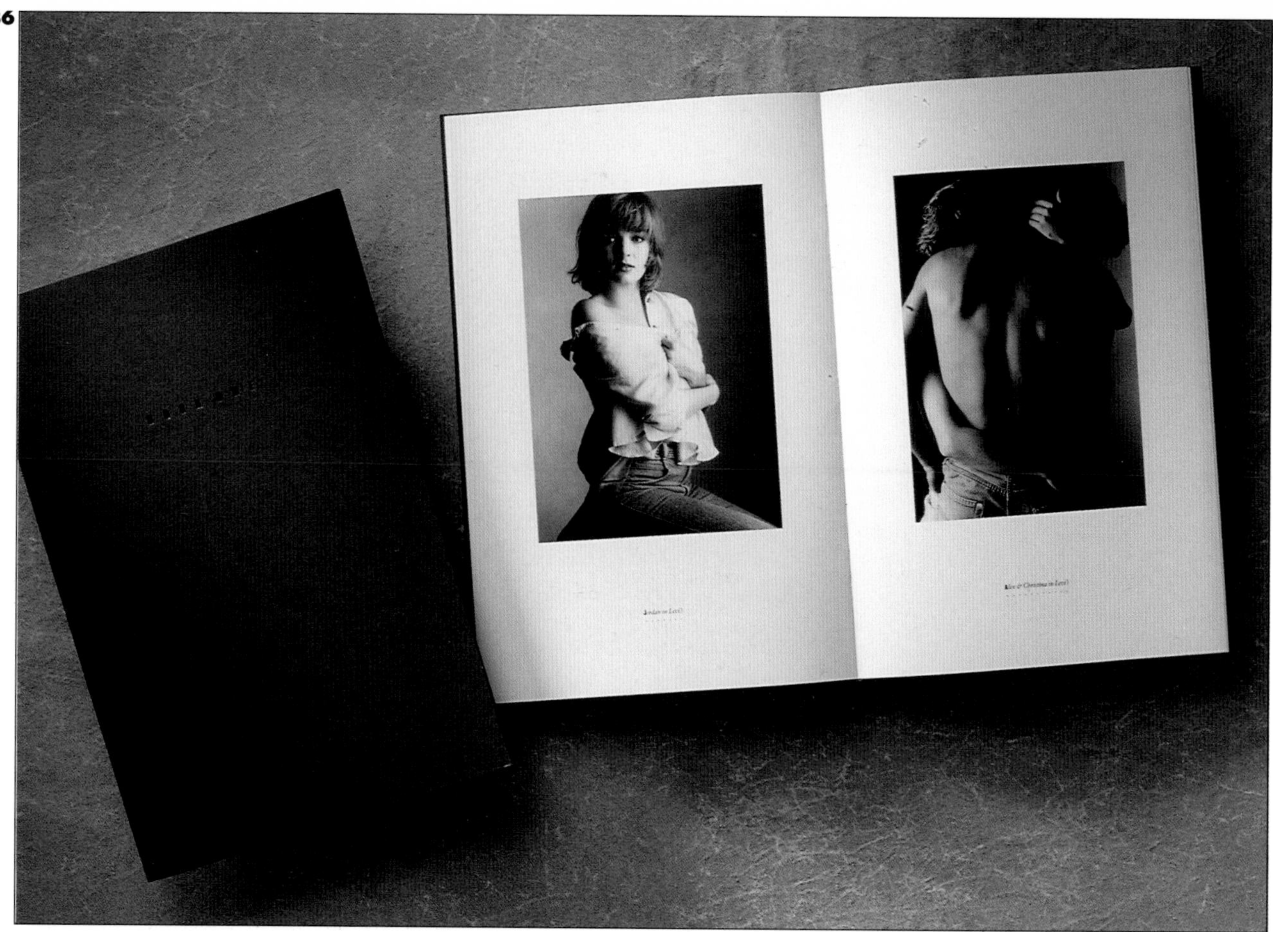

37

36
DESIGN FIRM: *Adrian Parry*
DESIGNER: *Adrian Pulfer and Jeff Streeper*
HEADLINE TYPEFACE: *Folio Bold Condensed*
TEXT TYPEFACE: *Janson Italic*
CLIENT: *ByBee Studios*

37
DESIGN FIRM: *Lisa Levin Design*
DESIGNER: *Lisa Levin*
TEXT TYPEFACE: *Trade Gothic Condensed*
CLIENT: *Cole Martinez Curtis*

38

39

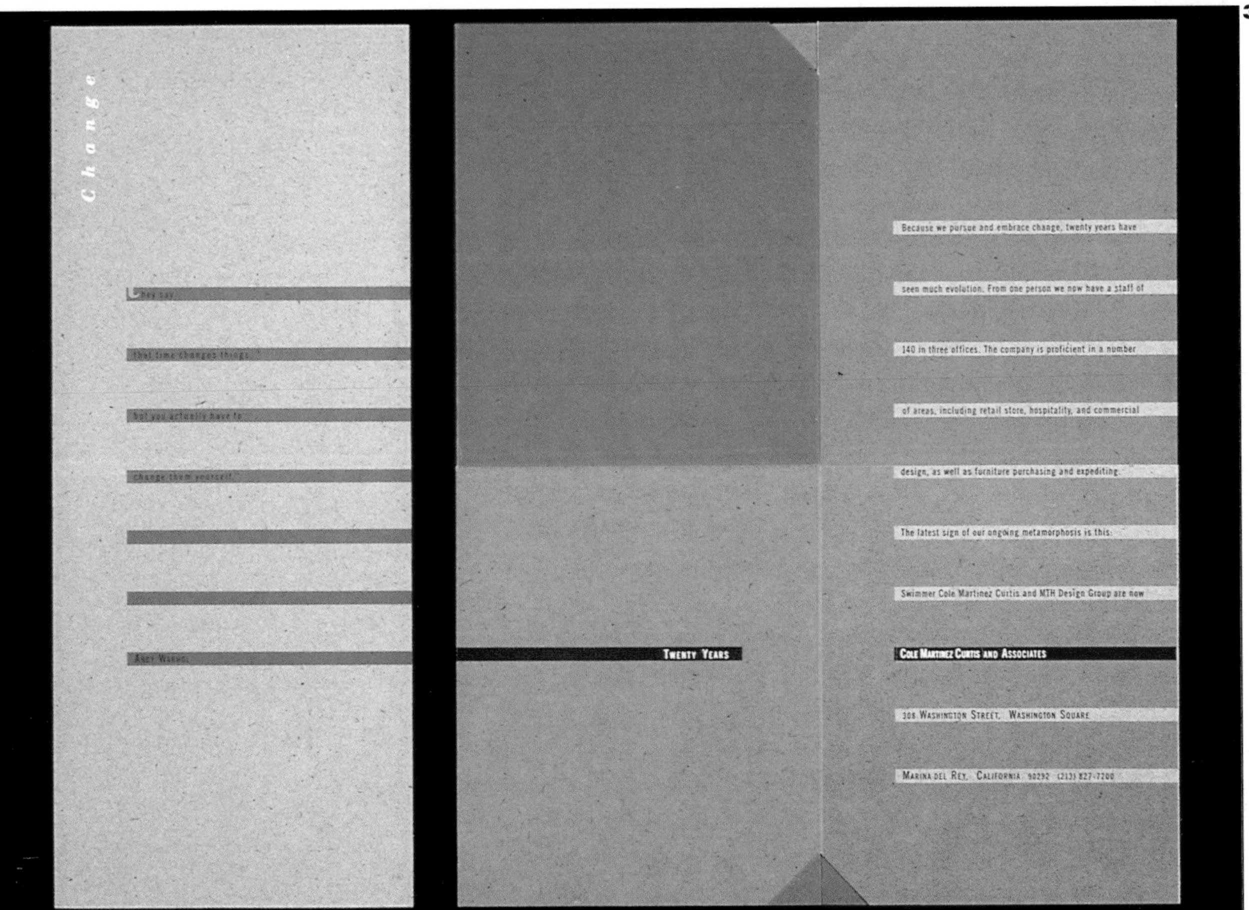

38/39
DESIGN FIRM: *Lisa Levin Design*
DESIGNER: *Lisa Levin*
TEXT TYPEFACE: *Trade Gothic Condensed*
CLIENT: *Cole Martinez Curtis*

40
DESIGN FIRM: *Northeastern University Publication*
DESIGNER: *Corey McPherson*
HEADLINE TYPEFACE: *Trade Gothic*
TEXT TYPEFACE: *Times Roman*
CLIENT: *Art Directors Club of Boston*

41
DESIGN FIRM: *Peterson & Company*
DESIGNER: *Scott Ray*
TEXT TYPEFACE: *Futura*
CLIENT: *Peterson & Company*

42
DESIGN FIRM: *The North Charles Street Design Organization*
HEADLINE TYPEFACE: *Goudy Oldstyle*
CLIENT: *Vassar College*

40

41

42

43
DESIGN FIRM: *The Duffy Design Group*
DESIGNER: *Charles S. Anderson*
HEADLINE TYPEFACE: *Garamond and Handlettering*
CLIENT: *Wenger Corp.*

44

45

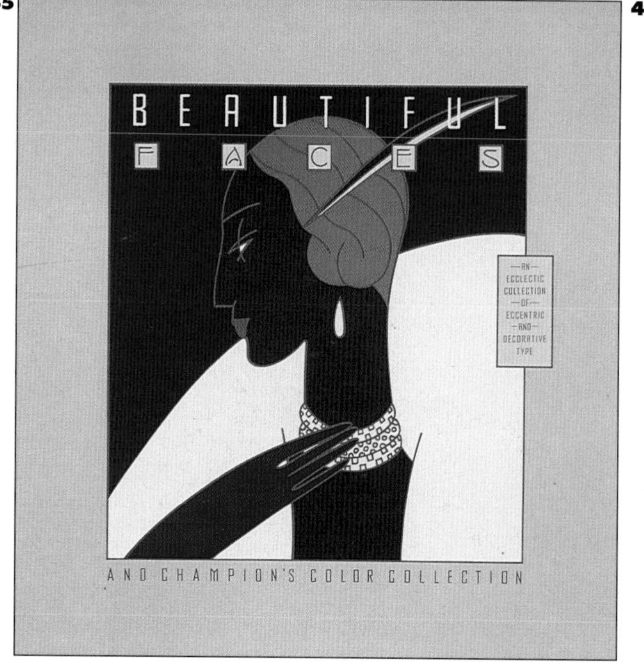

46

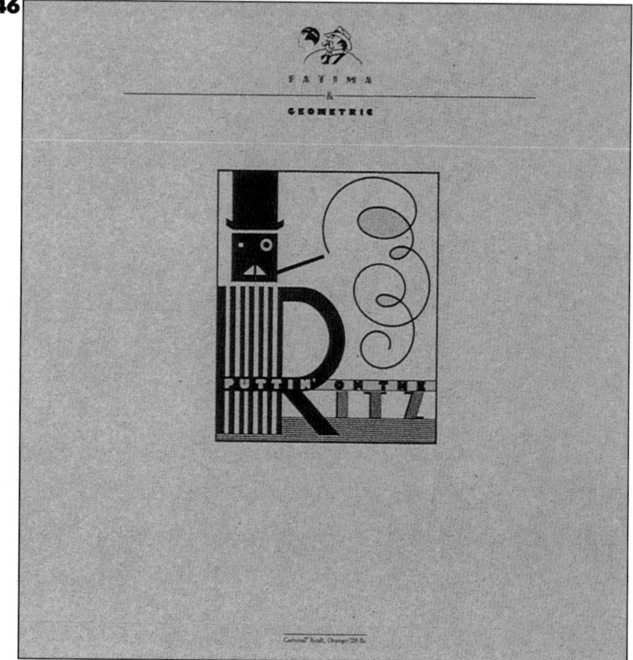

44
DESIGN FIRM: *The North Charles Street Design Organization*
CLIENT: *Vassar College*

45/46
DESIGN FIRM: *Pentagram Design*
DESIGNER: *Paula Scher*
HEADLINE TYPEFACE: *Various*
TEXT TYPEFACE: *Bodoni Book*
CLIENT: *Champion International*

47

T I M E

MAKING NEWS

MERIDIAN SL-100 GIVES TIME INC. THE POWER TO COMMUNICATE.

America's appetite for information is insatiable. World and national news. Sports. Pop culture. Business and finance. Tips on raising children. Ideas for home entertainment. We want to know it all. And one company—Time Inc.—has been satisfying this need to know longer and more completely than many news organizations in the United States.

Sixty-four years ago, the company published the nation's first newsmagazine, *Time*. It followed with *Life*, the icon of photojournalism, now in its 51st year of publication. Today Time Inc. reaches 100 million readers with a portfolio of 17 magazines, among them *Sports Illustrated*, *People*, *McCall's*, *Fortune*, *Parenting* and *Southern Living*. Add Home Box Office (HBO) and Cinemax cable television, Time-Life Books, Book-of-the-Month Club and various other enterprises to its list of activities, and you get an even broader picture of the impact Time Inc. wields in informing, entertaining and influencing our society.

Headquartered in the Time & Life Building in New York City, Time Inc. is a tower of information. The 47-story building at Rockefeller Center is where the communication network is managed and where news from around the globe is filed, written, edited and published. The magazines are printed in plants throughout the U.S.

THE POWER TO COMMUNICATE

With so many Americans—and legions of foreign subscribers—relying on Time Inc. for quick and accurate communications, it is imperative that the company itself maintain quick and accurate communications within the organization and with the outside world.

Much of Time Inc.'s power to communicate comes from a new telecommunication system at its New York headquarters—Northern Telecom's Meridian SL-100 integrated services network. (Four of the company's regional offices are equipped with smaller Meridian SL-1s.)

After two years of extensive collaboration between Time Inc.'s communications department and Northern Telecom, the installation of the SL-100 in the Time & Life Building was completed in January 1987. Says Assistant Communications Manager Frank Ferrara, "Northern Telecom was very good during installation. They worked very well with the additional contractors. When you're dealing with six or seven different types of trades, problems do come up." Currently the system is equipped with 4,500 phones and wired for 8,000.

With the SL-100, the corporation has a system it may never outgrow. The SL-100 has a capacity for up to 30,000 lines, but "there is no way we would ever get 30,000 lines in this building," says Bob Varisco, Time Inc.'s director of communications. He adds that everything is in place—a reliable and powerful switch, fiber optics cable, environmental specs—to handle as much growth as the building can accommodate.

"NORTHERN TELECOM WAS VERY GOOD DURING INSTALLATION. THEY WORKED WELL WITH ADDITIONAL CONTRACTORS."

Time Inc.'s magazines and books are religiously read by millions of subscribers around the world.

12

48

49

47
DESIGN FIRM: *Peterson & Company*
DESIGNER: *Bryan L. Peterson*
LETTERER: *Bryan L. Peterson*
HEADLINE TYPEFACE: *Handlettering*
TEXT TYPEFACE: *Baskerville and Frutiger*
CLIENT: *Northern Telecom*

48
DESIGN FIRM: *Pentagram Design*
DESIGNER: *Paula Scher*
HEADLINE TYPEFACE: *Various*
TEXT TYPEFACE: *Bodoni Book*
CLIENT: *Champion International*

49
DESIGN FIRM: *Pentagram Design*
DESIGNER: *Paula Scher*
HEADLINE TYPEFACE: *Various*
TEXT TYPEFACE: *Bodoni Book*
CLIENT: *Champion International*

50

DESIGN FIRM: *Tyler Smith*
DESIGNER: *Laura Kelly*
HEADLINE TYPEFACE: *Futura*
TEXT TYPEFACE: *Futura*
CLIENT: *Toyo Ink*

50

51

51
DESIGN FIRM: *The Duffy Design Group*
DESIGNER: *Charles S. Anderson*
HEADLINE TYPEFACE: *Bodoni Bold Condensed*
TEXT TYPEFACE: *Garamond*
CLIENT: *French Paper Co.*

52

52
DESIGN FIRM: *The Duffy Design Group*
DESIGNER: *Charles S. Anderson*
HEADLINE TYPEFACE: *Garamond Book*
CLIENT: *Rolling Stone Magazine*

53

53
DESIGN FIRM: *The Duffy Design Group*
DESIGNER: *Joe Duffy, Charles S. Anderson and Sharon Werner*
HEADLINE TYPEFACE: *Helvetica Bold Condensed*
TEXT TYPEFACE: *Century Schoolbook Italic*
CLIENT: *Dickson's, Inc.*

54
DESIGN FIRM: *The Duffy Design Group*
DESIGNER: *Joe Duffy*
LETTERER: *Lynn Schulte and Joe Duffy*
HEADLINE TYPEFACE: *Cheltenham Book Italic and Handlettering*
CLIENT: *Dickson's, Inc.*

55
DESIGN FIRM: *The Duffy Design Group*
DESIGNER: *Joe Duffy and Sharon Werner*
HEADLINE TYPEFACE: *Helvetica Bold Condensed*
TEXT TYPEFACE: *Century Schoolbook Italic*
CLIENT: *Dickson's, Inc.*

56
DESIGN FIRM: *The Duffy Design Group*
DESIGNER: *Joe Duffy and Sharon Werner*
LETTERER: *Lynn Schulte*
HEADLINE TYPEFACE: *Handlettering and Venus*
CLIENT: *Dickson's, Inc.*

54

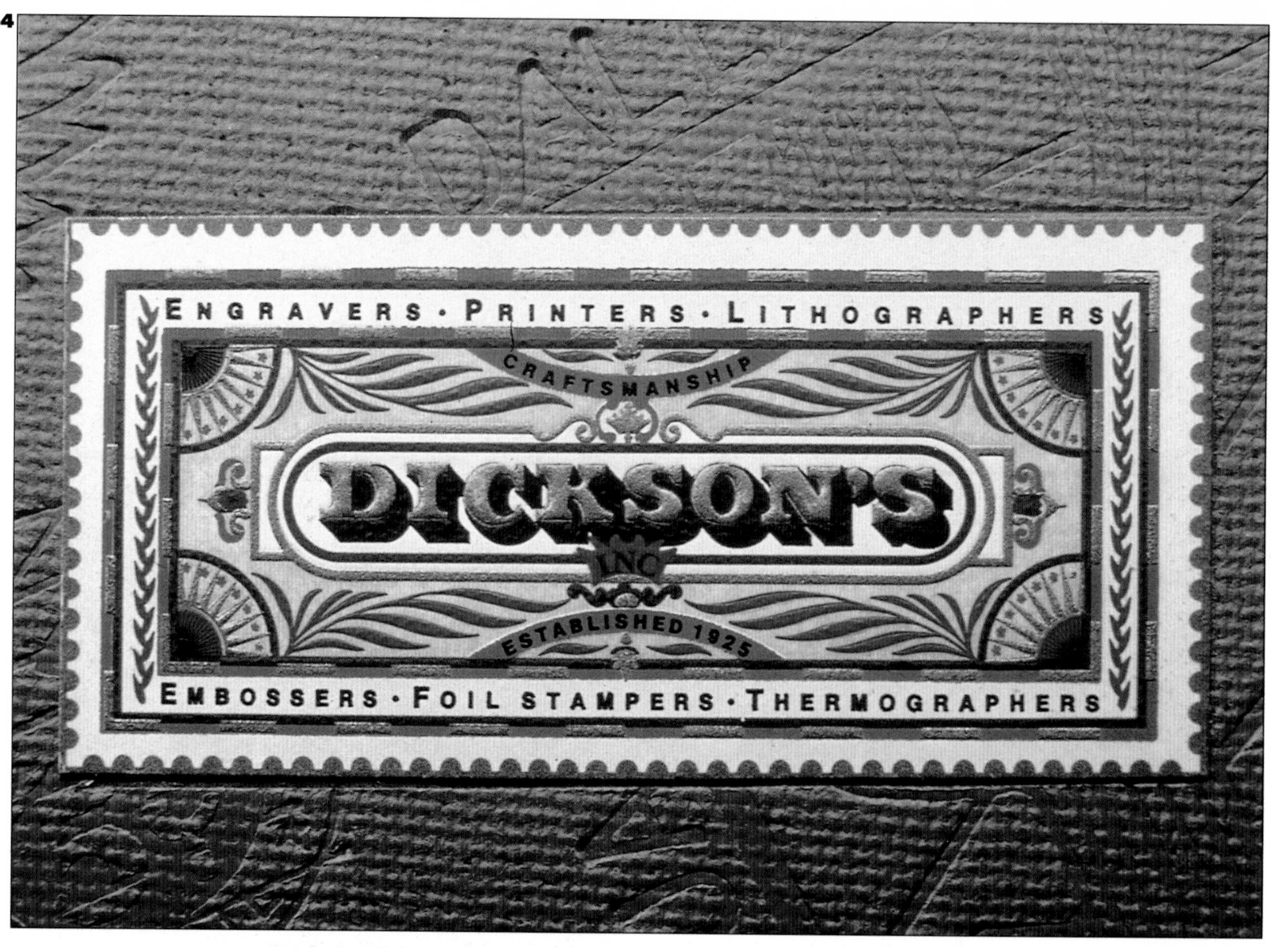

55

56

57

58

59

57
DESIGN FIRM: *The Duffy Design Group*
DESIGNER: *Joe Duffy and Sharon Werner*
LETTERER: *Lynn Schulte*
HEADLINE TYPEFACE: *Garamond and Handlettering*
CLIENT: *Dickson's, Inc.*

58
DESIGN FIRM: *The Duffy Design Group*
DESIGNER: *Joe Duffy and Sharon Werner*
LETTERER: *Lynn Schulte*
HEADLINE TYPEFACE: *Bodoni*
CLIENT: *Dickson's, Inc.*

59
DESIGN FIRM: *The Duffy Design Group*
DESIGNER: *Charles S. Anderson and Joe Duffy*
HEADLINE TYPEFACE: *Weiss Bold*
TEXT TYPEFACE: *Bodoni*
CLIENT: *French Paper Co.*

60

60
DESIGN FIRM: *The Duffy Design Group*
DESIGNER: *Charles S. Anderson*
HEADLINE TYPEFACE: *Eagle Bold*
CLIENT: *First Banks*

61

62

63

64

61
DESIGN FIRM: *Morla Design*
DESIGNER: *Jennifer Morla*
HEADLINE TYPEFACE: *Futura Bold*
CLIENT: *Levi Strauss & Co.*

62
DESIGN FIRM: *Isely and/or Clark Design*
DESIGNER: *Liz Clark and Pat Hornberger*
HEADLINE TYPEFACE: *Caslon 540*
TEXT TYPEFACE: *Caslon 224 Book*
CLIENT: *State of Maryland*

63
DESIGN FIRM: *Design Team One, Inc.*
DESIGNER: *Dan Bitman*
HEADLINE TYPEFACE: *Various*
CLIENT: *Mead Paper Company*

64
DESIGN FIRM: *Morla Design*
DESIGNER: *Jennifer Morla*
TEXT TYPEFACE: *Kabel Bold and Kabel Ultra Bold*
CLIENT: *Bradmill, Inc.*

65/66

DESIGN FIRM: *Samata Associates*

DESIGNER: *Pat Samata and Greg Samata*

HEADLINE TYPEFACE: *Garamond Oldstyle*

TEXT TYPEFACE: *Garamond Oldstyle*

CLIENT: *Samata Associates*

65

66

67

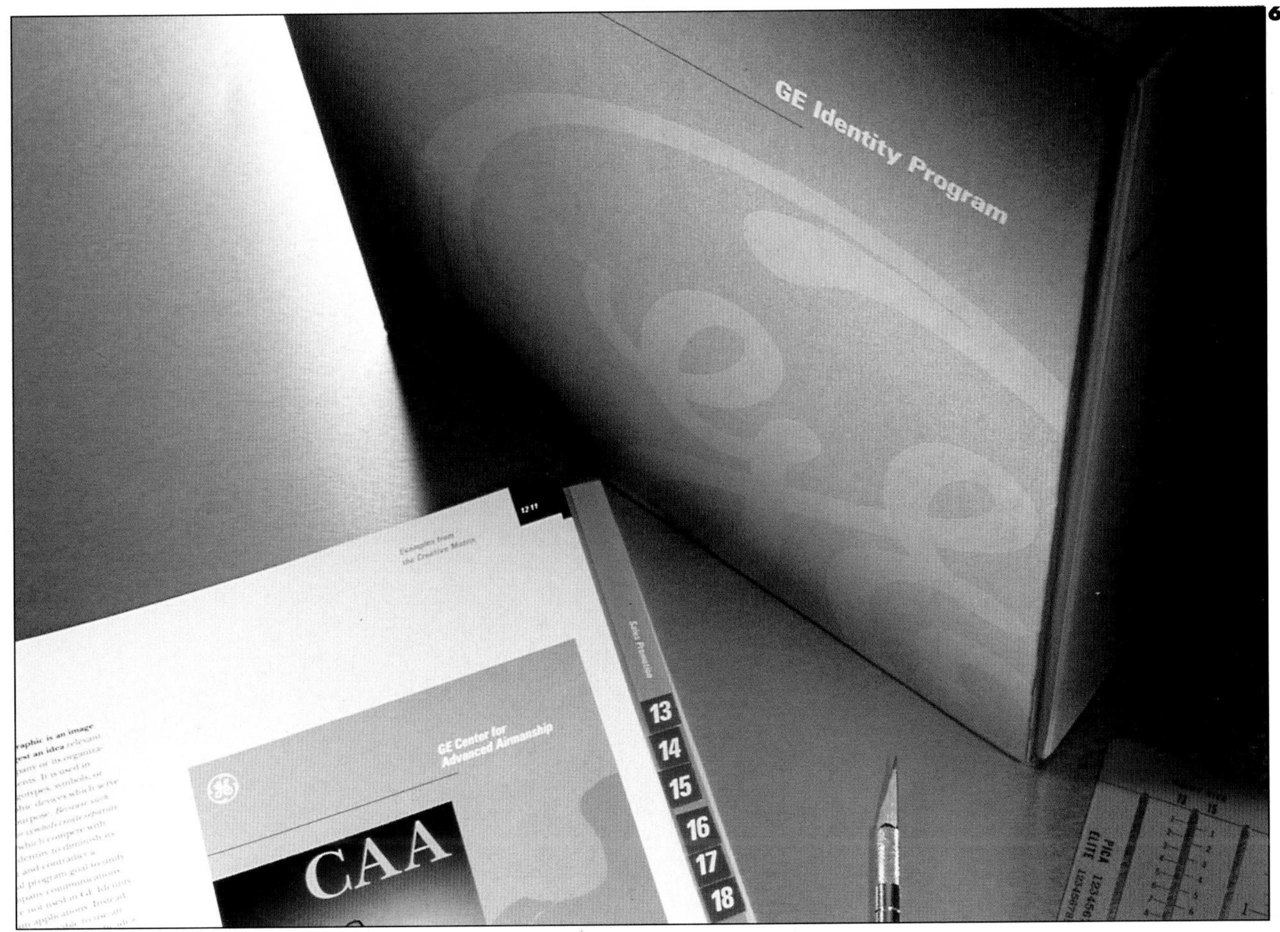

68

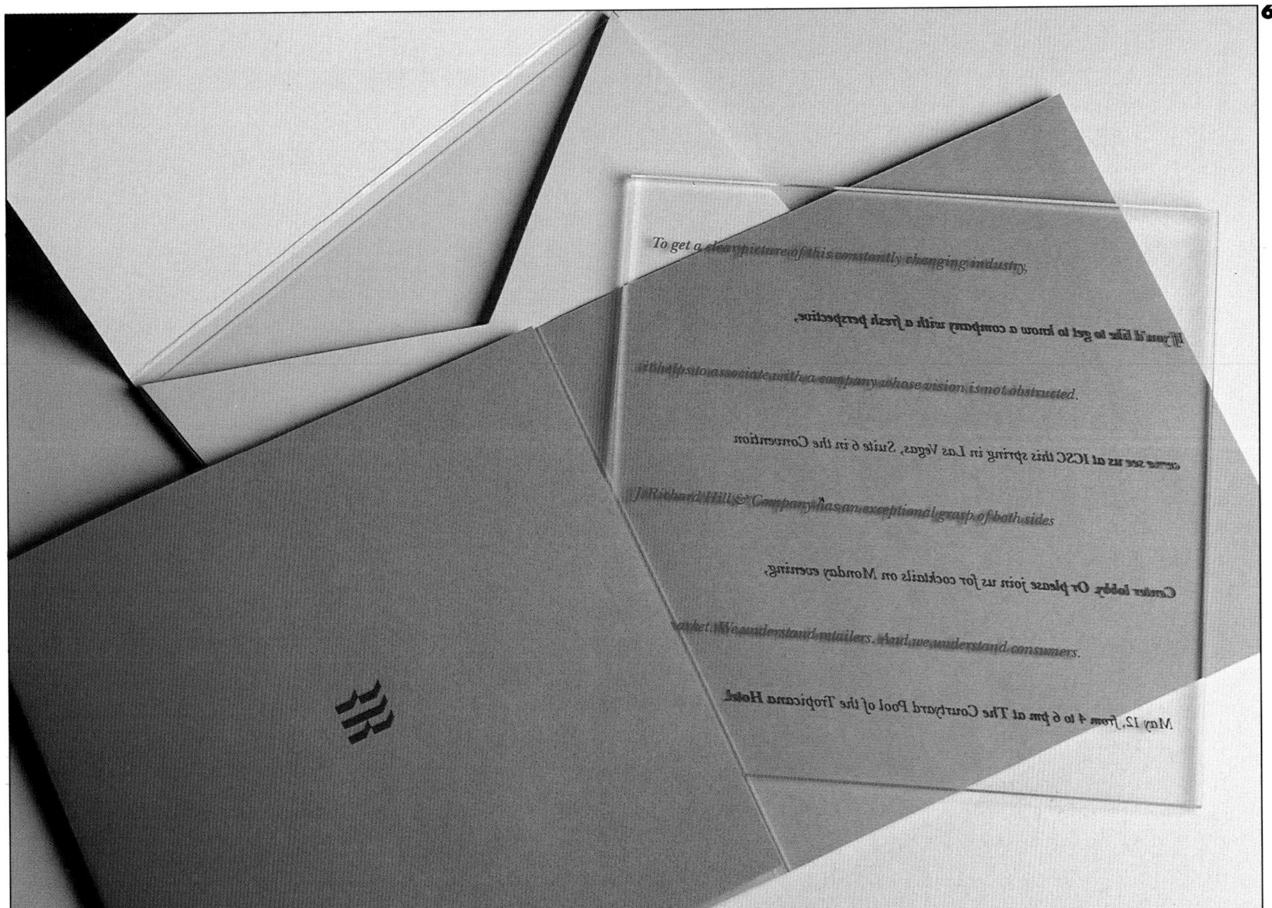

67
DESIGN FIRM: *Landor Associates*
DESIGNER: *Don Bartels, Karl Martens, Rebecca Livermore, Randall O'Dowd, and Virginia Zimmerman*
HEADLINE TYPEFACE: *ITC New Baskerville*
TEXT TYPEFACE: *ITC New Baserville*
CLIENT: *General Electric Co.*

68
DESIGN FIRM: *Richards Brock Miller Mitchell and Associates*
DESIGNER: *Ken Shafer*
TEXT TYPEFACE: *New Baskerville Semi-Bold Italic*
CLIENT: *J. Richard Hill*

69
DESIGN FIRM: *Tenazas Design*
DESIGNER: *Lucille Tenazas*
HEADLINE TYPEFACE: *Univers 75*
TEXT TYPEFACE: *Sabon and Univers 75*
CLIENT: *James River Corp.*

70/71
DESIGN FIRM: *Pentagram Design*
DESIGNER: *Woody Pirtle and Joe Rattan*
LETTERER: *Joe Rattan*
HEADLINE TYPEFACE: *Palatino*
TEXT TYPEFACE: *Palatino*
CLIENT: *Champion International*

69

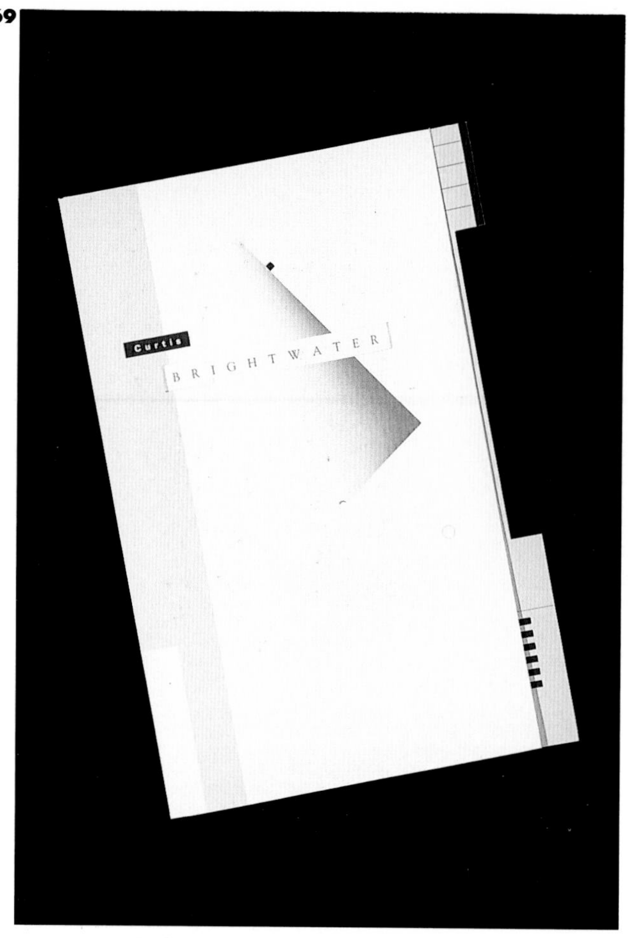

70

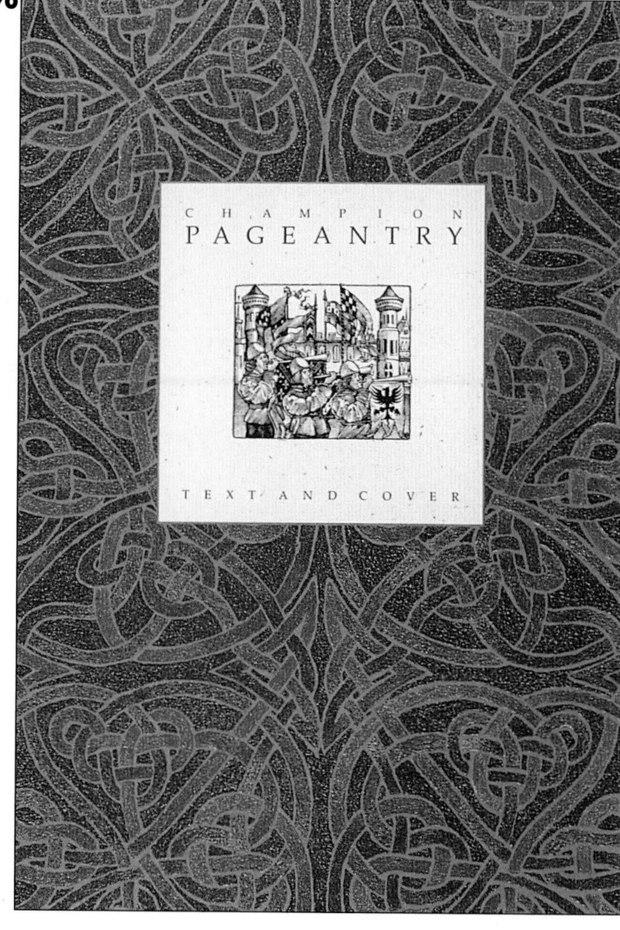

71

75

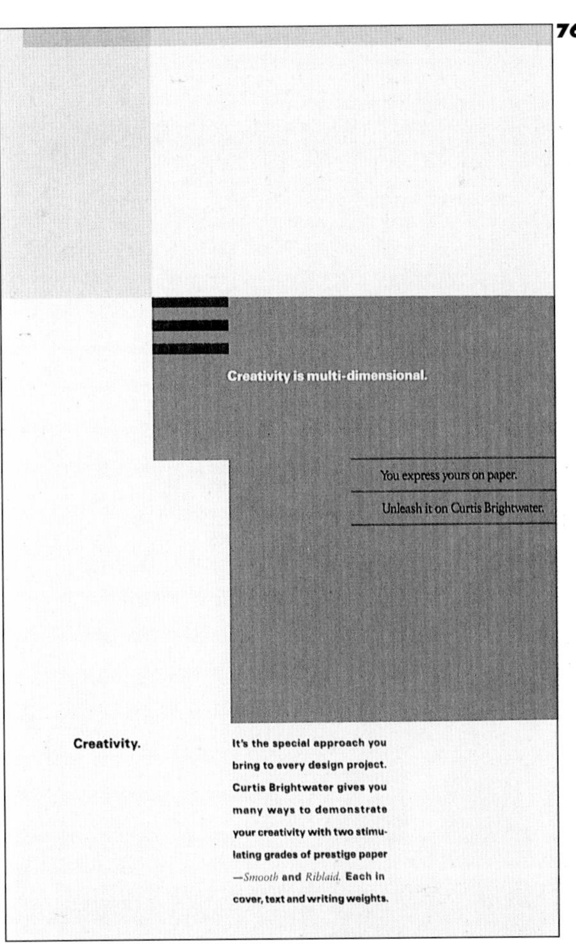

76

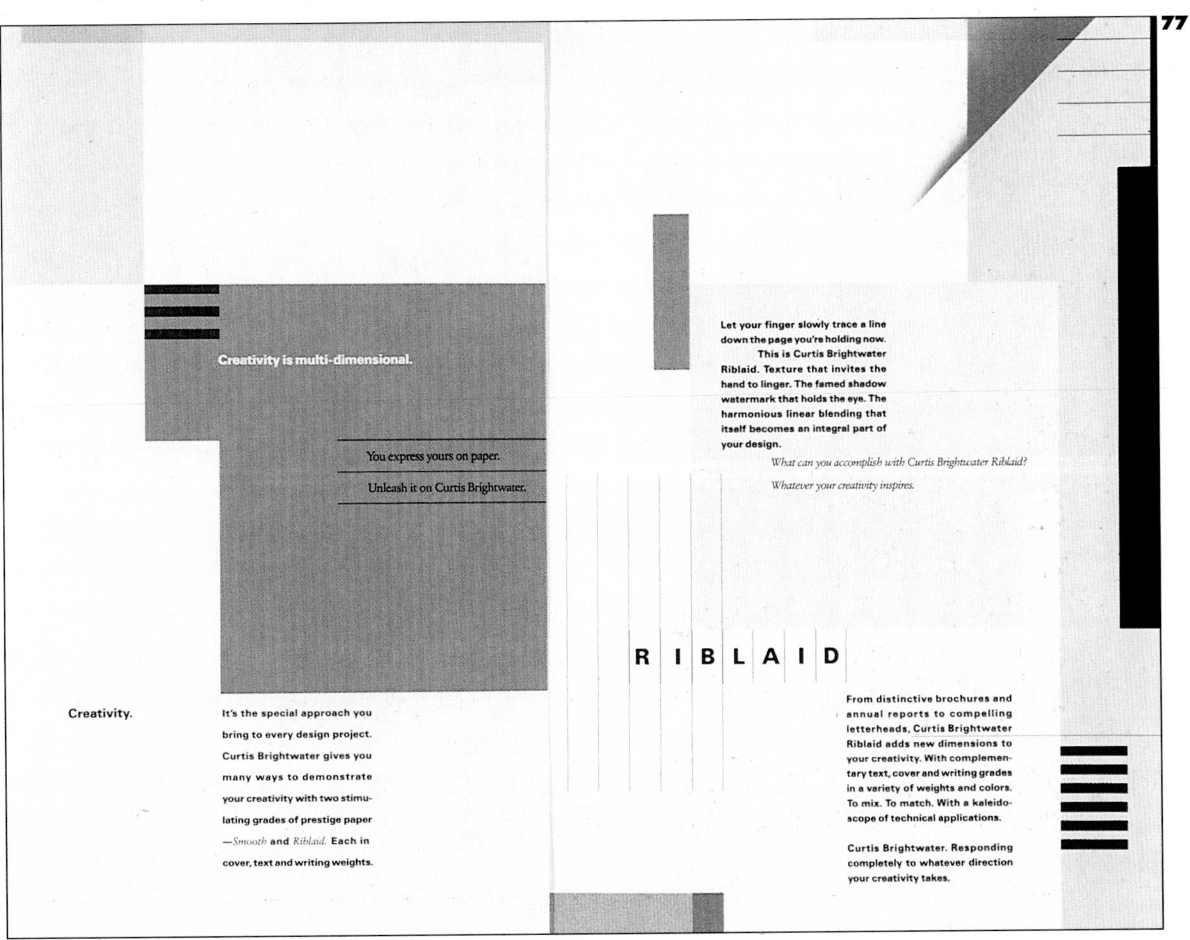

77

75
DESIGN FIRM: *The Duffy Design Group*
DESIGNER: *Charles S. Anderson*
HEADLINE TYPEFACE: *San Serif Bold*
TEXT TYPEFACE: *Bodoni*
CLIENT: *Shade*

76
DESIGN FIRM: *Tenazas Design*
DESIGNER: *Lucille Tenazas*
HEADLINE TYPEFACE: *Goudy Oldstyle*
TEXT TYPEFACE: *Sabon and Univers 75*
CLIENT: *James River Corp.*

77
DESIGN FIRM: *Tenazas Design*
DESIGNER: *Lucille Tenazas*
HEADLINE TYPEFACE: *Goudy Oldstyle*
TEXT TYPEFACE: *Sabon and Univers 75*
CLIENT: *James River Corp.*

78
DESIGN FIRM: *The Duffy Design Group*
DESIGNER: *Charles S. Anderson*
HEADLINE TYPEFACE: *Handlettering*
TEXT TYPEFACE: *Karnak Medium*
CLIENT: *French Paper Company*

79/80
DESIGN FIRM: *Mauk Design*
HEADLINE TYPEFACE: *Univers 75 and Spencerian Script*
TEXT TYPEFACE: *Univers 75*
CLIENT: *Entertainment Technologies*

81

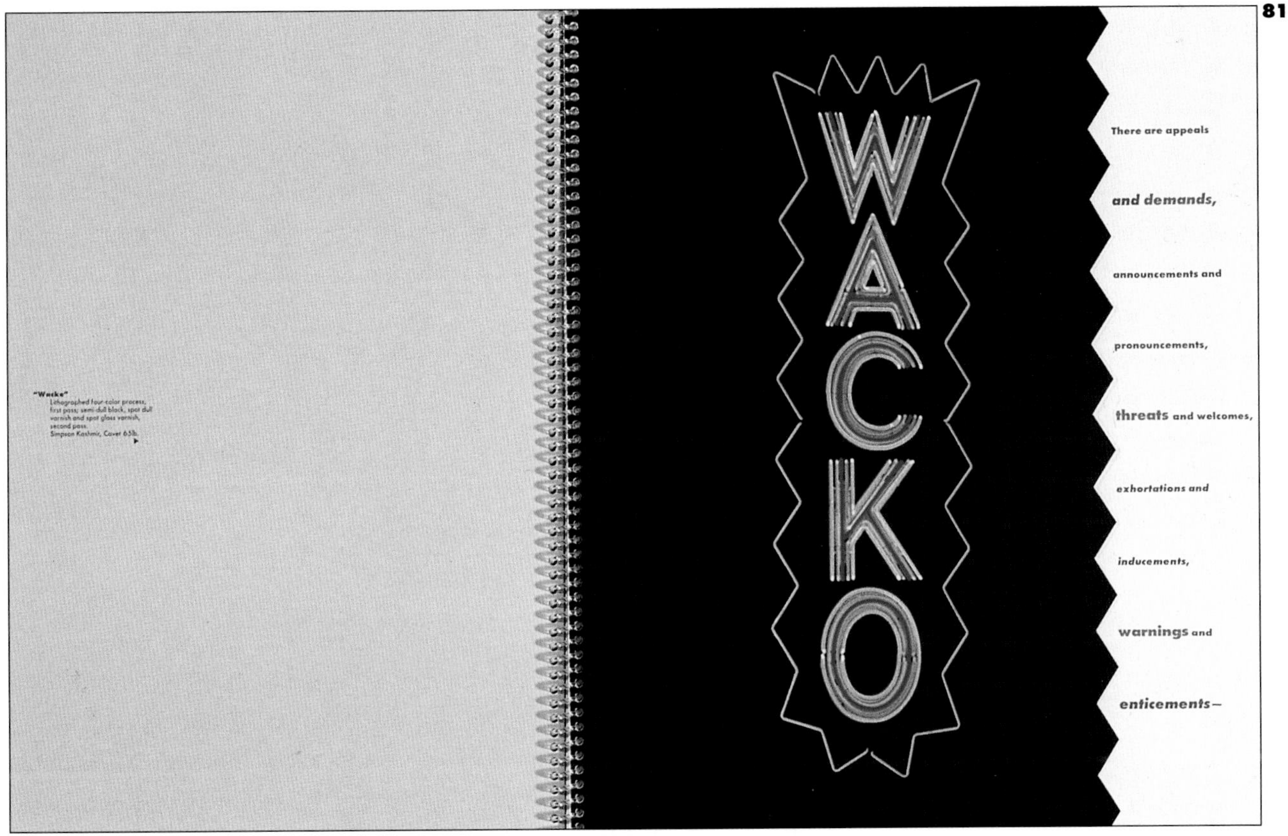

82

81
DESIGN FIRM: *Cross Associates*
DESIGNER: *John Clark and Paul Langland*
HEADLINE TYPEFACE: *Neon Sign and Futura Black*
TEXT TYPEFACE: *Futura Bold and Futura Book*
CLIENT: *Simpson Paper Company*

82
DESIGN FIRM: *Mauk Design*
HEADLINE TYPEFACE: *Univers 75 and Spencerian Script*
TEXT TYPEFACE: *Univers 75*
CLIENT: *Entertainment Technologies*

83
DESIGN FIRM: *Adrian Parry*
DESIGNER: *Adrian Parry and Cliff Morgan*
TEXT TYPEFACE: *Metro*
CLIENT: *Bybee Studios*

84
DESIGN FIRM: *Samata Associates*
DESIGNER: *Greg Samata*
HEADLINE TYPEFACE: *Garamond*
TEXT TYPEFACE: *Garamond*
CLIENT: *27 Chicago Designers*

85

THE ART DIRECTORS CLUB, INC.

ELIGIBILITY:
Entries must be received at the Club by the deadline date of November 30, 1988. Any material fitting the listed categories is eligible if it has been produced in the United States or Canada and published only in those markets. Material produced for foreign markets is not eligible.
¶ The entries must have been printed, published or broadcast for the first time between January 1 and December 31, 1988. Entries first published prior to January 1, 1988 will not be judged.

ENTRY PREPARATION:
Do not submit original artwork. Entries cannot be returned.

CATEGORIES:
Print: Submit tearsheets or proofs, unmounted and trimmed as published. Send supplements, inserts, sections, brochures, catalogs, or books in bound form. All posters must be submitted on 35mm slides. Point-of-purchase displays may be sent on slide. Tape an entry form to the back of each single entry.
¶ *A Campaign* or *Series* is a minimum of 3 and a maximum of 5 pieces from the same strategy or a multi-page story. A campaign of tearsheets, proofs or jackets must be taped together, accordian-style, with one control tag taped to the back. List the titles of each component of the campaign on the entry form. When a campaign cannot be taped together, tape a control tag to the back of each component and mark as "1 of 3," "2 of 3," etc.
¶ *Television:* Submit each single 16mm film entry on a separate reel with no academy leader or tail markings. Indicate the title of the spot on the control tag. Tape the entry form to the outside of the film box.
¶ Submit each single tape entry on a separate ¾" video tape. Include only a 10 second countdown. Do not include color bars. Indicate the title of the spot on the control tag. Tape the entry form to the outside of the cassette box.
Note: Should a tape entry be accepted for an award it may be necessary to provide a 16mm film conversion for use at the awards ceremony.
¶ A television campaign consists of 3 spots only. To submit a campaign, splice together, on one reel or one cassette, all three spots. Remove head and tail markings so that the spots run uninterrupted. Indicate on the entry form the title of each of the 3 spots in the order which they appear. Tape the entry form to the outside of the film box or tape cassette.

There is New York's *second* Statue of Liberty—the obscure, almost unnoticed statue that stands on top of the Liberty-Pac warehouse at 43 West Sixty-fourth Street. This reasonable facsimile, erected in 1902 at the request of William H. Flatteau, a patriotic warehouse owner, stands 55 feet high above its pedestal as compared with Bartholdi's 151-footer on Liberty Island. This smaller Liberty also had a lighted torch, and spiral staircase.

2

3

86

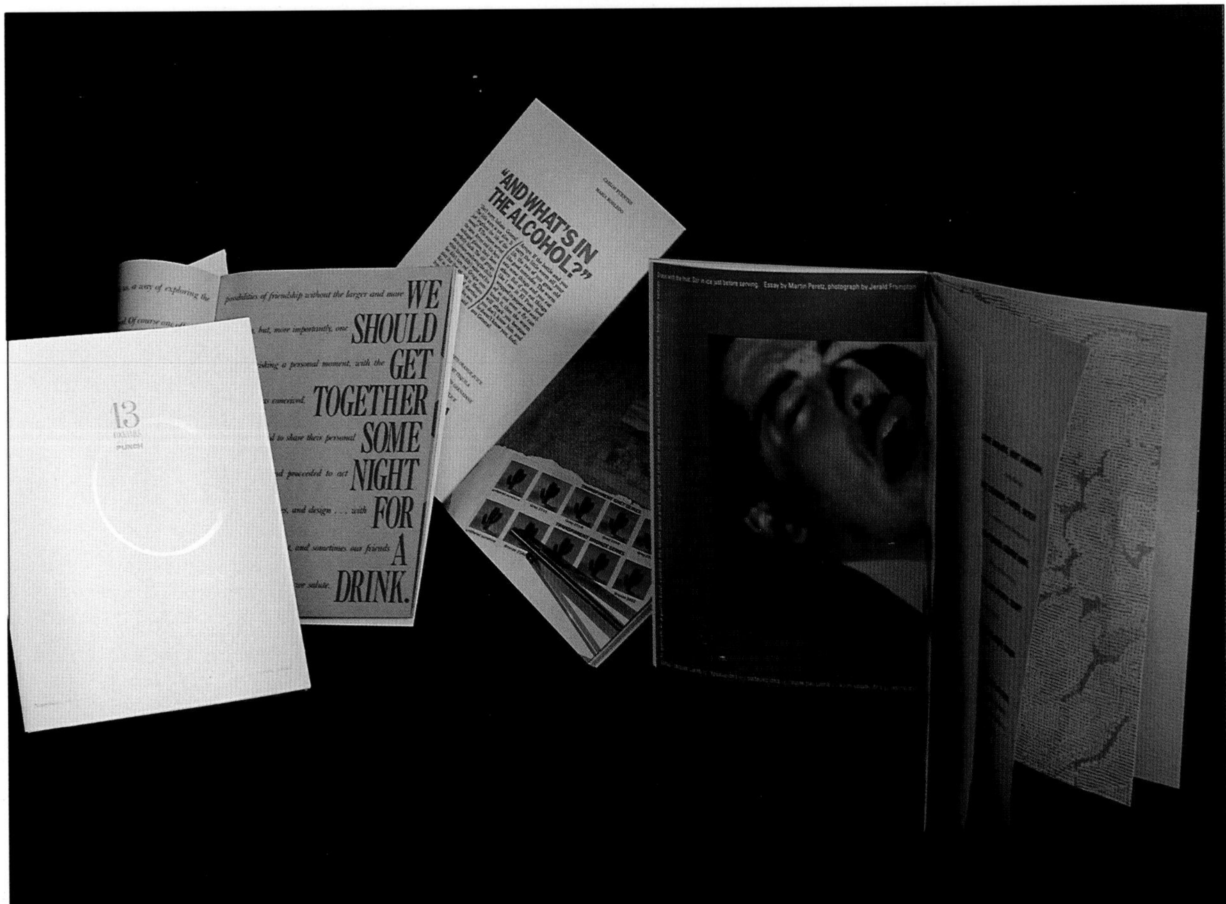

85
DESIGN FIRM: *Pentagram Design*
DESIGNER: *Kit Hinrichs and Karen Boone*
HEADLINE TYPEFACE: *Univers 67*
TEXT TYPEFACE: *Bodoni*
CLIENT: *New York Art Directors Club*

86
DESIGN FIRM: *Drenttel Doyle Partners*
DESIGNER: *Tom Kluepfel, Stephen Doyle, Rosemary Turk, and Katie Delahany*
HEADLINE TYPEFACE: *Various*
TEXT TYPEFACE: *Various*
CLIENT: *Drenttel Doyle Partners*

87

88

89

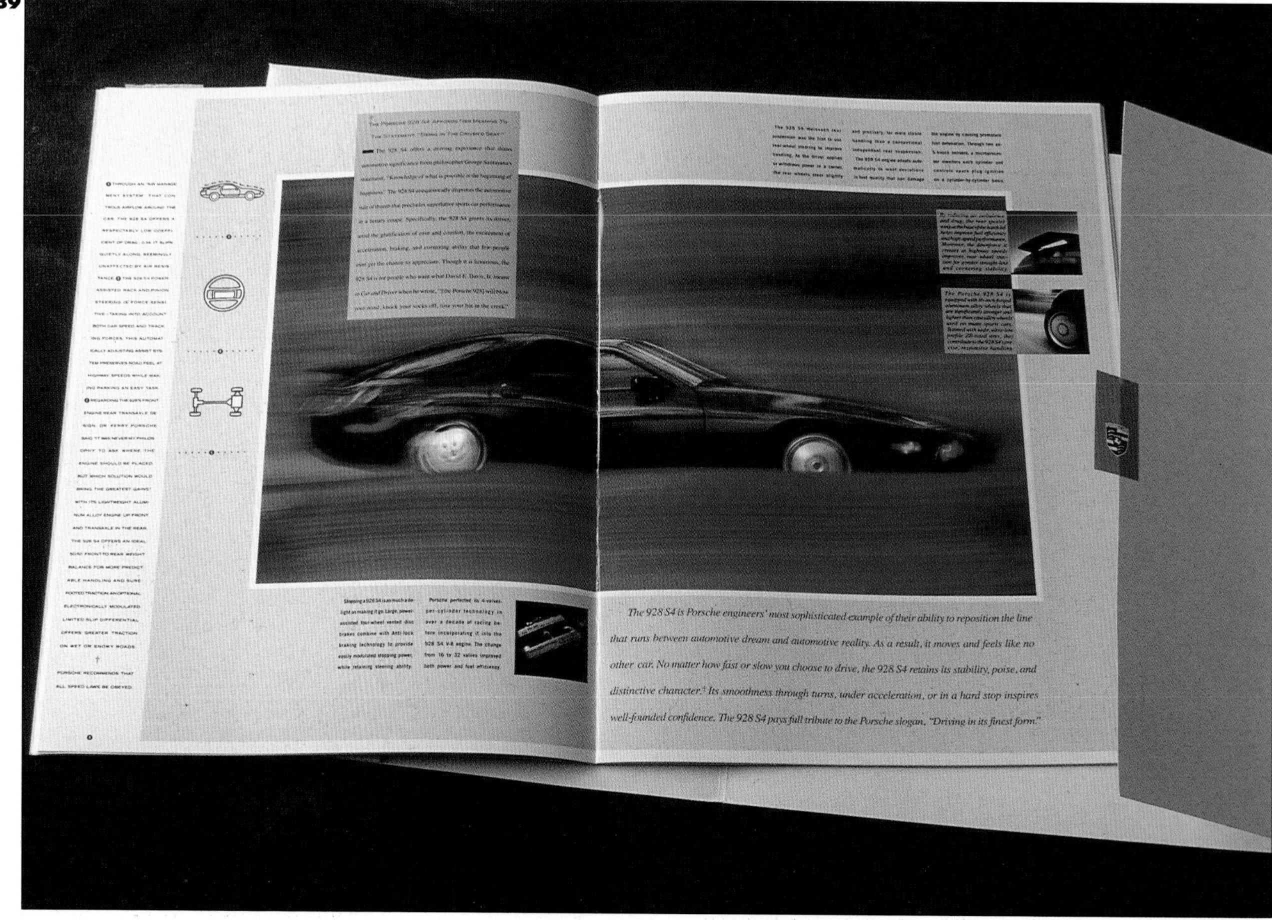

87
DESIGN FIRM: *The Duffy Design Group*
DESIGNER: *Charles S. Anderson and Haley Johnson*
HEADLINE TYPEFACE: *Handlettering and Futura Bold Condensed*
CLIENT: *French Paper Company*

88/89
DESIGN FIRM: *The Duffy Design Group*
DESIGNER: *Joe Duffy, Haley Johnson, and Charles S. Anderson*
HEADLINE TYPEFACE: *Trade Gothic*
TEXT TYPEFACE: *Times Italic*
CLIENT: *Porsche Cars of North America*

90

91

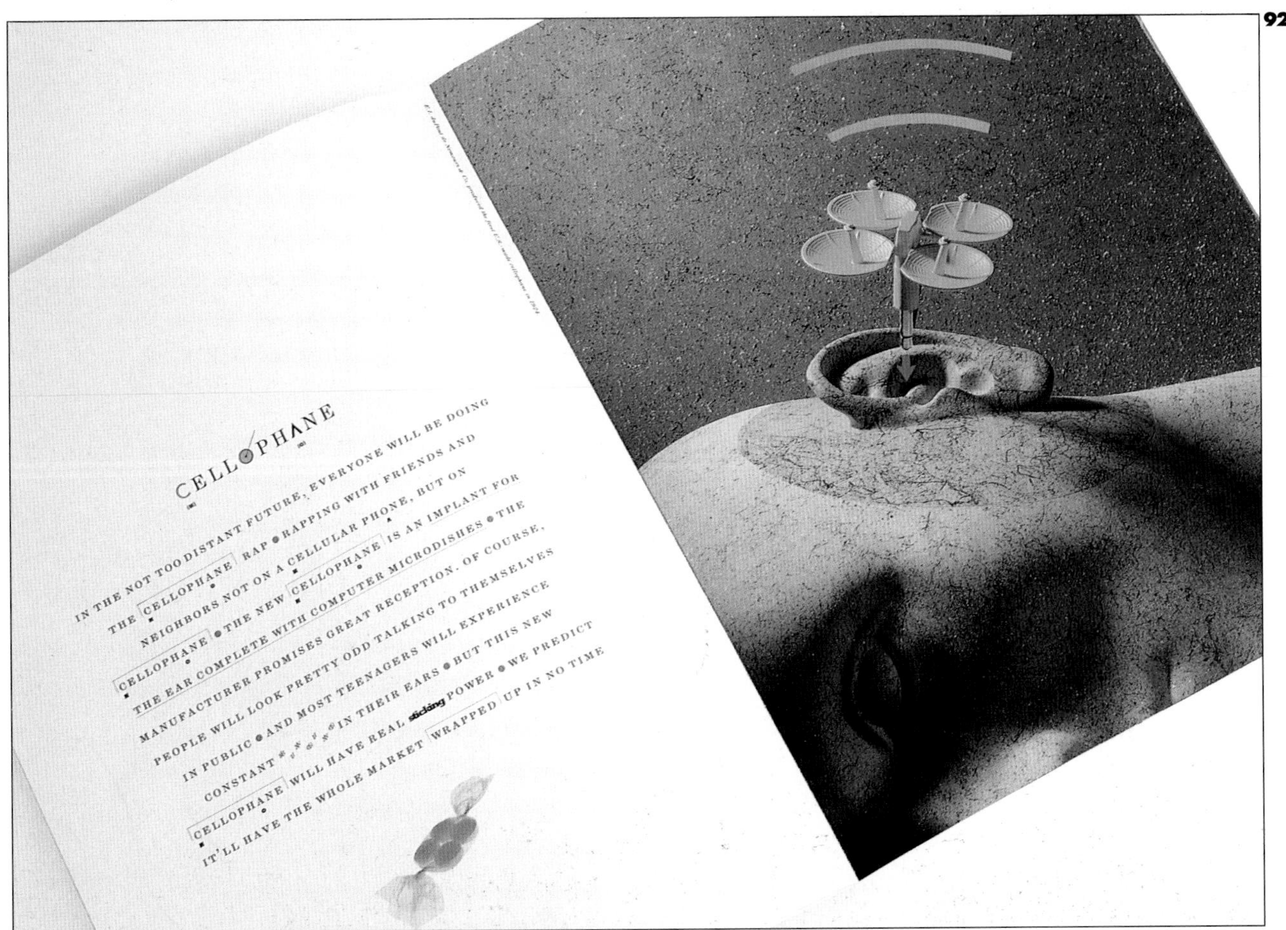

92

90
DESIGN FIRM: *The Duffy Design Group*
DESIGNER: *Charles S. Anderson*
LETTERER: *Lynn Schulte*
HEADLINE TYPEFACE: *Handlettering*
CLIENT: *French Paper Company*

91/92
DESIGN FIRM: *Thirst*
DESIGNER: *Rick Valicenti*
HEADLINE TYPEFACE: *Various*
TEXT TYPEFACE: *Various*
CLIENT: *Consolidated Papers, Inc.*

93

94

93/94
DESIGN FIRM: *Pentagram Design*
DESIGNER: *Peter Harrison and Susan Hochbaum*
HEADLINE TYPEFACE: *City*
TEXT TYPEFACE: *City*
CLIENT: *Mead & Gilbert Papers*

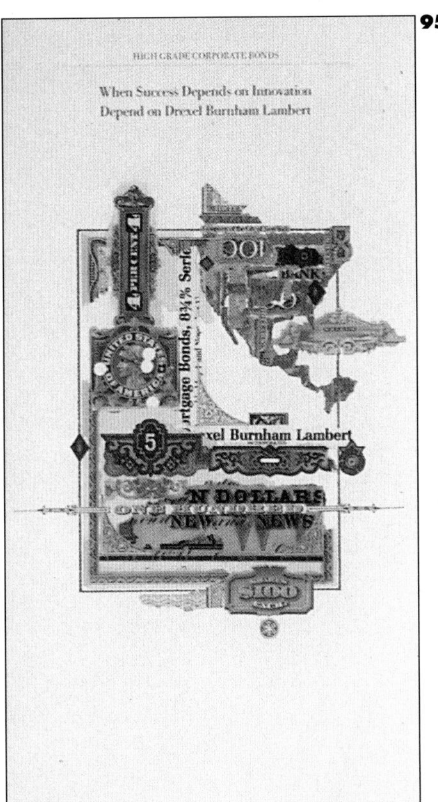
HIGH GRADE CORPORATE BONDS

When Success Depends on Innovation
Depend on Drexel Burnham Lambert

95

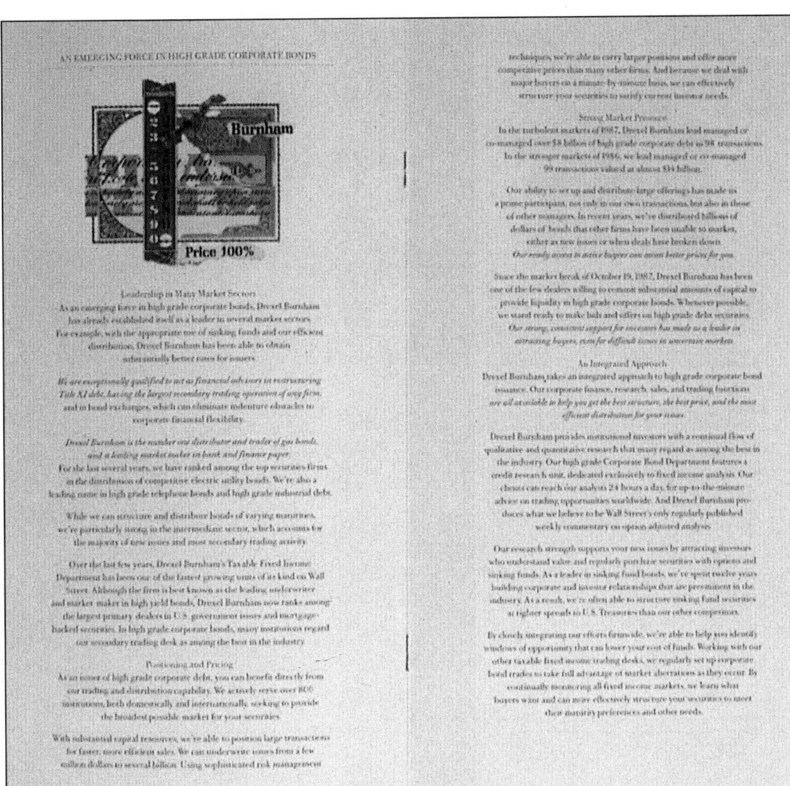
AN EMERGING FORCE IN HIGH GRADE CORPORATE BONDS

Leadership in Many Market Sectors

Strong Market Presence

An Integrated Approach

Positioning and Pricing

96

97

98

95/96
DESIGN FIRM: *Pentagram Design*
DESIGNER: *Michael Gericke and Colin Forbes*
HEADLINE TYPEFACE: *Bodoni Antiqua*
TEXT TYPEFACE: *Bodoni Antiqua*
CLIENT: *Drexel Burnham Lambert*

97
DESIGN FIRM: *The Duffy Design Group*
DESIGNER: *Charles S. Anderson*
LETTERER: *Lynn Schulte*
HEADLINE TYPEFACE: *Radiant Heavy*
TEXT TYPEFACE: *Futura Bold Condensed and Handlettering*
CLIENT: *French Paper Company*

98
DESIGN FIRM: *Wallace Church Associates, Inc.*
DESIGNER: *Stanley Church*
HEADLINE TYPEFACE: *Handlettering and Custom Design*
TEXT TYPEFACE: *Futura*
CLIENT: *Wallace Church Associates, Inc.*

99

99

DESIGN FIRM: *David Carter Graphics Design Associates*
DESIGNER: *Randall Hill*
HEADLINE TYPEFACE: *Garamond #3 Italic*
TEXT TYPEFACE: *Garamond #3*
CLIENT: *David Carter Graphic Design Associates*

100
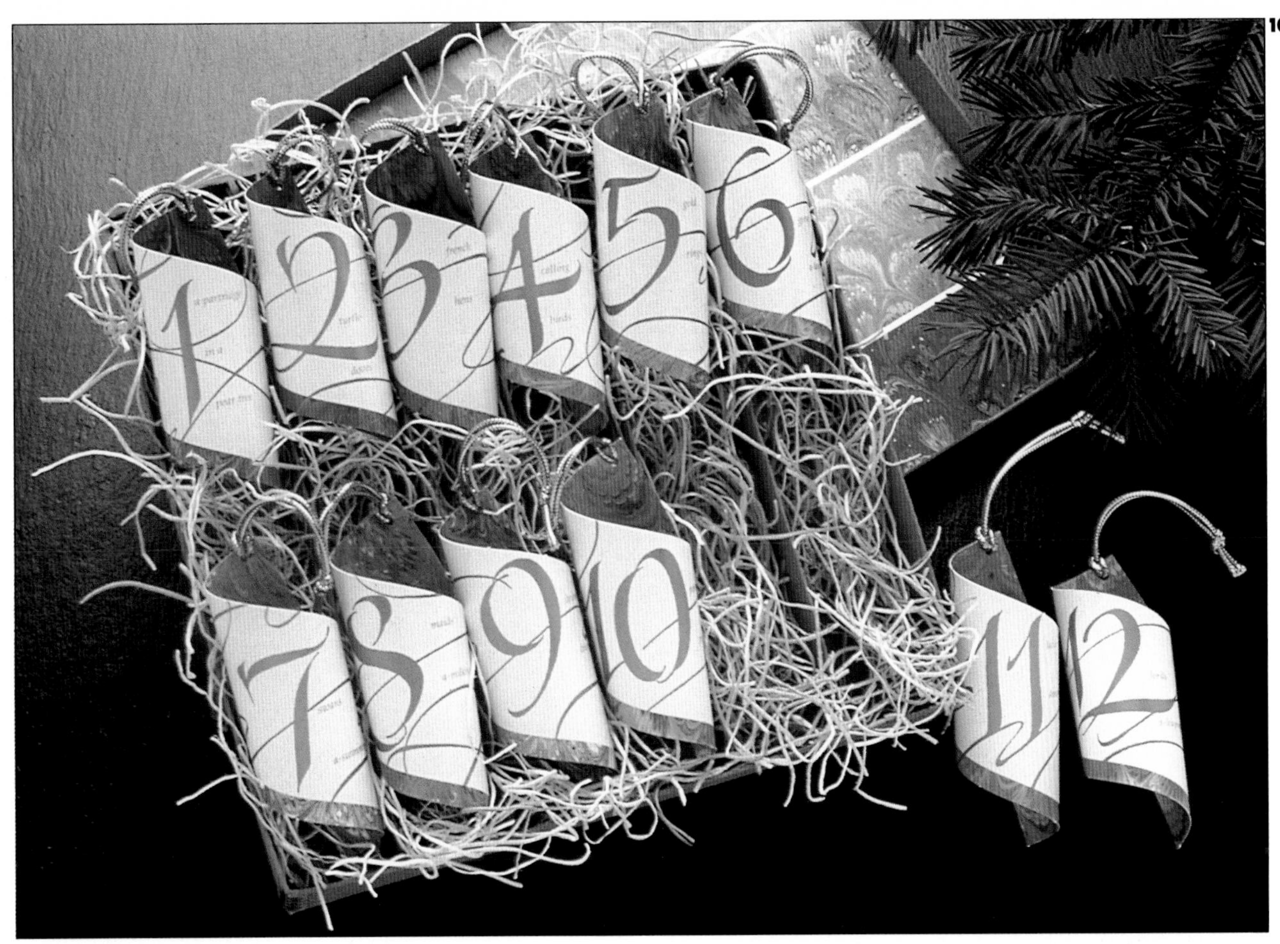

101

102

100
DESIGN FIRM: *Hornall Anderson Design Works*
LETTERER: *Glenn Yoshiyama*
TEXT TYPEFACE: *Palatino Italic*
CLIENT: *Hornall Anderson Design Works*

101
DESIGN FIRM: *The Duffy Design Group*
DESIGNER: *Joe Duffy*
LETTERER: *Joe Duffy and Lynn Schulte*
HEADLINE TYPEFACE: *Handlettering*
CLIENT: *The Duffy Design Group*

102
DESIGN FIRM: *Morla Design*
DESIGNER: *Jennifer Morla*
LETTERER: *Jeanette Aramboru*
HEADLINE TYPEFACE: *Handlettering*
TEXT TYPEFACE: *Bernhard Modern*
CLIENT: *Morla Design*

103

104

103
DESIGN FIRM: *Tenazas Design*
DESIGNER: *Lucille Tenazas*
HEADLINE TYPEFACE: *Goudy Oldstyle*
TEXT TYPEFACE: *Sabon and Univers 75*
CLIENT: *James River Corp.*

104/105
DESIGN FIRM: *Pentagram Design*
DESIGNER: *Harold Burch*
HEADLINE TYPEFACE: *Typewriters and Various*
TEXT TYPEFACE: *Univers, Futura, and Century*
CLIENT: *Warner Communications*

105

LEKTRA

106

107

108

Andy Warhol's most famous painting, the Campbell's Soup can, completely undid assumptions about what art was supposed to be. In May, Warner Books undid many assumptions about Warhol himself with its publication of *The Diaries of Andy Warhol*.

Warhol, whose paintings launched the 1960s art movement Pop Art, produced numerous underground films and created Interview magazine before his death in 1988. He encircled himself with hordes of celebrities, movie stars, political movers and shakers. His office in Manhattan, known as The Factory, was populated with exotic amphetamine-driven creatures assuming such identities as "Ondine," "Billy Name," and "International Velvet." In this milieu of the Pop esthetic, which was all about surface and the appearance of things, Warhol claimed to be turning himself into a cold and unfeeling art-making machine.

But *The Diaries*, according to Warhol's diarist Pat Hackett, will reveal him to the world as a sensitive man easily hurt by others. Hackett, starting as his personal diarist in 1972, has had more than 20,000 pages of entries transcribed from tapes, notes, and regular morning telephone conversations: "He was everything that the Pop image assumed he was not, his artistic ideal wasn't human reality. He had all of the problems that everybody else has, Pop was an artistic way of handling them."

Widely regarded as a man entranced with glamour, the painter-impresario of *The Diaries* comes across as very level-headed and honest, unafraid to make fun of himself, or others. "There was always an implicit understanding that the diaries would be published, " said Hackett in a recent interview. "But Andy didn't want them made public until after he died. He would ask me: 'What are you going to do with the diaries after I pop off?' I never thought about it much because he was in such good health I thought he would live forever."

Knowing the diaries would have a posthumous publication, Warhol called the shots exactly as he saw them. Thus he declared about the source of his own preeminence: "I'm so tired of the Campbell's Soup can I could throw up." He seemed always to be staring at life with a certain naivete; his public utterances were often replete with the astonishment of eight-year-olds. Surrounded by stars, for example, he would exclaim: "Gosh." In *The Diaries*, on the other hand, he proffers such revelations as: "Liz (Taylor) looked like a belly-button. Like a fat little kewpie doll.

Warhol's book, in Hackett's opinion, is sure to embarrass certain celebrities: "I don't think there's anything that will actually send them out the windows, but a few people will really be groaning and grabbing the phone to cry to friends."

A sample of entries:

WEDNESDAY SEPTEMBER 24, 1980
...And then Liz Taylor came in with John Warner and she came over and was really sweet and then later she came back to our table and had dinner with us. John would bring me a full glass of wine but he'd bring Liz a thimbleful, and she'd say, "Well, what happened?" and he would say, "Oh I don't know, it was the bartender, he just didn't give me enough."

MONDAY, FEBRUARY 23, 1981
Well, Mary Tyler Moore is trying to be a new woman. Brigid told Mary she loved her crow's feet, which she does, but its sounded insulting. Brigid was trying to get the conversation around to plastic surgery but...she didn't pursue it.

WARHOL ON HIS EMOTIONS:
I've got these desperate feelings that nothing means anything. And then I decide that I should try to fall in love, and that's what I'm doing now with Jon Gould, but then it's just too hard. I mean, you think about a person constantly and it's just a fantasy, it's not real, and then it gets so involved, you have to see them all the time and then it winds up that it's just a job like everything else, so I don't know.

WEDNESDAY, APRIL 8, 1981 VIENNA
I'd dreamt about Billy Name, that he was living under the stairs at my house and doing somersaults...his friends sort of invaded my house and were acting crazy in colorful costumes and jumping up and down and having so much fun and they took over, they took over my life...It was like clowns...they were just living there without letting me know, they'd come out in the morning when I wasn't there and they'd have a lot of fun and then they'd go back and live in the closet.

AT A WHITE HOUSE DINNER FOR THE MARCOSES:
I said, "Oh, I'm from Pittsburgh and my poor brother is out of work from the steel mill" – I was lying like crazy, – "and he's lost his mill job and what you should do is put one of those unused buildings to use and make it into a Disney World and give tours and charge people ten dollars to get a little coal on their faces and see hot lava being poured" and he said, "Oh, what a great idea, why didn't I think of that?" The Vice President Bushes were at our table...

ABOUT TRUMAN CAPOTE:
And he was talking about the article, it said the word "decline," and he said, "Decline?? What decline? I'm the most written about writer in the world." I guess he's confusing written about with writing.

According to Warner Books president Larry Kirshbaum, the company will print 100,000 copies of *The Diaries* initially. "It's a large print run for a book that retails at $29.95," says Kirshbaum. "We anticipate that it will stay hardcover for about two years." Warner Books also holds paperback rights to the book.

The company won rights to the Warhol manuscript in an auction held by literary agent Lynn Nesbitt at International Creative Management. "We knew it was a major commitment," says Kirshbaum, "and were prepared to spend a significant amount of money to get it. We thought it was an interesting project because Warhol was not only an internationally known artist, but he also chronicled a whole generation, several generations."

Warhol's diaries began as a defensive move against the Internal Revenue Service, which initiated regular audits of his business returns in 1972. His meticulous expense records included cab fares, luncheon and club receipts, even the number of dimes he dropped in public phones for business calls. In 1976, when diarist Hackett informed Warhol that she wanted to begin working at home, he suggested that she telephone him daily to record not only his public utterances but the truth of the day or night before. From that point, log entries for *The Diaries of Andy Warhol* became his personal initiative.

Warner Books Editor Jamie Raab, in charge of *The Diaries*, used special messengers and ordered all manuscript copying to be done in-house. "We kept the thing top secret," she said. "Andy Warhol was the ultimate voyeur, and the diaries contain what he never wanted to show people while he was alive." *By Kim Wozencraft*

106
DESIGN FIRM: *Tenazas Design*
DESIGNER: *Lucille Tenazas*
HEADLINE TYPEFACE: *Goudy Oldstyle*
TEXT TYPEFACE: *Sabon and Univers 75*
CLIENT: *James River Corp.*

107/108
DESIGN FIRM: *Pentagram Design*
DESIGNER: *Haold Burch*
HEADLINE TYPEFACE: *Various*
TEXT TYPEFACE: *Helvetica, Bembo, and Times Roman*
CLIENT: *Warner Communications*

109

VALLEY FORGE PARCHMENT

109/110
DESIGN FIRM: *Morla Design*
DESIGNER: *Jennifer Morla*
HEADLINE TYPEFACE: *6-Line Block Gothic*
TEXT TYPEFACE: *6 Line Block Gothic, 4 Line Block Gothic and Typoscript*
CLIENT: *Simpson Paper Company*

110

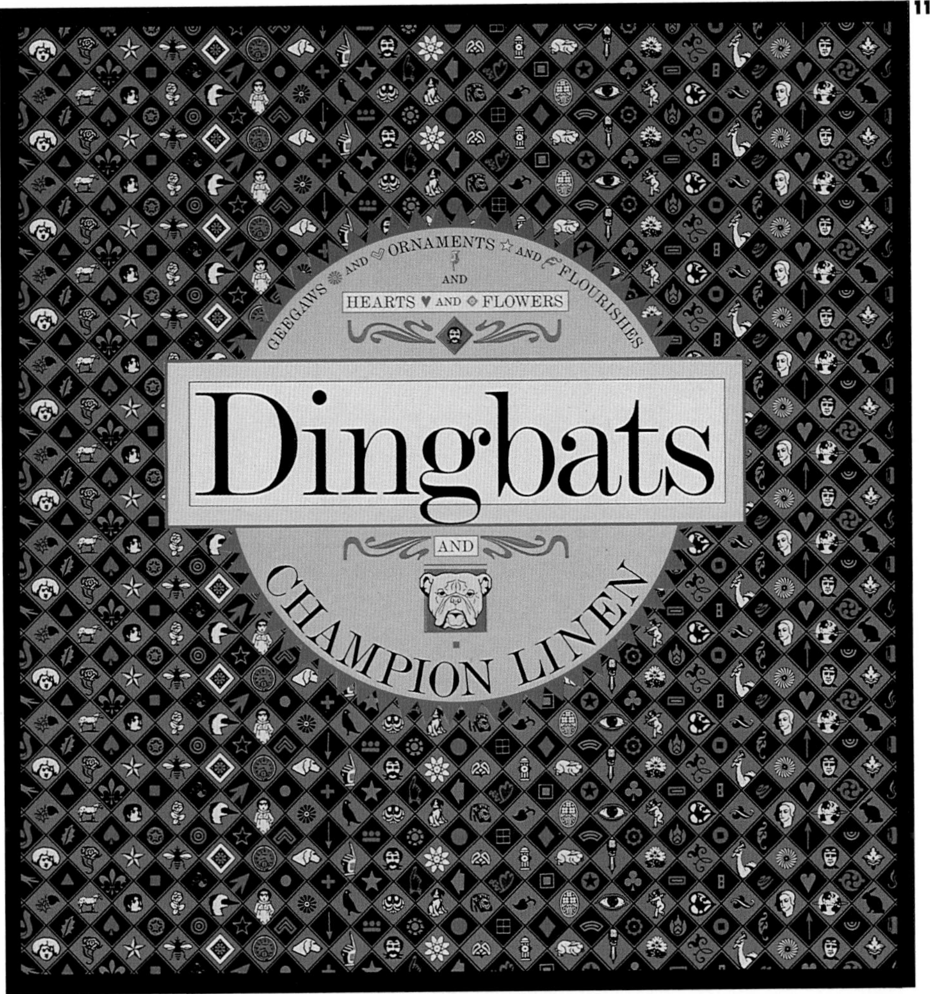

111

112

111/112
DESIGN FIRM: *Pentagram Design*
DESIGNER: *Paula Scher*
HEADLINE TYPEFACE: *Devinne*
TEXT TYPEFACE: *Bodoni Book*
CLIENT: *Champion International*

113

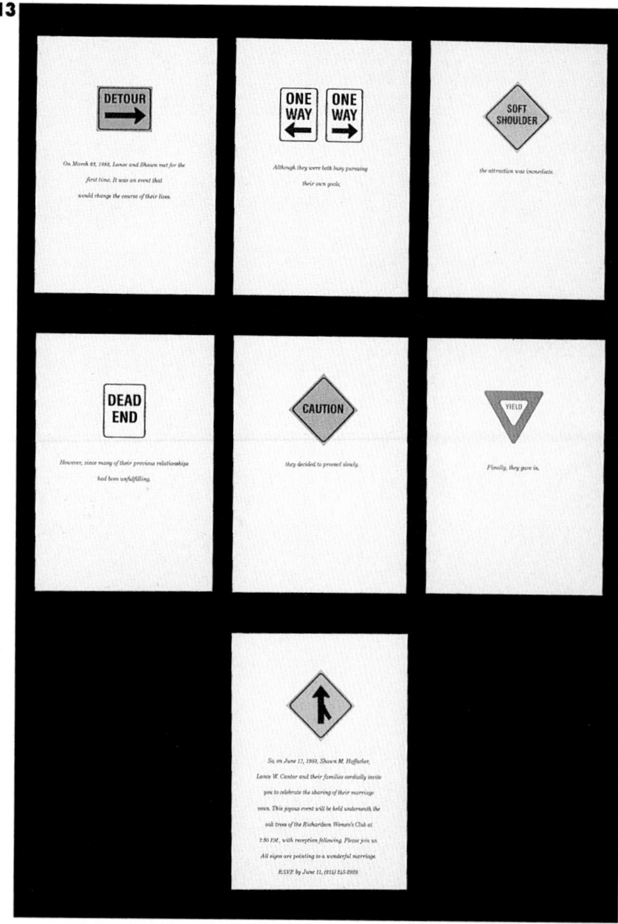

114

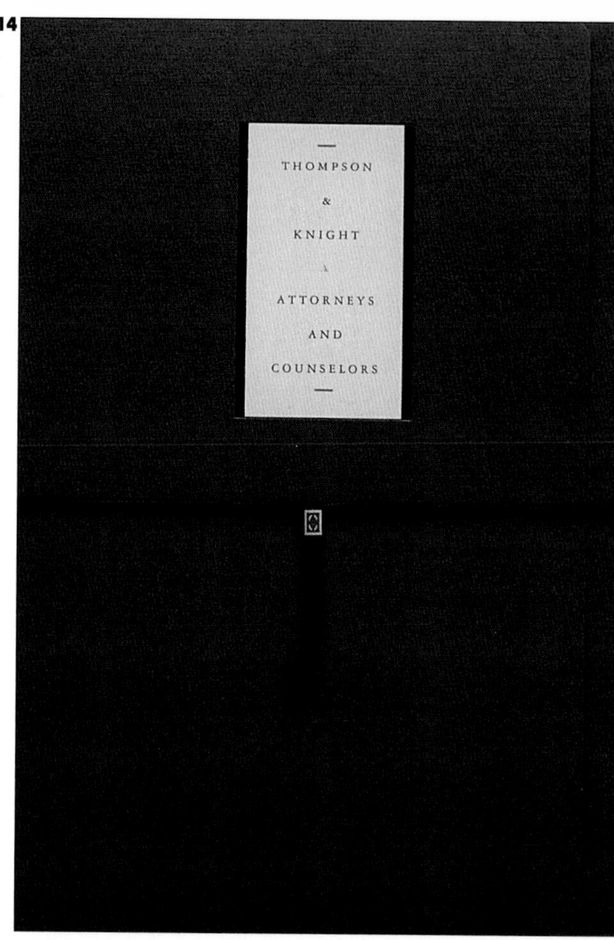

113
DESIGN FIRM: *Knape & Knape*
DESIGNER: *Willie Baronet*
TEXT TYPEFACE: *Baskerville Italic*
CLIENT: *Shawn Hoffacker*

114/115
DESIGN FIRM: *Dennard Creative, Inc.*
DESIGNER: *Bob Dennard, Chuck Johnson, and Marcie Doane*
HEADLINE TYPEFACE: *Erbar and Garamond*
TEXT TYPEFACE: *Garamond #3*
CLIENT: *Thompson & Knight Law Firm*

115

116

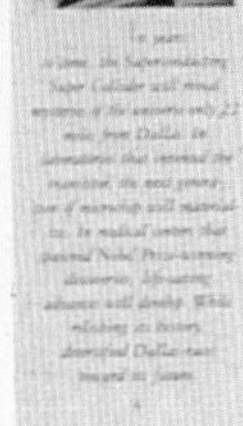

117

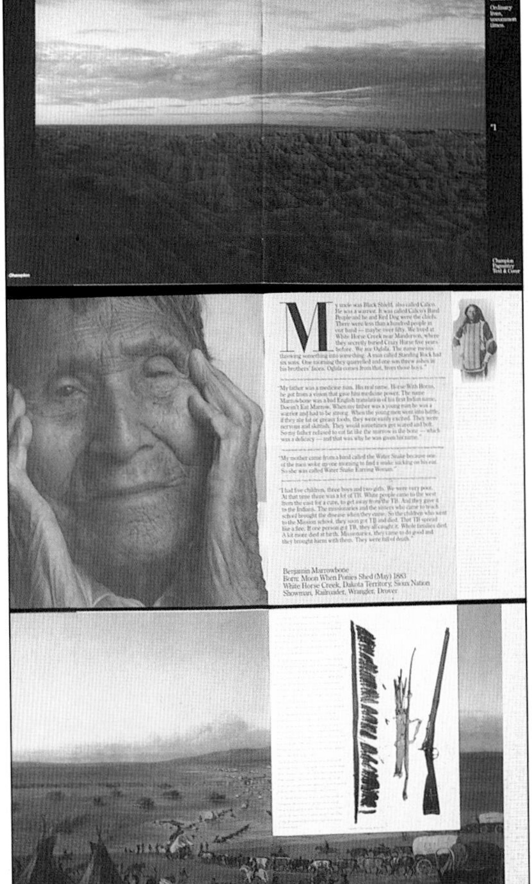

118

116
DESIGN FIRM: *Dennard Creative, Inc.*
DESIGNER: *Bob Dennard, Chuck Johnson, and Marcie Doane*
HEADLINE TYPEFACE: *Erbar and Garamond*
TEXT TYPEFACE: *Garamond #3*
CLIENT: *Thompson & Knight Law Firm*

117
DESIGN FIRM: *Hess & Hess*
DESIGNER: *Richard C. Hess*
CLIENT: *Champion International*

118
DESIGN FIRM: *Hess & Hess*
DESIGNER: *Richard C. Hess*
CLIENT: *Champion International*

119
DESIGN FIRM: *Studio Guarnaccia*
DESIGNER: *Steven Guarnaccia*
LETTERER: *Steven Guarnaccia*
HEADLINE TYPEFACE: *Handlettering*
CLIENT: *Aspen Design Conference*

119

120 

121 

122 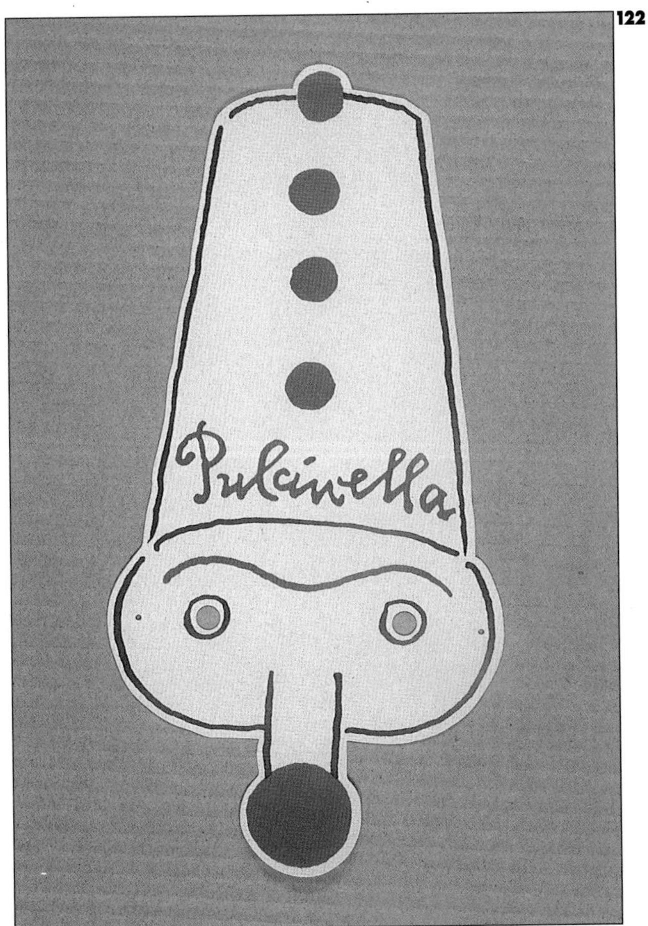

123 

120/121/122/123
DESIGN FIRM: *Studio Guarnaccia*
DESIGNER: *Steven Guarnaccia*
LETTERER: *Steven Guarnaccia*
HEADLINE TYPEFACE: *Handlettering*
CLIENT: *Aspen Design Conference*

124

125

124
DESIGN FIRM: *Cipriani Kremer Design*
DESIGNER: *Robert Cipriani*
HEADLINE TYPEFACE: *Franklin Gothic Condensed*
TEXT TYPEFACE: *ITC Berkeley Oldstyle Book*
CLIENT: *Bitstream*

125
DESIGN FIRM: *Concrete Design Communications*
DESIGNER: *Diti Katona*
HEADLINE TYPEFACE: *Cominus Antiqua*
TEXT TYPEFACE: *Cominus Antiqua*
CLIENT: *First Mercantile Currency Fund*

126

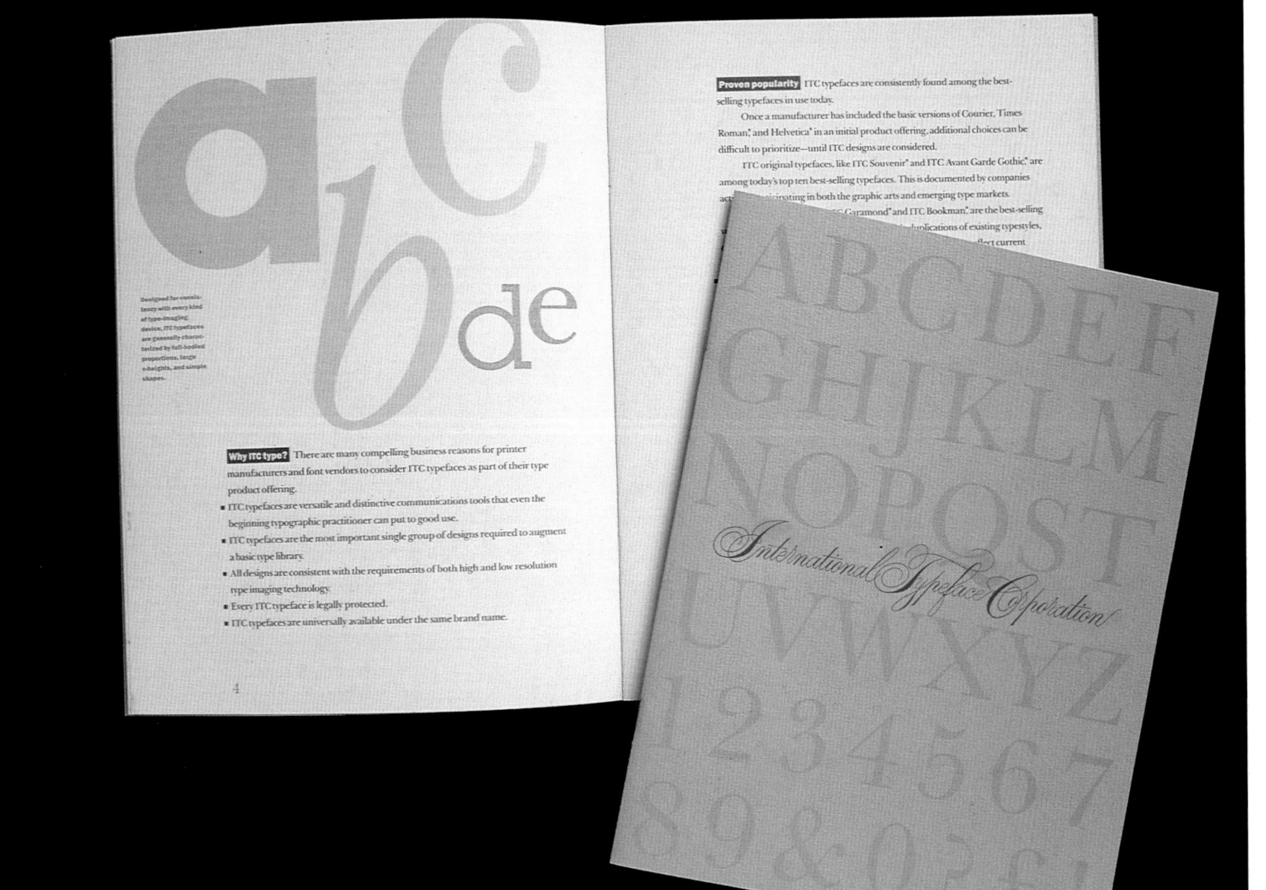

127

126
DESIGN FIRM: *Knape & Knape*
DESIGNER: *Michael Connors*
HEADLINE TYPEFACE: *Bodoni*
TEXT TYPEFACE: *Helvetica*
CLIENT: *City of Garland*

127
DESIGN FIRM: *Shapiro Design Associates*
DESIGNER: *Ellen Shapiro*
HEADLINE TYPEFACE: *ITC Franklin Gothic Heavy*
TEXT TYPEFACE: *ITC Baskerville Roman*
CLIENT: *International Typeface Corp.*

128
DESIGN FIRM: *Anton C. Kimball Graphic Design*
DESIGNER: *Anton C. Kimball*
LETTERER: *Anton C. Kimball*
HEADLINE TYPEFACE: *Handlettering*
CLIENT: *Anton C. Kimball Graphic Design*

128

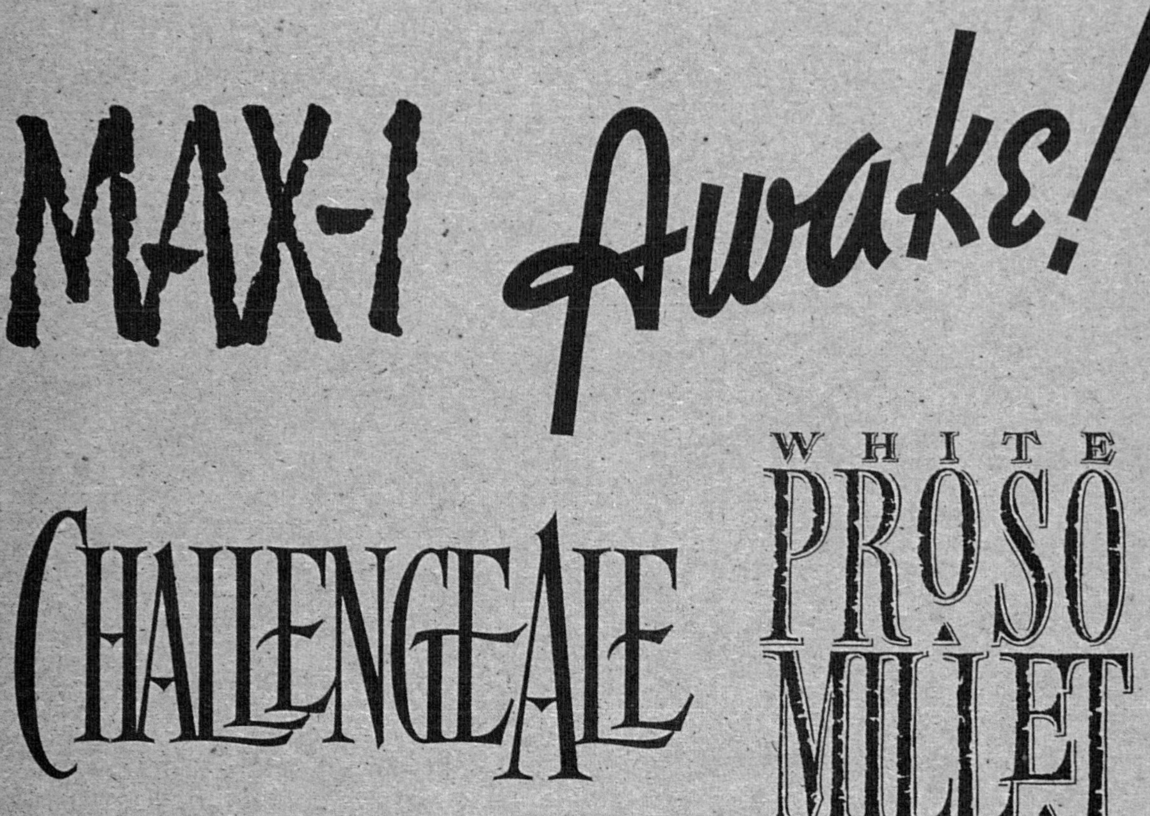

129

ANTON C. KIMBALL
820 S.E. SANDY BLVD.
PORTLAND, OR 97214
503 234-4777
FAX 234-4687

129
DESIGN FIRM: *Anton C. Kimball Graphic Design*
DESIGNER: *Anton C. Kimball*
LETTERER: *Anton C. Kimball*
HEADLINE TYPEFACE: *Handlettering*
CLIENT: *Anton C. Kimball Graphic Design*

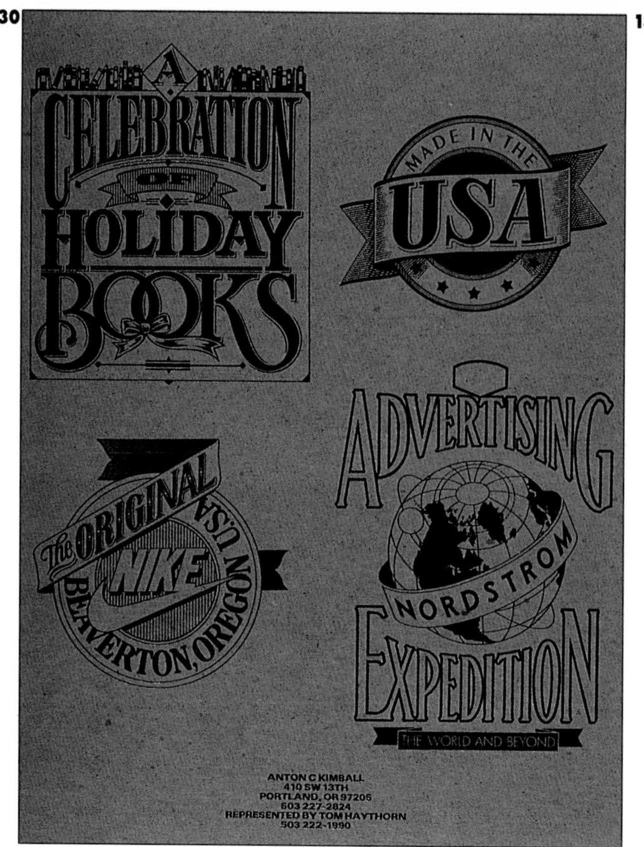

130/131
DESIGN FIRM: *Anton C. Kimball Graphic Design*
DESIGNER: *Anton C. Kimball*
LETTERER: *Anton C. Kimball*
HEADLINE TYPEFACE: *Handlettering*
CLIENT: *Anton C. Kimball Graphic Design*

132
DESIGN FIRM: *Thirst*
DESIGNER: *Rick Valicenti*
HEADLINE TYPEFACE: *Various*
TEXT TYPEFACE: *Various*
CLIENT: *American Center for Design*

133

134

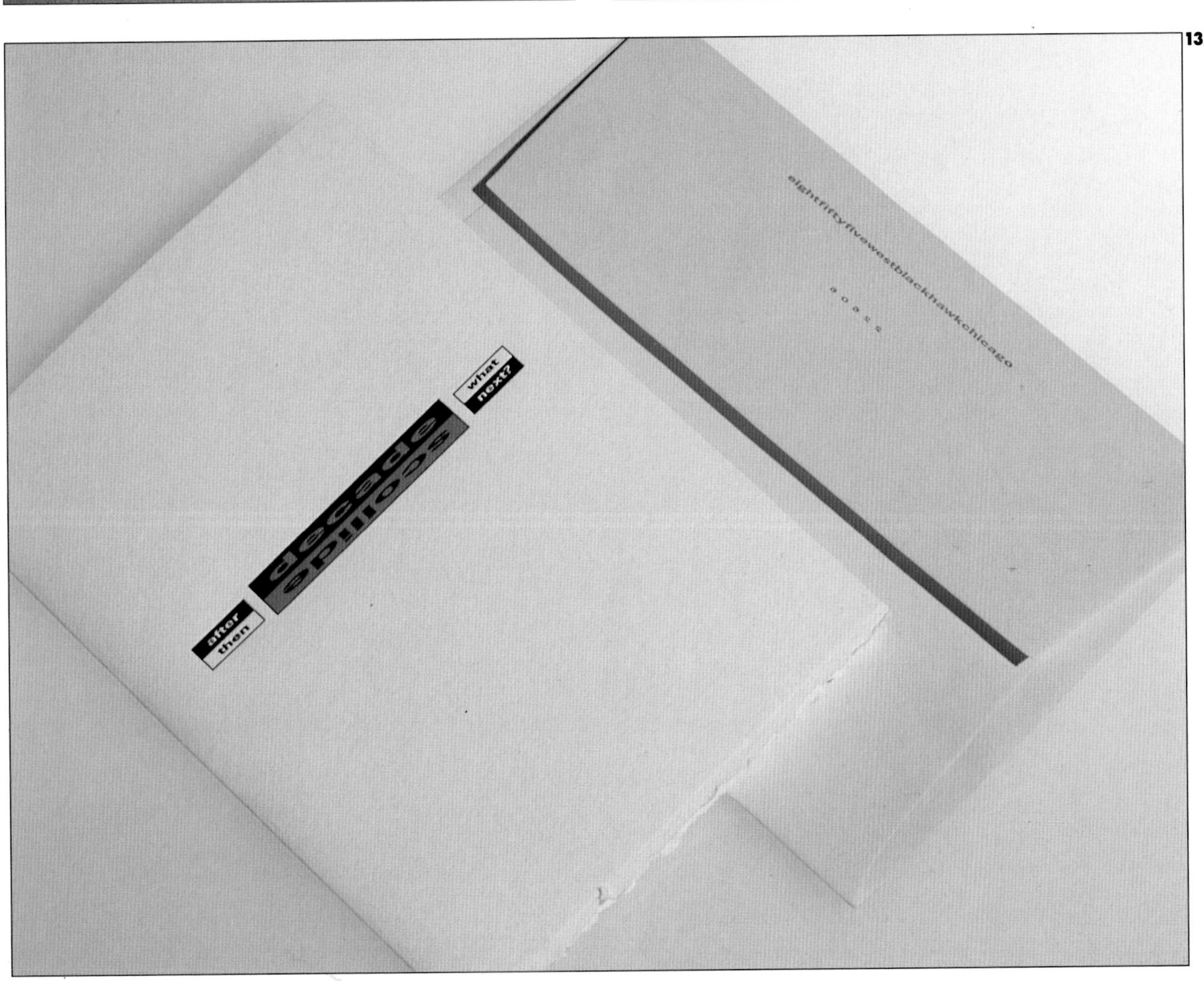

135

133/134
DESIGN FIRM: *Anton C. Kimball Graphic Design*
DESIGNER: *Anton C. Kimball*
HEADLINE TYPEFACE: *Handlettering*
CLIENT: *Anton C. Kimball Graphic Design*

135
DESIGN FIRM: *Cross Associates*
DESIGNER: *Ken Cook, James Cross, and Yee-Ping Cho*
HEADLINE TYPEFACE: *Helvetica Medium Condensed*
TEXT TYPEFACE: *Stempel Garamond, Helvetica Bold Expanded, and Helvetica Light Condensed*
CLIENT: *Simpson Paper Company*

136
DESIGN FIRM: *Anton C. Kimball Graphic Design*
DESIGNER: *Anton C. Kimball*
HEADLINE TYPEFACE: *Handlettering*
CLIENT: *Anton C. Kimball Graphic Design*

136

BOARD WARRIOR
Lake Washington
Marcella
BOYD'S BONUS DOLLARS
PORTLAND BREWING COMPANY ALE
LONG HOT SUMMER
ZONE
ROCK CREEK TAVERN RESTAURANT & BAR
LOOK WEST
HEARD THE NEWS AT NORDSTROM?
SPACE OCCUPIED

ANTON C KIMBALL
410 SW 13TH
PORTLAND, OR 97205
503 227-2824

137

matrixmetals

the NERVe

Pacific Ballet Theatre
NUTCRACKER

ANTON C KIMBALL
410 SW 13TH
PORTLAND, OR 97205
503 227-2824

137
DESIGN FIRM: *Anton C. Kimball Graphic Design*
DESIGNER: *Anton C. Kimball*
HEADLINE TYPEFACE: *Handlettering*
CLIENT: *Anton C. Kimball Graphic Design*

138/139

DESIGN FIRM: *Anton C. Kimball Graphic Design*
DESIGNER: *Anton C. Kimball*
HEADLINE TYPEFACE: *Handlettering*
CLIENT: *Anton C. Kimball Graphic Design*

140

DESIGN FIRM: *Cross Associates*
DESIGNER: *Ken Cook, James Cross and Yee-Ping Cho*
HEADLINE TYPEFACE: *Futura*
TEXT TYPEFACE: *Univers 67 and Caslon*
CLIENT: *Simpson Paper Company*

138

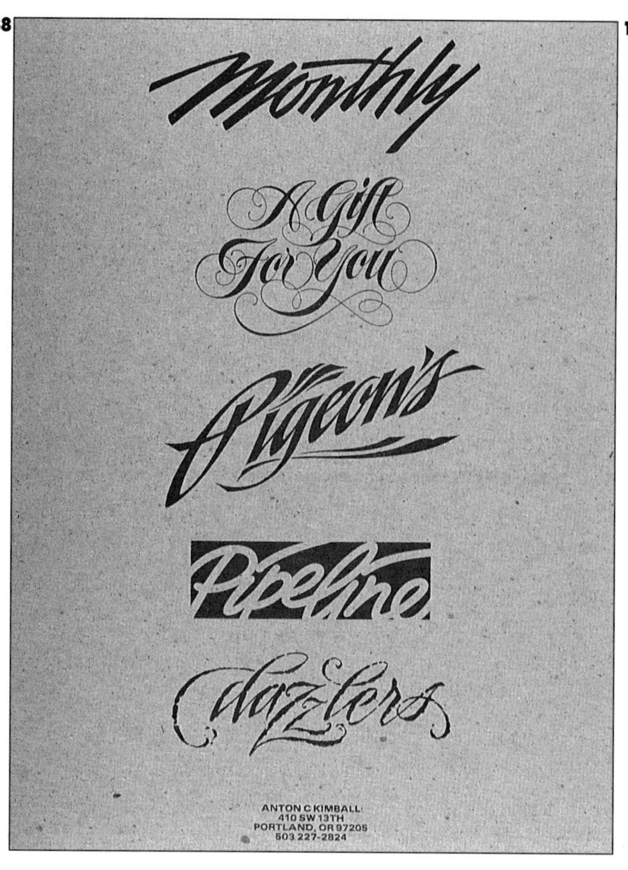

139

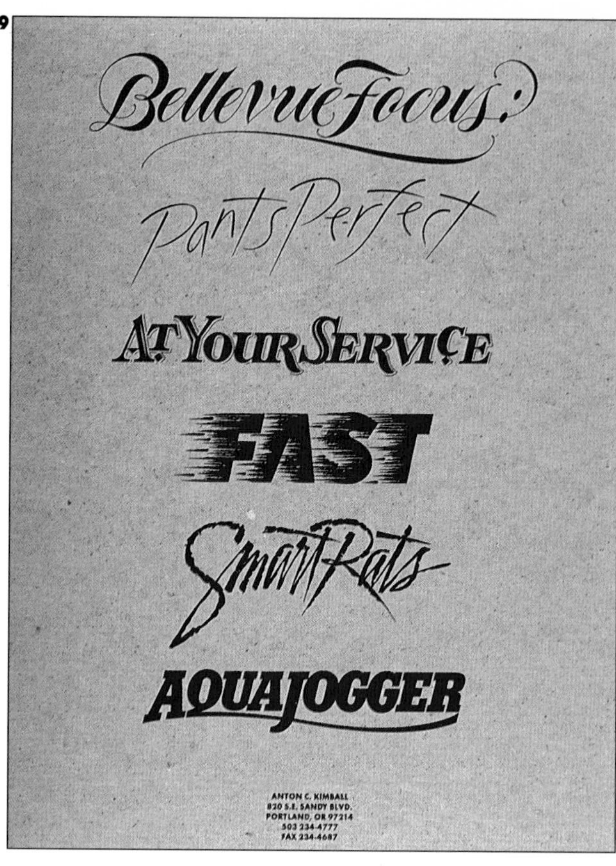

140

141

142

141
DESIGN FIRM: *Cross Associates*
DESIGNER: *Ken Cook, James Cross and Yee-Ping Cho*
HEADLINE TYPEFACE: *Futura*
TEXT TYPEFACE: *Univers 67 and Caslon*
CLIENT: *Simpson Paper Company*

142
DESIGN FIRM: *Vrontikis Design Office*
HEADLINE TYPEFACE: *Futura Bold*
TEXT TYPEFACE: *Bodoni Antiqua*
CLIENT: *AIGA, LA*

143

143
DESIGN FIRM: *Morla Design*
DESIGNER: *Jennifer Morla*
HEADLINE TYPEFACE: *Handlettering*
TEXT TYPEFACE: *6-Line Block, Coronet Bold, and Engravers Bold*
CLIENT: *Levi Strauss & Co.*

144

145

146

147

144
DESIGN FIRM: *Little & Company*
DESIGNER: *Paul Wharton and Ellen Huber*
HEADLINE TYPEFACE: *Sabon and Various*
TEXT TYPEFACE: *Sabon and Various*
CLIENT: *Gilbert Paper*

145
DESIGN FIRM: *GrandPre' and Whaley, Ltd.*
DESIGNER: *Kevin Whaley*
HEADLINE TYPEFACE: *Futura Bold*
TEXT TYPEFACE: *Univers*
CLIENT: *Chargo Printing, Inc.*

146
DESIGN FIRM: *David Carter Graphic Design Associates*
DESIGNER: *Gary Lobue*
HEADLINE TYPEFACE: *Berkeley Medium*
TEXT TYPEFACE: *Berkeley Book*
CLIENT: *David Carter Graphic Design Associates*

147
DESIGN FIRM: *Barshun Design*
DESIGNER: *Scott Barshun*
LETTERER: *Scott Barshun*
HEADLINE TYPEFACE: *Handlettering*
TEXT TYPEFACE: *Radiant and Century*
CLIENT: *Minneapolis College of Art and Design Gallery*

148
DESIGN FIRM: *Peterson & Company*
DESIGNER: *Bryan L. Peterson and David Lerch*
HEADLINE TYPEFACE: *Handlettering*
TEXT TYPEFACE: *Copperplate 33 BC*
CLIENT: *Southern Methodist University*

149
DESIGN FIRM: *The Duffy Design Group*
DESIGNER: *Sharon Werner*
LETTERER: *Lynn Shulte*
HEADLINE TYPEFACE: *Handlettering, Spartan Black, and Trade Gothic*
CLIENT: *Fallon McElligott*

150
DESIGN FIRM: *Letterform Design*
DESIGNER: *Terry Irwin and Leah Toby Hoffmitz*
LETTERER: *Leah Toby Hoffmitz*
HEADLINE TYPEFACE: *Various*
TEXT TYPEFACE: *Various*
CLIENT: *Characters and Color*

148

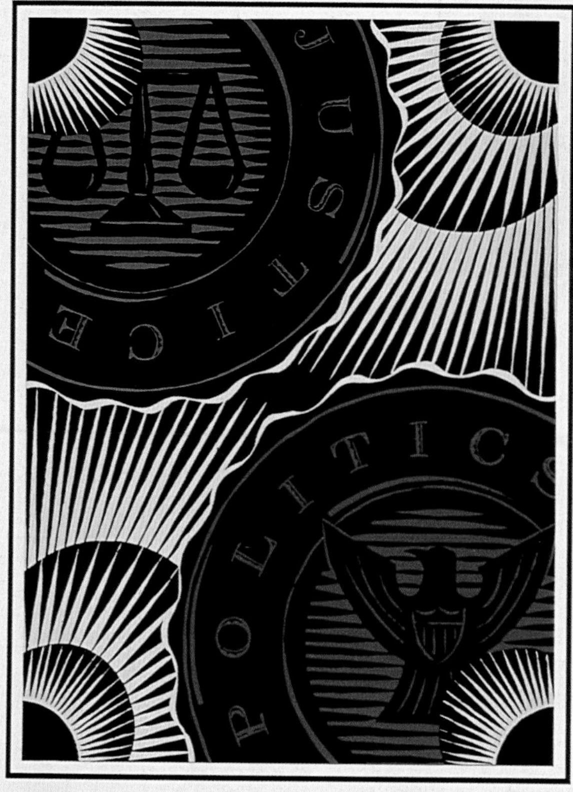

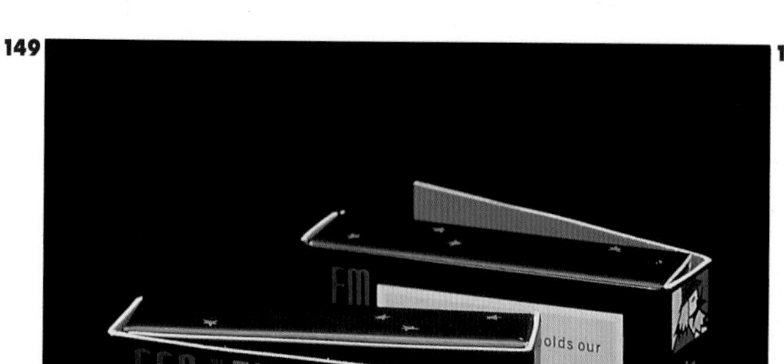

149

150

151

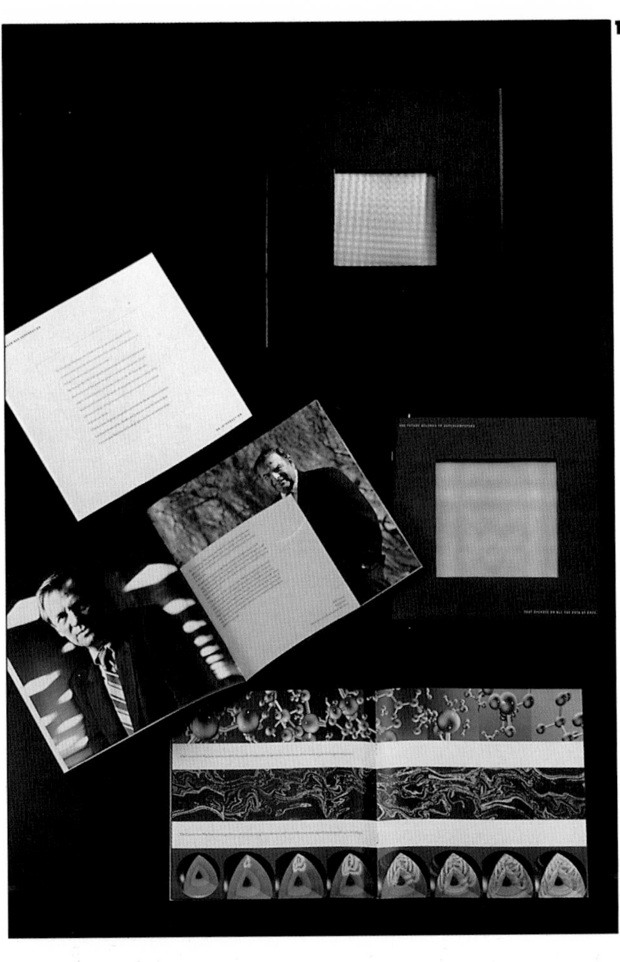

152

153

151
DESIGN FIRM: *Cipriani Kremer Design*
DESIGNER: *Robert Cipriani*
HEADLINE TYPEFACE: *Helvetica Medium Condensed*
TEXT TYPEFACE: *ITC New Baskerville*
CLIENT: *Thinking Machines, Corp.*

152/153
DESIGN FIRM: *Pentagram Design*
DESIGNER: *Kit Hinrichs and Belle How*
HEADLINE TYPEFACE: *Bernhard Schonschrifl*
TEXT TYPEFACE: *Futura Light and Bernhard Modern*
CLIENT: *Graphic Arts Center*

154

DESIGN FIRM: *Avchen and Associates, Inc.*
DESIGNER: *Leslee Avchen*
HEADLINE TYPEFACE: *Stone*
TEXT TYPEFACE: *Stone*
CLIENT: *The Science Museum of Minnesota*

155

DESIGN FIRM: *Avchen and Associates, Inc.*
DESIGNER: *Leslee Avchen*
HEADLINE TYPEFACE: *Cloister Antiqua*
TEXT TYPEFACE: *Various*
CLIENT: *Consolidated Papers, Inc.*

154

FIRST NATIONAL LEAGUE GAME
THE THIRTIES

On the heels of the 1927 Yankees entered the 1929-31 Philadelphia A's. The A's were overwhelming for three seasons, but in 1931, the A's had six Hall of Famers on the field: Grove, Simmons, Cochrane and Foxx. Mix those talents with a solid support team and it's no wonder they seemed destined to win their third consecutive World Series title. Yet one man, St. Louis Cardinal center fielder Pepper Martin, almost singlehandedly destroyed Philadelphia in the World Series collecting 12 hits in his first 18 at bats to help St. Louis take the series, 4 games to 3. In the National League, the Giants' "meal-ticket" of the 1930s, Carl Hubbell, led them to three pennants and two near-misses in five years. Noted for his screwball, he compiled a 46 scoreless inning streak in 1933 and won 16 straight in 1936. He is remembered for his 1934 All Star Game Performance when he fanned Ruth, Gehrig, Foxx, Simmons and Cronin!

Clay Bryant's homemade belt buckle

Night game ticket c. late 30's

Game 5, 1938 World Series ticket and press pin

11

155

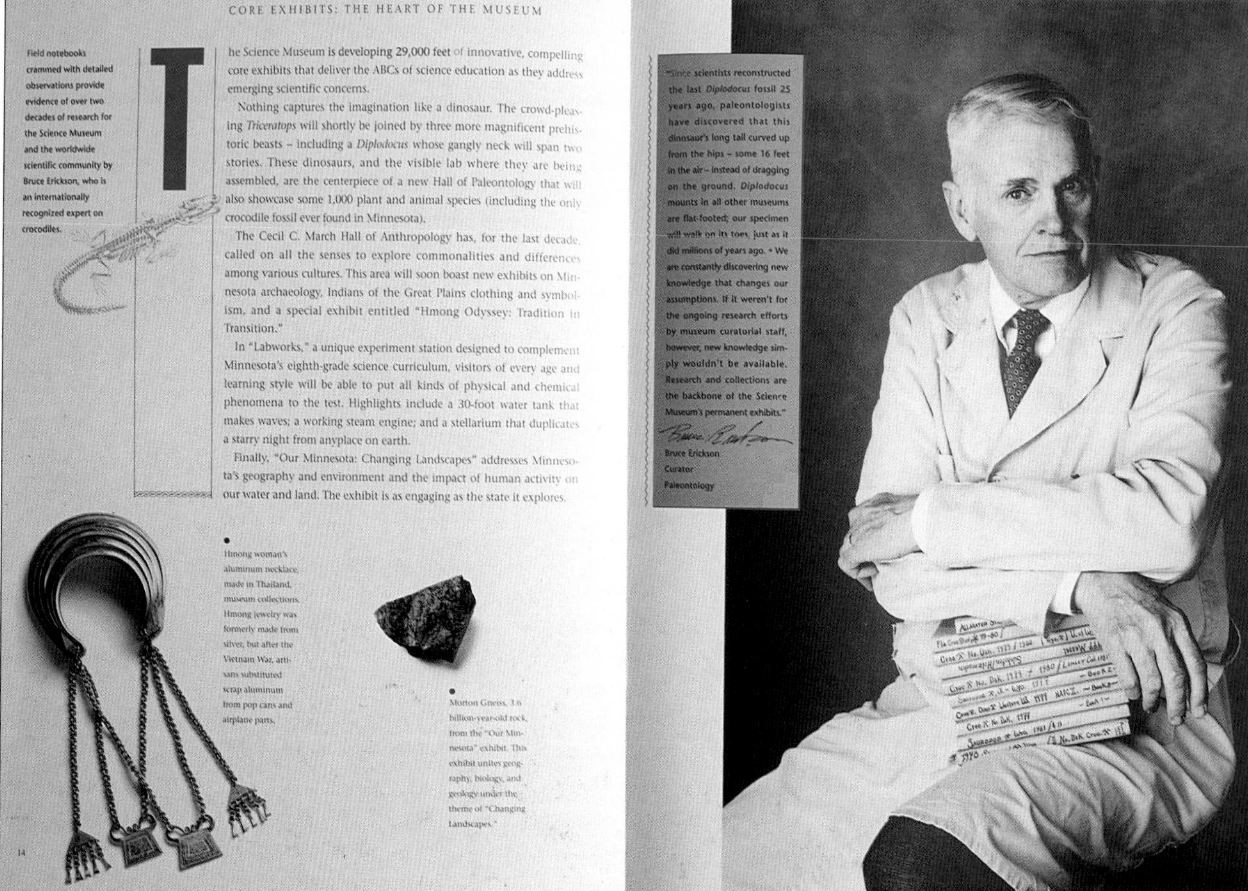
CORE EXHIBITS: THE HEART OF THE MUSEUM

Field notebooks crammed with detailed observations provide evidence of over two decades of research for the Science Museum and the worldwide scientific community by Bruce Erickson, who is an internationally recognized expert on crocodiles.

The Science Museum is developing 29,000 feet of innovative, compelling core exhibits that deliver the ABCs of science education as they address emerging scientific concerns.

Nothing captures the imagination like a dinosaur. The crowd-pleasing *Triceratops* will shortly be joined by three more magnificent prehistoric beasts – including a *Diplodocus* whose gangly neck will span two stories. These dinosaurs, and the visible lab where they are being assembled, are the centerpiece of a new Hall of Paleontology that will also showcase some 1,000 plant and animal species (including the only crocodile fossil ever found in Minnesota).

The Cecil C. March Hall of Anthropology has, for the last decade, called on all the senses to explore commonalities and differences among various cultures. This area will soon boast new exhibits on Minnesota archaeology, Indians of the Great Plains clothing and symbolism, and a special exhibit entitled "Hmong Odyssey: Tradition in Transition."

In "Labworks," a unique experiment station designed to complement Minnesota's eighth-grade science curriculum, visitors of every age and learning style will be able to put all kinds of physical and chemical phenomena to the test. Highlights include a 30-foot water tank that makes waves; a working steam engine; and a stellarium that duplicates a starry night from anyplace on earth.

Finally, "Our Minnesota: Changing Landscapes" addresses Minnesota's geography and environment and the impact of human activity on our water and land. The exhibit is as engaging as the state it explores.

Hmong woman's aluminum necklace, made in Thailand, museum collections. Hmong jewelry was formerly made from silver, but after the Vietnam War, artisans substituted scrap aluminum from pop cans and airplane parts.

Morton Gneiss, 3.6 billion-year-old rock, from the "Our Minnesota" exhibit. This exhibit unites geography, biology, and geology under the theme of "Changing Landscapes."

14

"Since scientists reconstructed the last *Diplodocus* fossil 25 years ago, paleontologists have discovered that this dinosaur's long tail curved up from the hips – some 16 feet in the air – instead of dragging on the ground. *Diplodocus* mounts in all other museums are flat-footed; our specimen will walk on its toes, just as it did millions of years ago. • We are constantly discovering new knowledge that changes our assumptions. If it weren't for the ongoing research efforts by museum curatorial staff, however, new knowledge simply wouldn't be available. Research and collections are the backbone of the Science Museum's permanent exhibits."

Bruce Erickson
Curator
Paleontology

156

BY PERRY GARFINKEL

A TASTE OF INDIA

India is like the parable of the elephant and the 10 blind men. As the tale goes, each man is asked to feel a different part of the animal and then describe it. Naturally, they all describe 10 unique beasts.

That's the diversity in this country of more than 700 million people, living in 20 different states in a region the size of Europe. There is no way for even a sighted person to fathom the whole beast, except maybe through its food.

A person could describe with surprising accuracy what part of India he or she was in simply by tasting that region's food. A well-cultured palate could distinguish among Gujarati, Malayali, Assamese, Punjabi, Maharashtrian, Sindhi, Bengali, Kashmiri, Goan, and Hyderabadi foods – to name just a few. In some states, like Kerala, Bengal, and Andhra Pradesh, the staple is rice; in others, like Punjab and Uttar Pradesh, where rice is not grown, wheat becomes the center of the diet, used most frequently in breads. In the Valley of Kashmir, in the northernmost part of India, the cool climate is perfect for raising sheep, which explains the frequency of lamb dishes.

"Indian food is the reflection of the heritage of its people," writes Julie Sahni in *Classic Indian Cooking* (William Morrow, 1980). "It represents its historical development, religious beliefs, cultural practices, and, above all, its geographical attributes."

For delicious proof, walk the streets of any city in any part of this vast polyglot nation, and you will be assaulted by sights, sounds, and particularly smells of foods that will follow you forever. The aromas of exotic spices – cardamom and cumin, saffron and the world famous curries – bombard the traveler's nose and palate. The spices and other ingredients used in each region depend entirely on what grows best there. For example, coconuts are prevalent in southern India, so you'll find most southern curries and sauces are coconut-based. You'll rarely encounter that sweet, milky flavor in northern India. Generally, southern foods are spicier than those in the north. One theory explains that hot chilies and peppers are more abundant and pungent in the south. Another suggests that the warmer southern weather demanded, in the days of scarce refrigeration, that food be more heavily spiced to preserve it better. Some suggest that hot and spicy foods raise the body temperature, thus lowering the difference between one's own heat and that of the environment. Whatever the reason, lovers of hot food will feel they have entered a state of bliss when they head south.

Lining every Indian city and village alleyway are food stalls and vendors hawking snacks, drinks, fruit, and various edibles of indistinguishable origin. Popular snacks are chutney and other forms of pickled fruit and vegetables. Regional variations of street foods depend on indigenous vegetables, grains, and spices. *Chevda* – fried lentils, nuts, and sweet raisins – can be bought by the same name on streets throughout India, but it will never taste the same in any two locales. The taste will depend upon which of the 40 varieties of lentils and dozens of nuts grow in the region. Beware – for some of these foods may assault your intestinal fortitude, as well. In most cases, however, you can safely follow on a Kipling-esque journey to the soulful stomach of India.

Speaking of soul, Westerners who assume the heart and soul of any meal is meat had better brush up on their Vedic readings before arriving in India. Religious practice and observance have played no small part in the country's dietary habits, and even the staunchest meat-and-potatoes devotee is likely to give some of India's many delectable vegetarian dishes a try.

8

9

157

156
DESIGN FIRM: *Pentagram Design*
DESIGNER: *Kit Hinrichs, Terri Driscoll, and Karen Berndt*
HEADLINE TYPEFACE: *Bodoni Book*
TEXT TYPEFACE: *Century Line*
CLIENT: *Royal Viking Line*

157
DESIGN FIRM: *Peterson & Company*
DESIGNER: *Scott Paramski*
CLIENT: *ASMP*

158
DESIGN FIRM: *Pentagram*
DESIGNER: *Kit Hinrichs and Belle How*
HEADLINE TYPEFACE: *Engravers Roman Bold*
TEXT TYPEFACE: *Garamond and Cheltenham Oldstyle*
CLIENT: *Simpson Paper Company*

159
DESIGN FIRM: *Little & Company*
DESIGNER: *Paul Wharton*
HEADLINE TYPEFACE: *Antiqua Open*
TEXT TYPEFACE: *Berkeley Oldstyle*
CLIENT: *Public Relations Society of America*

160

161

160
DESIGN FIRM: *The Duffy Design Group*
DESIGNER: *Joe Duffy, Sharon Werner, Haley Johnson, Glenn Tutssel, and Garrick Hamm*
HEADLINE TYPEFACE: *Bodoni Italic*
CLIENT: *The Duffy Design Group/Michael Peterson Group*

161
DESIGN FIRM: *Little & Company*
DESIGNER: *Paul Wharton*
HEADLINE TYPEFACE: *Futura Extra Bold*
TEXT TYPEFACE: *Emigré Matrix Wide*
CLIENT: *AIGA/Minnesota*

162

163

164

As part of the nationwide Junior Achievement program, IBM volunteers provide guidance and instruction on economics and other business-related subjects. The program gives groups of high school students the opportunity to develop entrepreneurial skills by establishing and managing their own small businesses.

We hire more than a thousand students each year as part-time employees through our High School Cooperative program. The students are generally secretarial and/or business students who receive paid experience in their field of study.

Encouraging parental involvement

Many of the more than 22,000 IBM employees who volunteer their time in U.S. K-12 programs are parents of school-age children. We encourage parental involvement in schools.

The IBM Fund for Community Service program is a major way for employees to participate in local community

22

projects. The program combines volunteerism with corporate contributions by providing money or IBM equipment to community organizations, as well as to qualified elementary and high schools, where IBM employees, retirees or their spouses work as volunteers.

In 1990, IBM announced a K-12 Matching Grants program that enables an employee or group of employees to buy IBM equipment for a school with IBM's help. The employees contribute 20 percent of the retail cost of IBM equipment and software – up to $5,000 per year, per school, per employee transaction. IBM contributes the balance.

A new school volunteer hotline in the San Francisco Bay area, conceived by an IBM employee and funded by IBM, provides information about local volunteer opportunities in K-12 schools. With the aid of a computer data base, the telephone hotline speeds the process of matching organizations supporting education with citizens, including local IBMers, who want to volunteer.

Supporting our teachers

Many IBM locations have established programs with local schools and school systems aimed at professional development of teachers and at helping them develop courses for their students.

IBM Grants for Technology in Education, announced in 1989, is a five-year, more than $25 million program to help improve U.S. elementary and secondary education through more effective use of technology. The grants, which focus on colleges of education throughout the United States,

23

162
DESIGN FIRM: *Morla Design*
DESIGNER: *Jennifer Morla*
HEADLINE TYPEFACE: *Torino*
TEXT TYPEFACE: *Univers 49*
CLIENT: *Levi Strauss & Co.*

163/164
DESIGN FIRM: *Pentagram Design*
DESIGNER: *Woody Pirtle and Jennifer Long*
HEADLINE TYPEFACE: *Helvetica Bold*
TEXT TYPEFACE: *Berthold Bodoni*
CLIENT: *IBM Corp.*

165

166

167

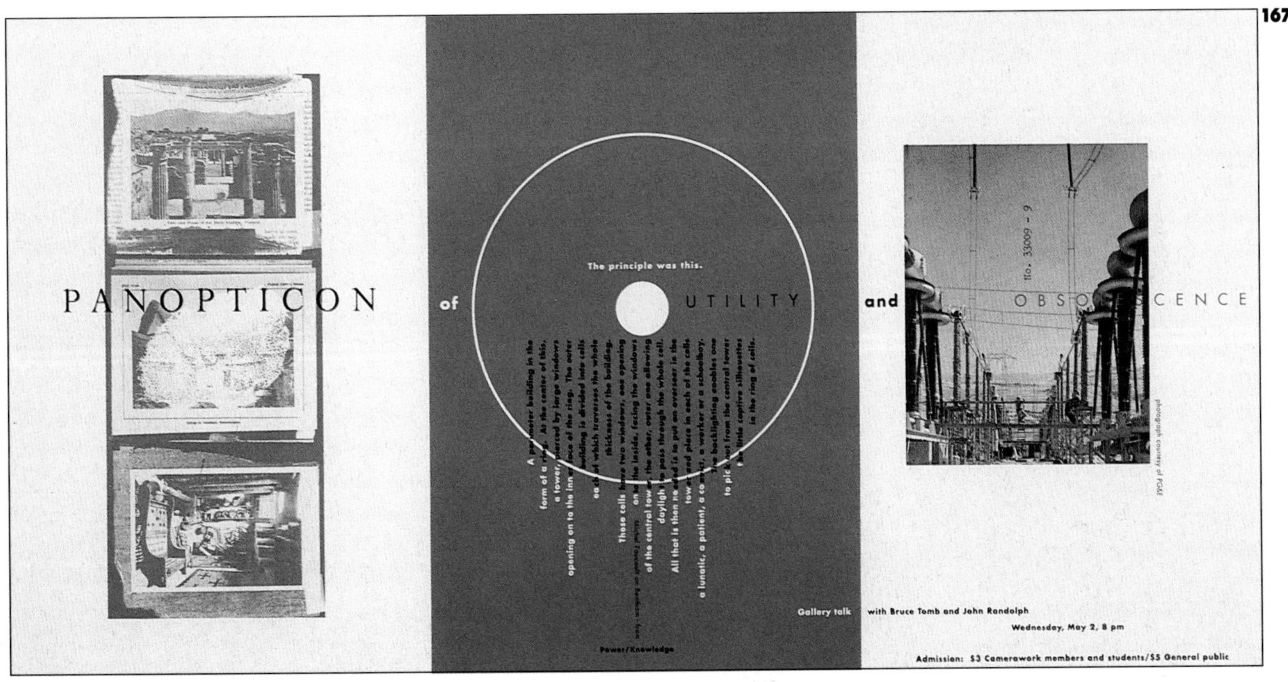

165
DESIGN FIRM: *Tenazas Design*
DESIGNER: *Lucille Tenazas*
HEADLINE TYPEFACE: *Perpetua and Univers*
TEXT TYPEFACE: *Futura*
CLIENT: *SF Camerawork*

166
DESIGN FIRM: *The Duffy Design Group*
DESIGNER: *Haley Johnson*
LETTERER: *Todd Waterbory*
HEADLINE TYPEFACE: *Venus Bold Extended*
TEXT TYPEFACE: *Uranus*
CLIENT: *D'Amico & Partners*

167
DESIGN FIRM: *Tenazas Design*
DESIGNER: *Lucille Tenazas*
HEADLINE TYPEFACE: *Perpetua and Univers*
TEXT TYPEFACE: *Futura*
CLIENT: *SF Camerawork*

168
DESIGN FIRM: *Thirst*
DESIGNER: *Rick Valicenti and Tony Klassen*
HEADLINE TYPEFACE: *Franklin Gothic Condensed*
CLIENT: *Consolidated Papers, Inc.*

169
DESIGN FIRM: *Thirst*
DESIGNER: *Rick Valicenti and Tony Klassen*
HEADLINE TYPEFACE: *Bronzo and News Gothic*
TEXT TYPEFACE: *Franklin Gothic Condensed*
CLIENT: *Gilbert Paper*

170
DESIGN FIRM: *Mark Oldach Design*
DESIGNER: *Mark Oldach*
HEADLINE TYPEFACE: *Bodoni*
TEXT TYPEFACE: *Helvetica Black Condensed*
CLIENT: *USG Interiors*

168

169

170

171

172

173

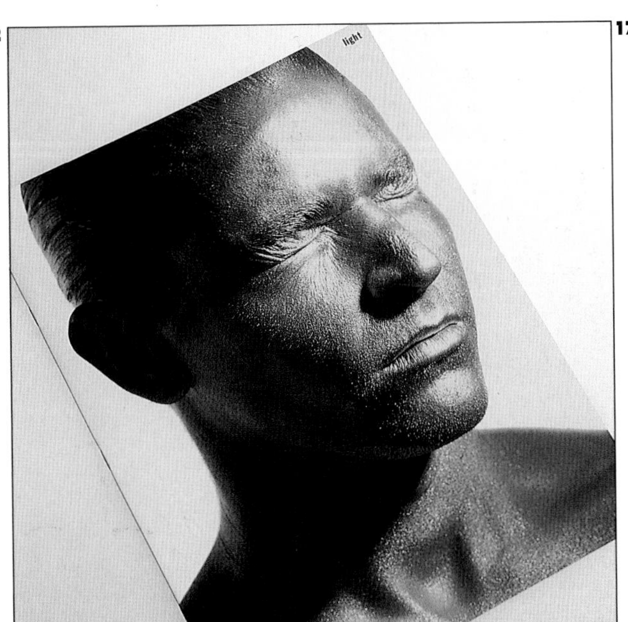

171
DESIGN FIRM: *Thirst*
DESIGNER: *Rick Valicenti and Tony Klassen*
HEADLINE TYPEFACE: *Franklin Gothic Condensed*
CLIENT: *Consolidated Papers, Inc.*

172
DESIGN FIRM: *Mark Oldach Design*
DESIGNER: *Mark Oldach*
HEADLINE TYPEFACE: *Bodoni*
TEXT TYPEFACE: *Helvetica Black Condensed*
CLIENT: *USG Interiors*

173
DESIGN FIRM: *Thirst*
DESIGNER: *Rick Valicenti and Tony Klassen*
HEADLINE TYPEFACE: *Franklin Gothic Condensed*
CLIENT: *Consolidated Papers, Inc.*

174

175

174

DESIGN FIRM: *Little & Company*

DESIGNER: *Paul Wharton, Karen Geiger, and Ellen Huber*

HEADLINE TYPEFACE: *Coronet and Gill Sans Bold*

TEXT TYPEFACE: *Gill Sans and Various*

CLIENT: *Cross Pointe Paper Corp.*

175

DESIGN FIRM: *Morla Design*

DESIGNER: *Jennifer Morla and Jeanette Aramburu*

HEADLINE TYPEFACE: *Copperplate 33 BC and Shelly Allegro*

TEXT TYPEFACE: *Copperplate 33 BC*

CLIENT: *Levi Strauss & Co.*

176

177

176
DESIGN FIRM: *Dunn and Rice Design, Inc.*
DESIGNER: *John Dunn*
TEXT TYPEFACE: *Linoscript and Sabon*
CLIENT: *Ashby Park Collection*

177
DESIGN FIRM: *Little & Company*
DESIGNER: *Paul Wharton, Ted Riley, and Ellen Huber*
HEADLINE TYPEFACE: *Emigré Elektrix Bold*
TEXT TYPEFACE: *Emigré Elektrix Light*
CLIENT: *Cross Pointe Paper Corp.*

178

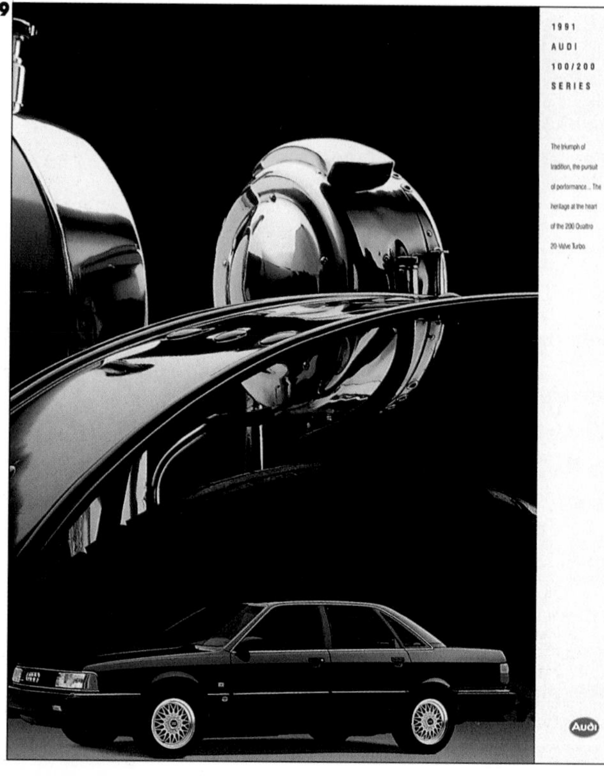

179

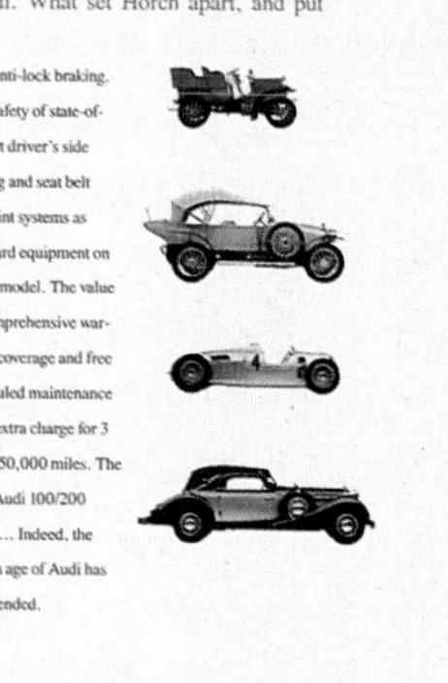

180

178
DESIGN FIRM: *The Duffy Design Group*
DESIGNER: *Sharon Werner*
LETTERER: *Lynn Shulte and Sharon Werner*
HEADLINE TYPEFACE: *Handlettering*
TEXT TYPEFACE: *Eurostyle Bold Extended*
CLIENT: *Fox River Paper Co.*

179/180
DESIGN FIRM: *SHR Design Communications*
DESIGNER: *Karin Burklein Arnold*
HEADLINE TYPEFACE: *Triumvirate Black Condensed*
TEXT TYPEFACE: *Times*
CLIENT: *Audi of America, Inc.*

181

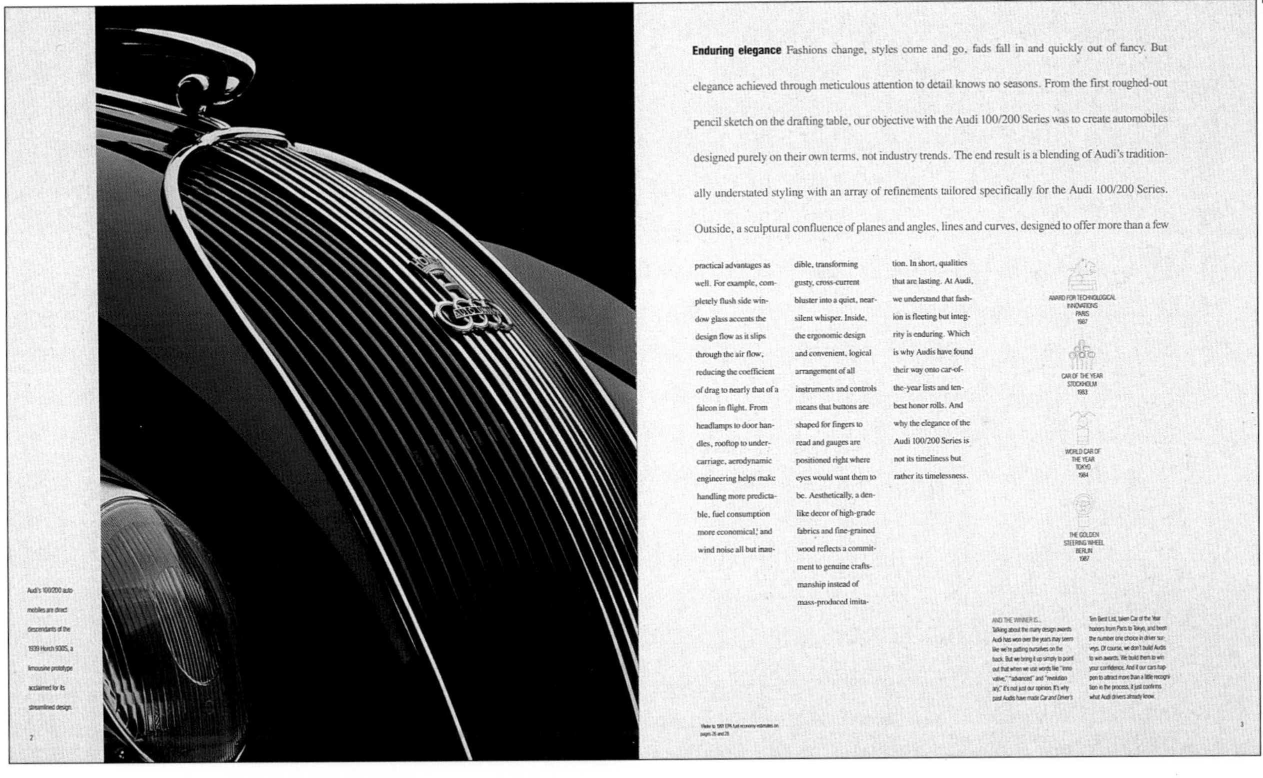

182

181/182

DESIGN FIRM: *SHR Design Communications*

DESIGNER: *Karin Burklein Arnold*

HEADLINE TYPEFACE: *Triumvirate Black Condensed*

TEXT TYPEFACE: *Times*

CLIENT: *Audi of America, Inc.*

183

DESIGN FIRM: *The Duffy Design Group*
DESIGNER: *Sharon Werner*
HEADLINE TYPEFACE: *Discus*
TEXT TYPEFACE: *Spartan Medium*
CLIENT: *D'Amico & Partners*

184/185

DESIGN FIRM: *SHR Design Communications*
DESIGNER: *Karin Burklein Arnold*
HEADLINE TYPEFACE: *Triumvirate Black Condensed*
TEXT TYPEFACE: *Times*
CLIENT: *Audi of America, Inc.*

183

184

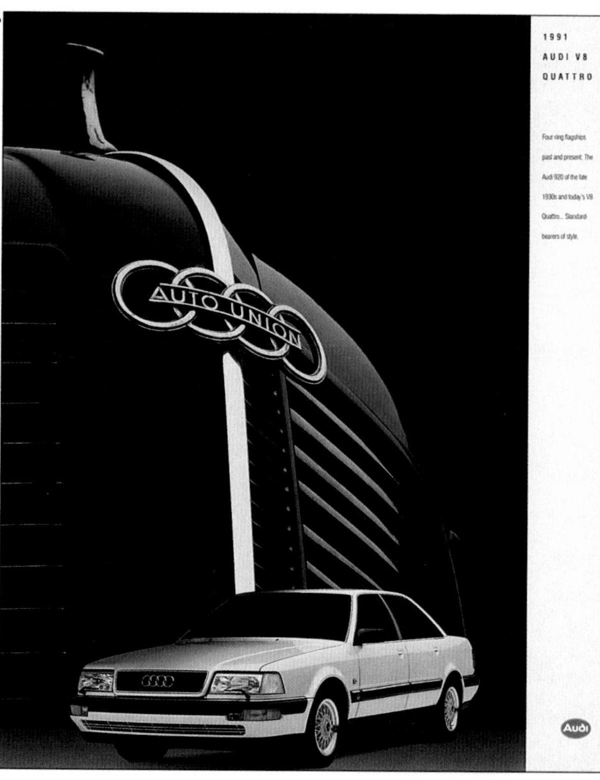

185

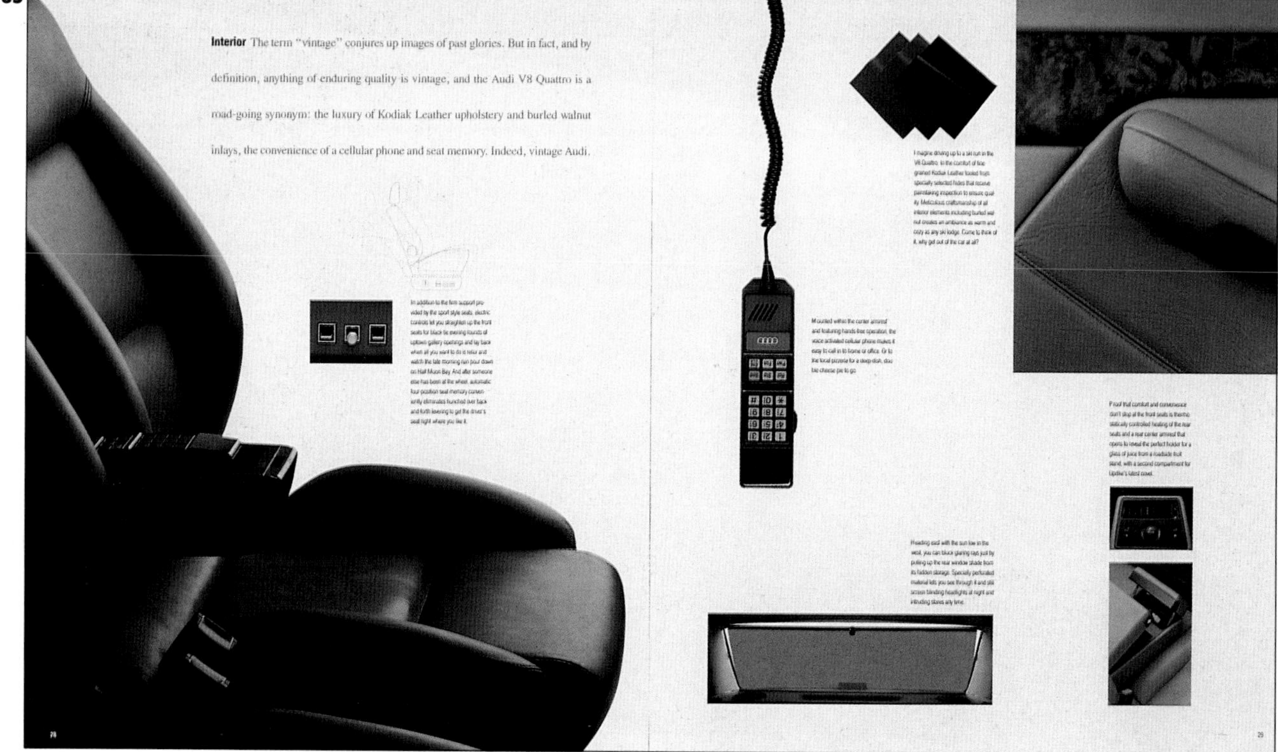

186

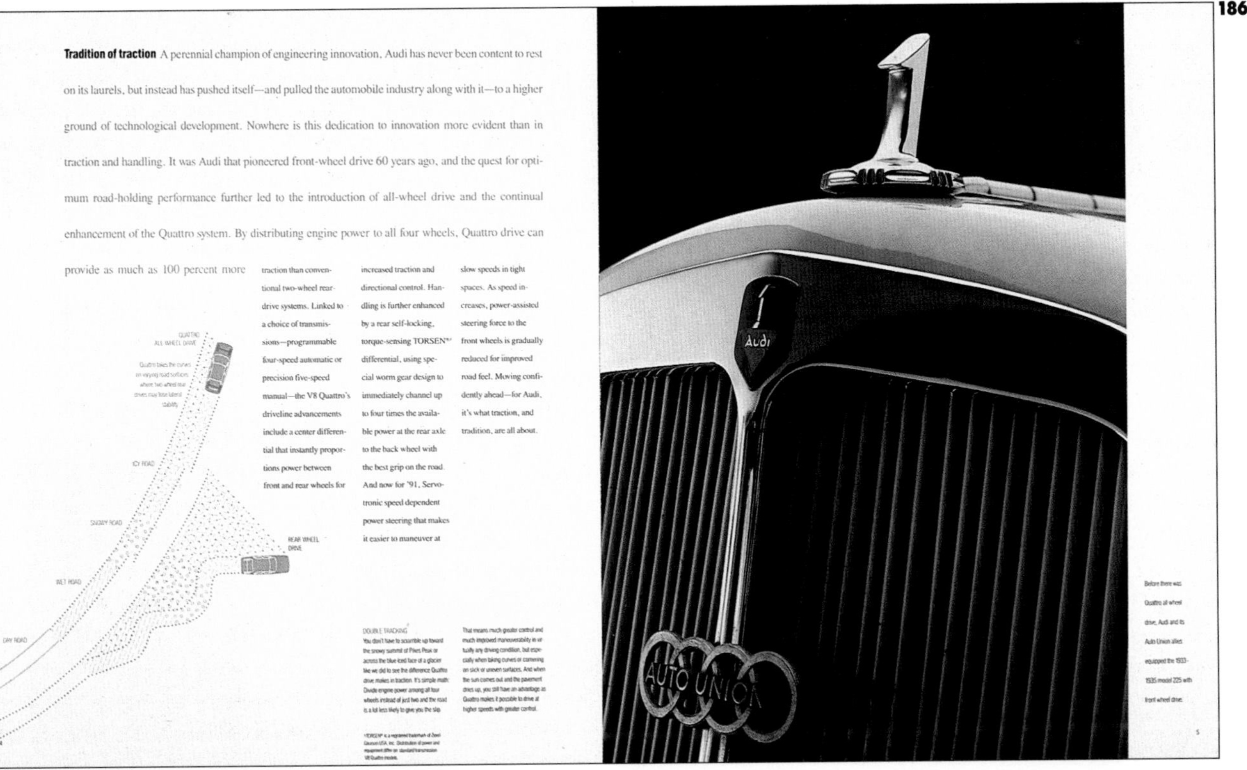

187

186/187
DESIGN FIRM: *SHR Design Communications*
DESIGNER: *Karin Burklein Arnold*
HEADLINE TYPEFACE: *Triumvirate Black Condensed*
TEXT TYPEFACE: *Times*
CLIENT: *Audi of America, Inc.*

188

President's Letter

Everywhere we look we see the work of designers. Their hands shape the products we buy, use, and value. Their sensibilities guide the look and content of the visual communication that surrounds us. We live and work in spaces they create. Their ideas change our ideas about the world and our place in it. Design is the intersection between commerce and culture, between the individual and the environment. At its best, design embodies respect between maker and materials, between maker and eventual user. Designing is more than a job or even a career, although our rapidly changing, increasingly international economy offers plenty of opportunity. Rather, designing is a commitment and, ultimately, a way of life.

189

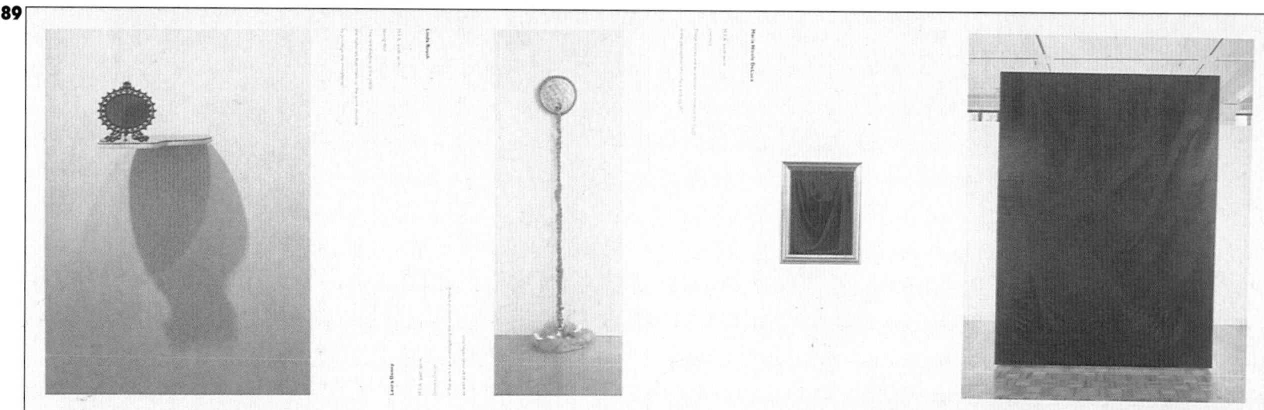

190

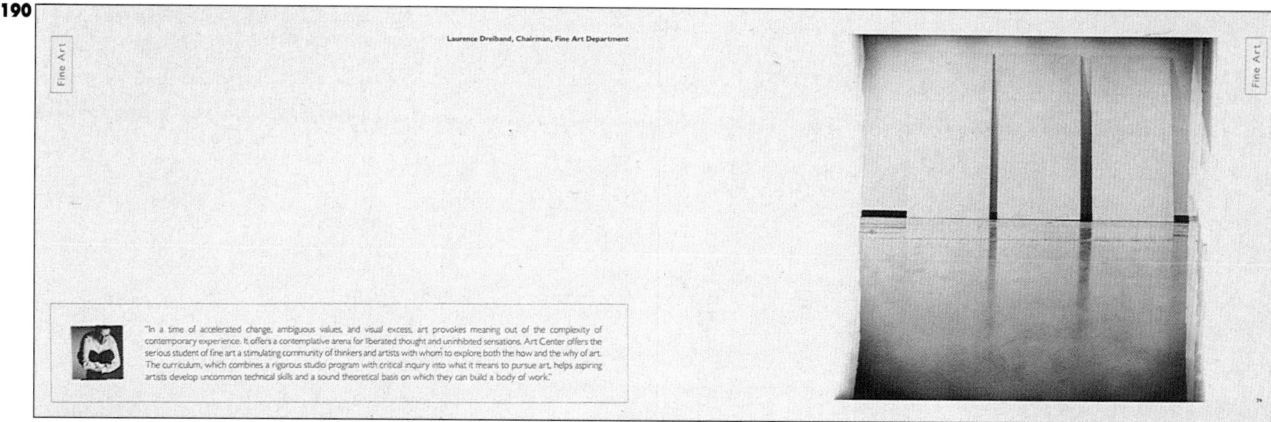

191

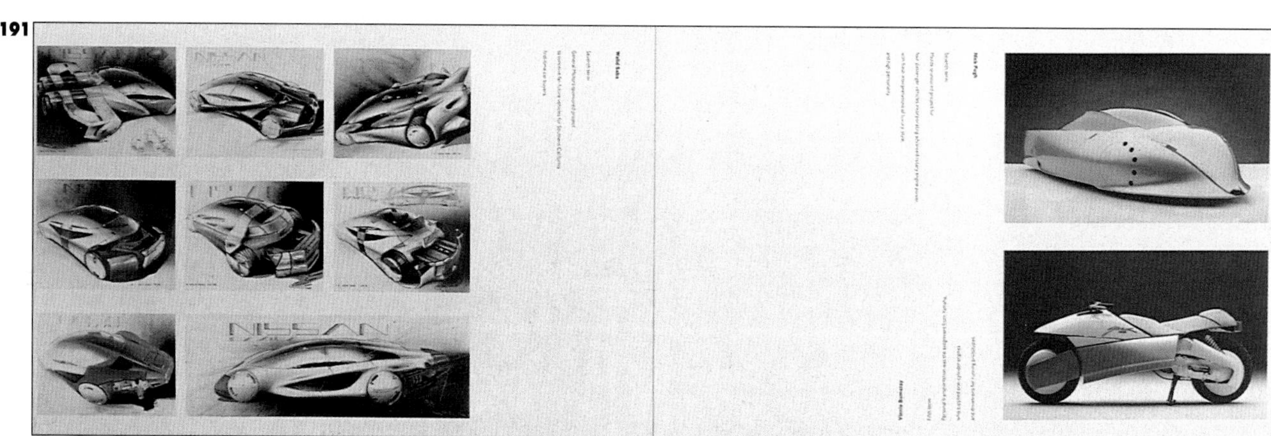

188/189/190/191
DESIGN FIRM: *Art Center Design Office*
DESIGNER: *Rebeca Mèndez and SzeTsung Leong*
HEADLINE TYPEFACE: *Gill Sans*
TEXT TYPEFACE: *Gill Sans*
CLIENT: *Art Center College of Design*

192

193

192
DESIGN FIRM: *The Bang Design Group*
DESIGNER: *Bill Douglas*
HEADLINE TYPEFACE: *Custom Designed Bang*
TEXT TYPEFACE: *Garamond Bold Extended*
CLIENT: *The Bang Design Group*

193
DESIGN FIRM: *Carlson Marketing Group*
DESIGNER: *Mike Thomas*
HEADLINE TYPEFACE: *Handlettering and Copperplate Gothic*
TEXT TYPEFACE: *Baskerville Italic*
CLIENT: *GE Capital*

194
DESIGN FIRM: *Pentagram Design*
DESIGNER: *Woody Pirtle and Susan Hochbaum*
HEADLINE TYPEFACE: *Copperplate Gothic*
TEXT TYPEFACE: *Bodoni*
CLIENT: *Champion International*

195
DESIGN FIRM: *Pentagram Design*
DESIGNER: *Woody Pirtle and Susan Hochbaum*
HEADLINE TYPEFACE: *Corvinus*
TEXT TYPEFACE: *Bodoni*
CLIENT: *Champion International*

196
DESIGN FIRM: *Pentagram Design*
DESIGNER: *Woody Pirtle and Nancy Hoefig*
HEADLINE TYPEFACE: *Copperplate and Invitation Script*
TEXT TYPEFACE: *Copperplate, Bodoni, and Helvetica*
CLIENT: *Champion International*

194

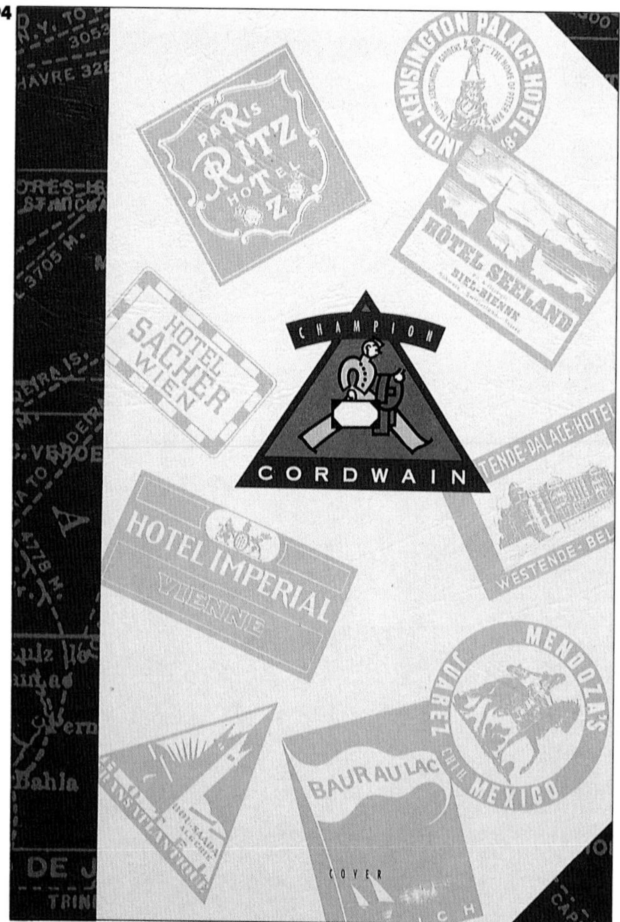

195

196

197

198

199

197/198

DESIGN FIRM: *Pentagram Design*
DESIGNER: *Woody Pirtle and Susan Hochbaum*
HEADLINE TYPEFACE: *Trio*
TEXT TYPEFACE: *Bodoni*
CLIENT: *Champion International*

199

DESIGN FIRM: *Pentagram Design*
DESIGNER: *Woody Pirtle and Susan Hochbaum*
HEADLINE TYPEFACE: *Futura Condensed*
TEXT TYPEFACE: *Bodoni*
CLIENT: *Champion International*

200

201

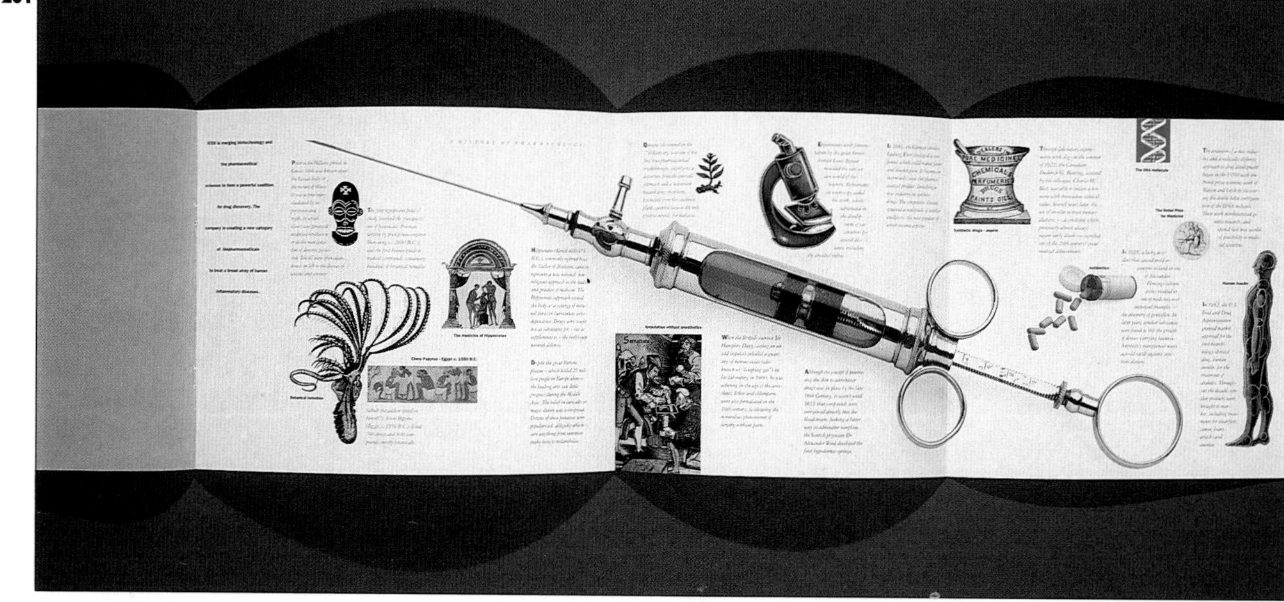

200/201
DESIGN FIRM: *Pentagram Design*
DESIGNER: *Woody Pirtle and Jennifer Long*
HEADLINE TYPEFACE: *Arrow, Helvetica Bold, and Garamond*
TEXT TYPEFACE: *Helvetica Bold and Garamond #3*
CLIENT: *ICOS Corporation/Noonan Russo*

202

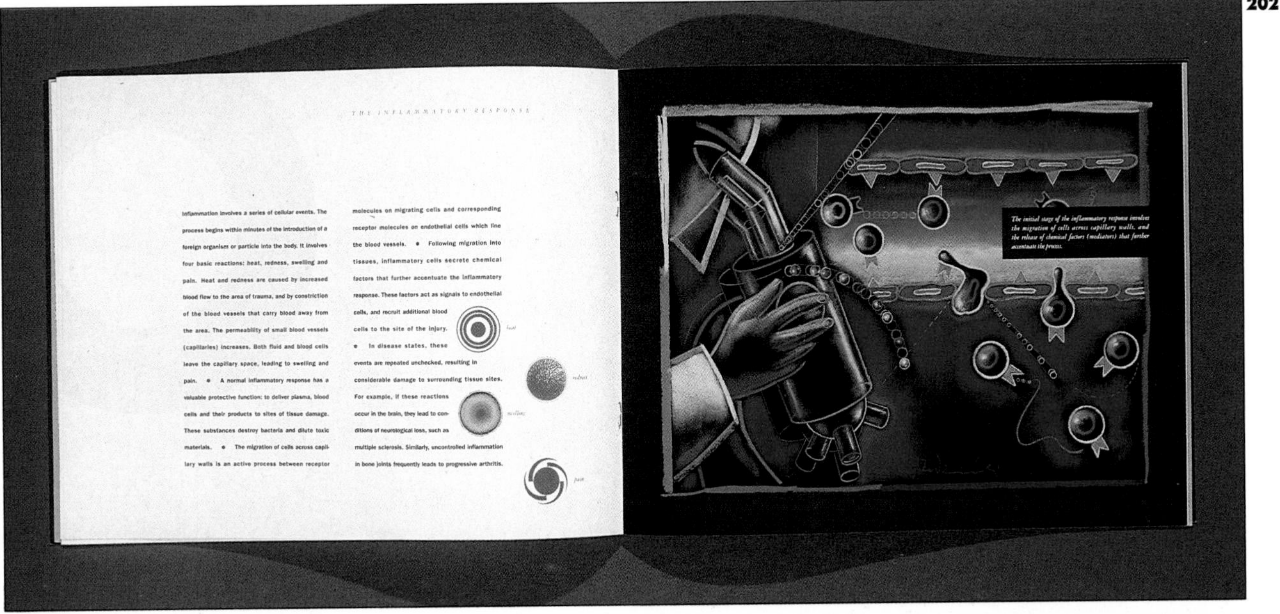

203

202
DESIGN FIRM: *Pentagram Design*
DESIGNER: *Woody Pirtle and Jennifer Long*
HEADLINE TYPEFACE: *Arrow, Helvetica Bold, and Garamond*
TEXT TYPEFACE: *Helvetica Bold and Garamond #3*
CLIENT: *ICOS Corporation/Noonan Russo*

203
DESIGN FIRM: *Ponzo Design*
DESIGNER: *Anthony Ponzo*
HEADLINE TYPEFACE: *Futura*
TEXT TYPEFACE: *Futura*
CLIENT: *Society of Graphic Designers of Canada*

204

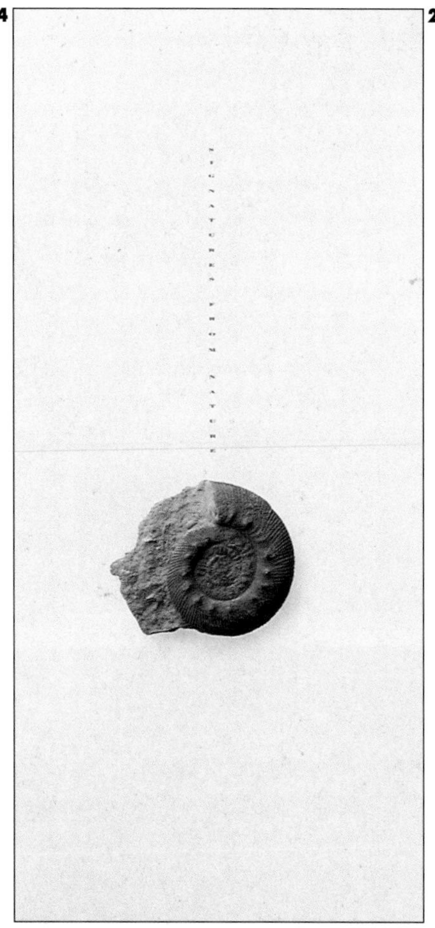

205

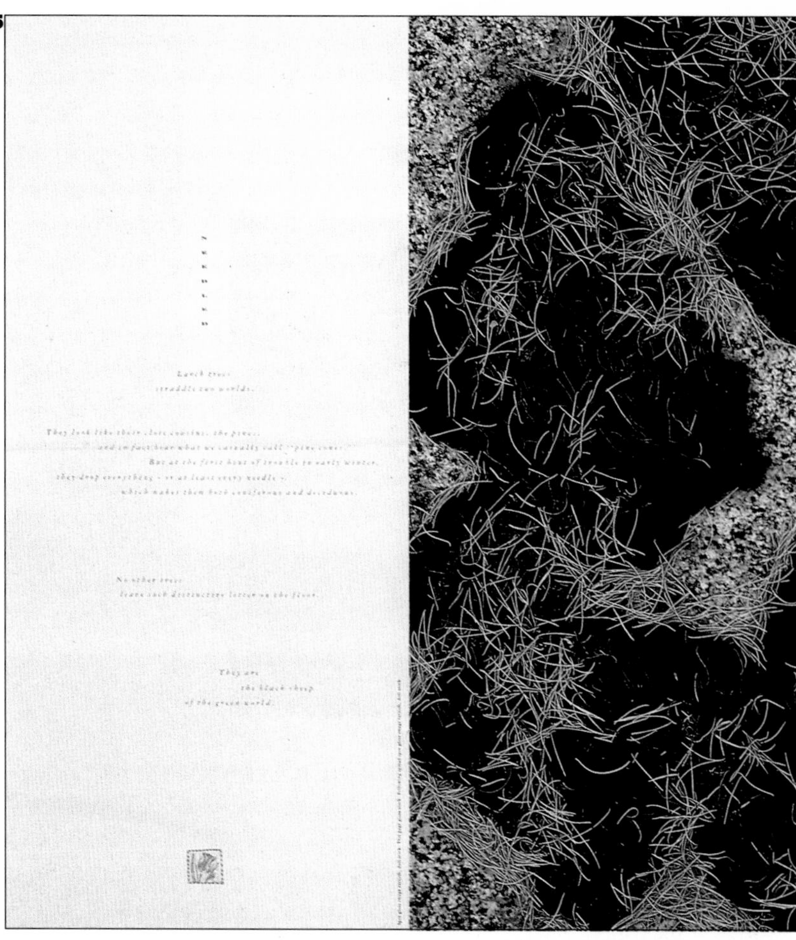

204/205
DESIGN FIRM: *Van Dyke Company*
DESIGNER: *John Van Dyke*
HEADLINE TYPEFACE: *Bodoni Bold*
TEXT TYPEFACE: *Garamond #3*
CLIENT: *Mead Corp.*

206

206
DESIGN FIRM: *Dunn and Rice Design, Inc.*
DESIGNER: *John Dunn and Cynthia Hummel*
TEXT TYPEFACE: *ITC Didi, Clarendon, Sabon, and Helvetica Black*
CLIENT: *Rochester Monotype*

207

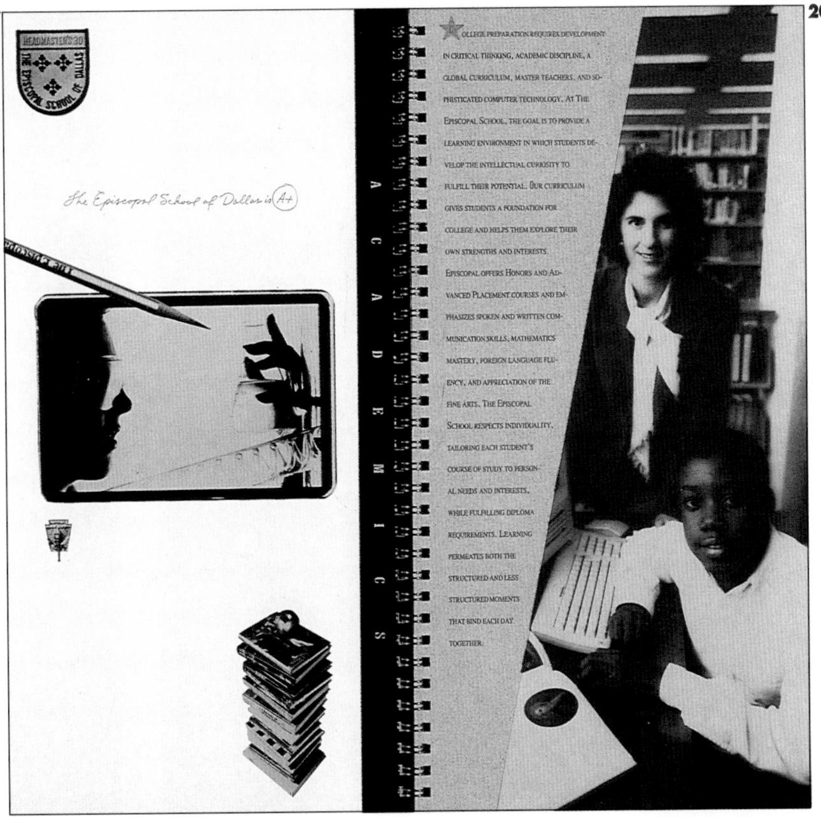

208

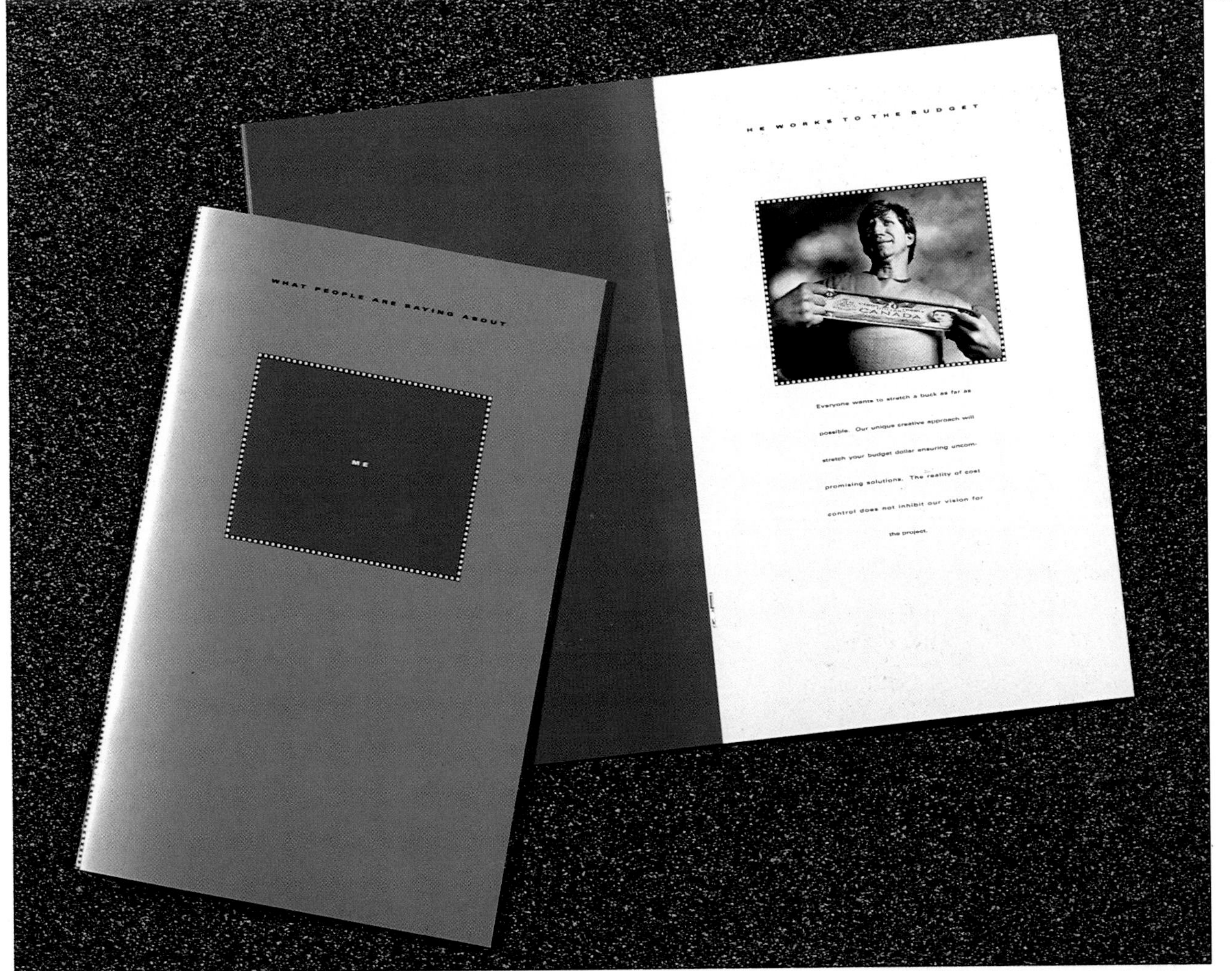

209

207/208
DESIGN FIRM: *RBMM/The Richards Group*
DESIGNER: *Brian Boyd*
TEXT TYPEFACE: *Times and Clarendon Bold Condensed*
CLIENT: *Episcopal School of Dallas*

209
DESIGN FIRM: *Landgraff Design Associates, Ltd.*
DESIGNER: *Michael Landgraff*
CLIENT: *Landgraff Design Associates, Ltd.*

210
DESIGN FIRM: *Cipriani Kremer Design*
DESIGNER: *Toni Bowerman*
HEADLINE TYPEFACE: *Univers 49*
TEXT TYPEFACE: *Copperplate Gothic 31 AB*
CLIENT: *Cole Hann*

211/212
DESIGN FIRM: *Altman & Manley/Eagle Advertising*
HEADLINE TYPEFACE: *Various*
TEXT TYPEFACE: *Various*
CLIENT: *Agfa Corp.*

210

211

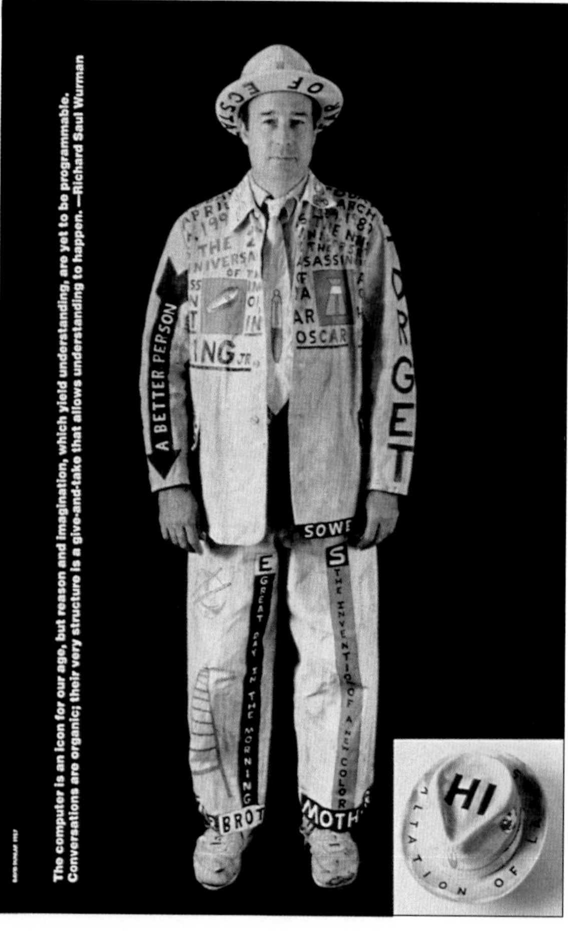

212

THE OBSCENE DISPARITY

A COUPLE SITS ON THE SIDEWALK NEAR FANEUIL HALL IN BOSTON. THEY'RE COLD AND HOMELESS. ALL THEY OWN IS STACKED UP BESIDE THEM. THEIR DOG AND CAT ARE CURLED UP NEXT TO THE SIGN THAT PLEADS FOR WORK— ANY WORK. NEXT DOOR PEOPLE ARE MUNCHING DOWN DESIGNER COOKIES, WHILE BUYING ELECTRIC TOOTHBRUSHES.

213

214

215

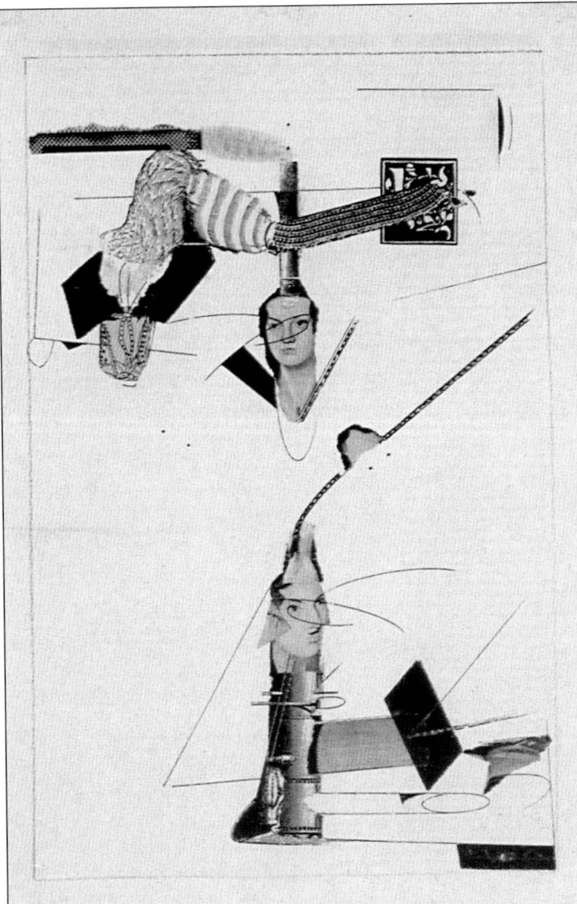

213
DESIGN FIRM: *Altman & Manley/ Eagle Advertising*
HEADLINE TYPEFACE: *Various*
TEXT TYPEFACE: *Various*
CLIENT: *Agfa Corp.*

214
DESIGN FIRM: *Cipriani Kremer*
DESIGNER: *Toni Bowerman*
HEADLINE TYPEFACE: *Univers 49*
TEXT TYPEFACE: *Copperplate Gothic 31 AB*
CLIENT: *Cole Haan*

215
DESIGN FIRM: *Altman & Manley/Eagle Advertising*
HEADLINE TYPEFACE: *Various*
TEXT TYPEFACE: *Various*
CLIENT: *Agfa Corp.*

216

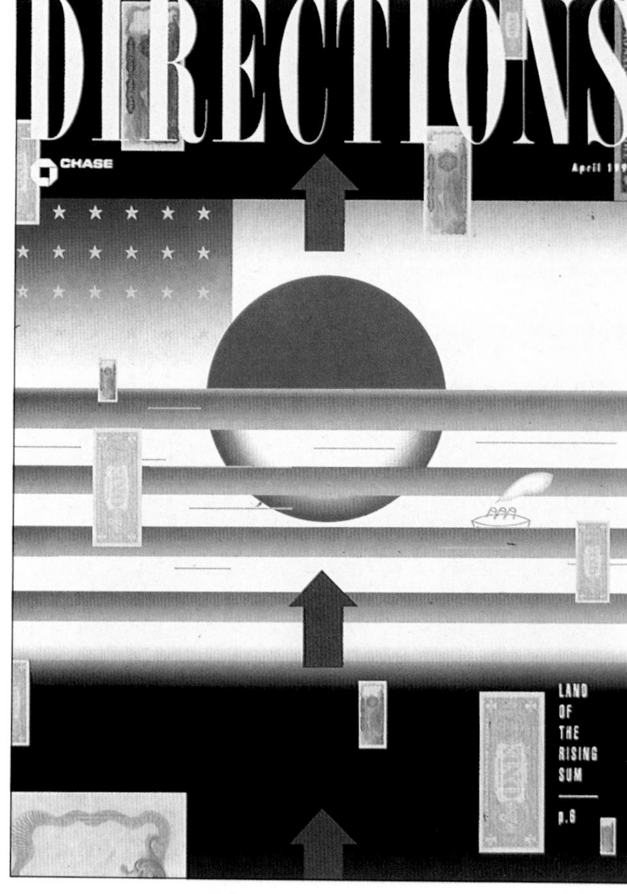

217

LAND OF THE RISING SUM

"Imagine that these are $1,000 bills," says Tim McGinnis as he places five ones on top of each other. "In Japan," he says, patting the sides of the pile to make sure they're perfectly aligned, "these five $1,000 bills won't pay for the land they're sitting on."

The Senior Chase Officer for Japan goes on to say that it's not unusual to see a half-dozen Ferraris in a span of six Tokyo blocks, that the Japanese may pay up to $4 million for one golf club membership, that a medium-sized company in Japan may have $3 billion in cash…

The message: There's money to be found in Japan – and money to be made. The problem: competing against the largest banks in the world on their own turf.

"You don't stand in the way of a Japanese bullet train," says Mr. McGinnis, "or Japanese banks. Instead of going head-to-head with them, you have to work the fringes."

This approach helped Chase Japan quadruple earnings in 1989, to $13 million (135 yen to the dollar) after taxes. It was the best year of the decade – a decade of great economic growth for Japan and of great change for Chase.

Chase first entered Japan at the end of World War II, bringing U.S. dollars to rebuild industries such as steel smelting,and shipbuilding. Japanese banks were prohibited by law from making these "impact" loans, and Chase quickly became one of the top three foreign commercial banks in the country.

Then in 1980 the Japanese government opened the dollar-lending business to Japan's banks. At the same time, Japanese companies – especially in up-and-coming industries like consumer electronics – began exporting more, bringing in more cash and thus borrowing less.

Mr. McGinnis describes the Chase Japan of the 1980s as "a supertanker being battered by storms but with enough momentum to keep moving."

When he took the helm again in 1988 (he was Japan country manager from 1980 to 1983), "Chase Japan had already changed course. If we couldn't lend money to the Japanese companies, we had to get the yen from their pockets by selling them fee-based products."

One thing Japanese companies need is a place to invest their extra cash. Chase is finding a home for their yen through private placements (arranging for investors to buy debt or equity directly instead of through a public offering). Last summer, for instance, Chase placed $100 million of subordinated debt in Thai Oil with 10 Japanese leasing companies. The deal was one of about a dozen private placements in 1989, compared with three the year before.

Tim McGinnis

YEN AT WORK

Japanese companies are also looking to make the most from the investments they've already made. A Japanese electronic parts manufacturer with factories in Brazil may opt to swap LDC debt for equity.

Says Mr. McGinnis, "We knew we had to be in this business, but we were absolutely not successful at it. Part of the solution was to build a bridge between Japan and the Western Hemisphere." In just five months, LDC Corporate Finance in Tokyo and the Japan Business Unit in Brazil worked together to bring in three swaps for seven-figure fees. To strengthen the "bridge" further, the heads of both units have also swapped jobs.

And in a country that imports virtually 100 percent of its petroleum, Chase Japan is drumming up business with commodity swaps, which help corporations hedge against fluctuating prices. In six months Chase Japan completed swaps for 3.1 million barrels.

Chase not only competes with the likes of The Mitsubishi Bank and The Bank of Tokyo, it also provides services to them.

"We're the bank for the banks," says Mr. McGinnis. "Any bank in Japan that has dollars to be moved can move them through Chase Tokyo Dollar Clearing." In fact, the dollar-clearing business has helped Chase Japan become one of the dominant correspondent banks in the country.

Overall, the turnaround in Japan has not been without cost. Chase Japan cut expenses by $6 million in 1989, reduced the number of employees by more than 100 to some 550, and restructured several operations. Treasury, for example, renovated accounting, systems and training to make way for risk management products such as options. Chase Japan's securities operation underwent a similar reconstruction.

"We went through trauma in the first six months of last year," says Mr. McGinnis, "and our earnings reflected that. But we started coming back last summer, and morale today is dramatically better."

Despite the cutbacks, Chase Japan is investing in areas like corporate finance, treasury and foreign exchange, which, says Mr. McGinnis, "is hiring staff to build up sales to customers outside of Japan."

CHASE ORIENT EXPRESS

Such employees are also well versed in doing business Japanese-style. It's a culture where you never arrive late, and where you always dress formally and place your business card on the table in front of you.

Where if you can't stand in the way of the bullet trains that are the Japanese banks, you can do quite nicely traveling alongside them.●

→ Chase Japan's talented Tokyo team: (clockwise from top) Jayme Garcia dos Santos, Capital/Investor Markets & Client Relations; Yoshi Hashimoto, Foreign Exchange; Chris Carlin, Chase InfoServ International; and Leo Janssen, Treasury.

6 CHASE DIRECTIONS

216/217
DESIGN FIRM: *Pentagram Design*
DESIGNER: *Harold Burch*
HEADLINE TYPEFACE: *Univers*
TEXT TYPEFACE: *Bembo*
CLIENT: *Chase Manhattan Bank*

223

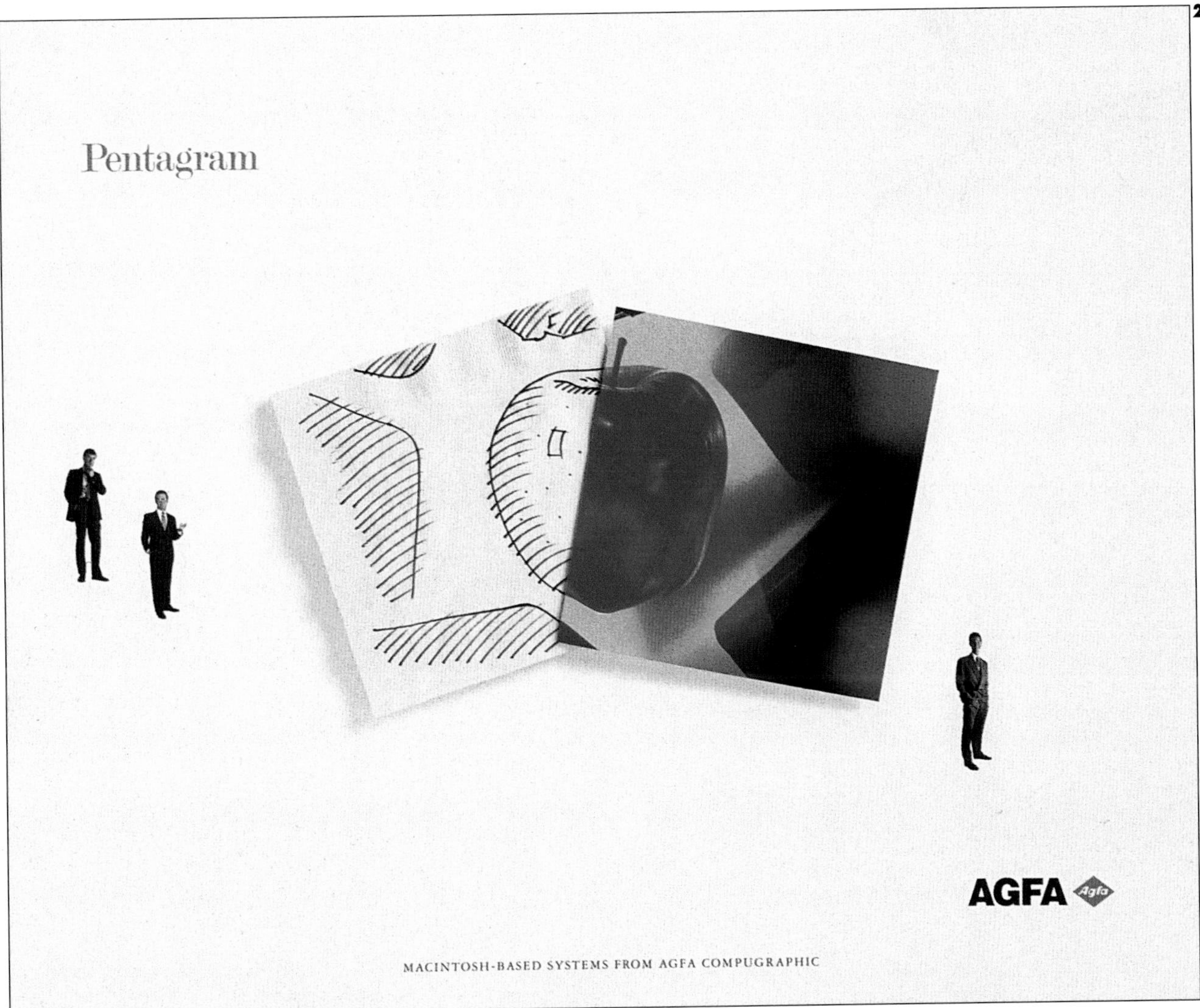

224

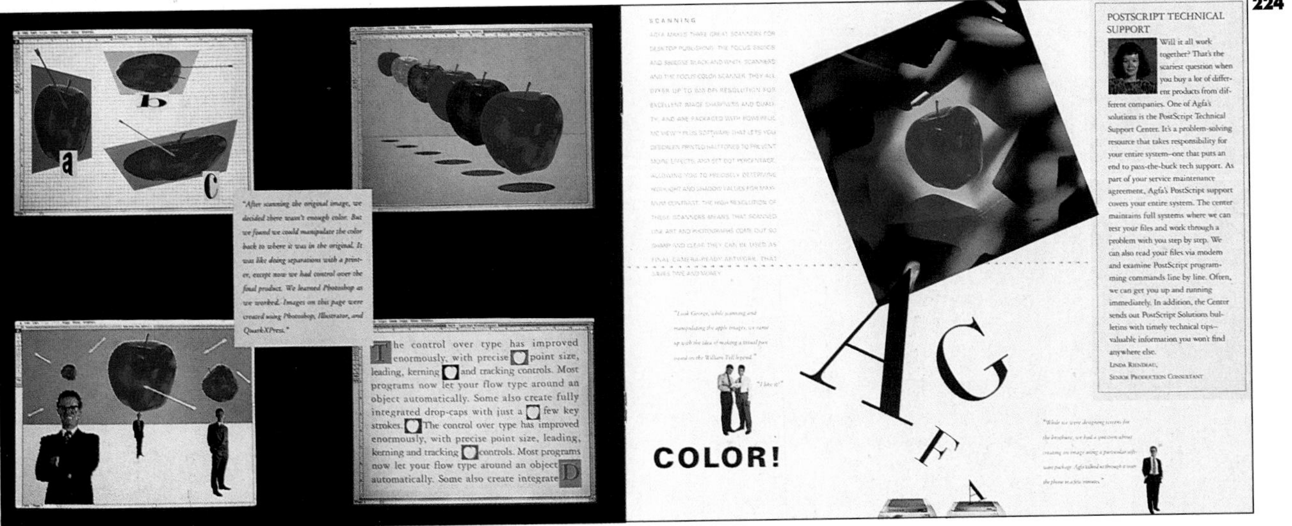

223/224
DESIGN FIRM: *Pentagram Design*
DESIGNER: *Harold Burch and Peter Harrison*
HEADLINE TYPEFACE: *Univers and Bodoni*
TEXT TYPEFACE: *Garamond #3 and Univers*
CLIENT: *Agfa/Compugraphic*

225

JASPER RIDGE
A STANFORD SANCTUARY

226

225/226

DESIGN FIRM: *Tom Lewis, Inc.*
DESIGNER: *Tom Lewis*
HEADLINE TYPEFACE: *Bauer Bodoni*
TEXT TYPEFACE: *Bodoni*
CLIENT: *Stanford Alumni Association*

227

228

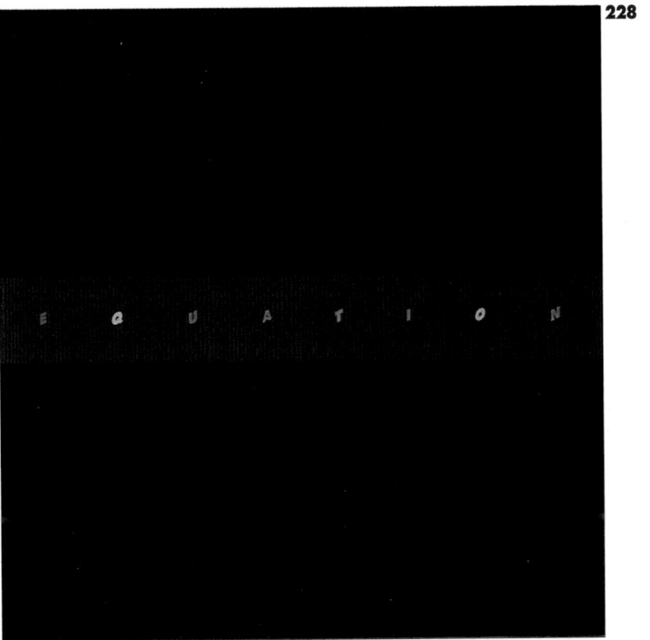

229

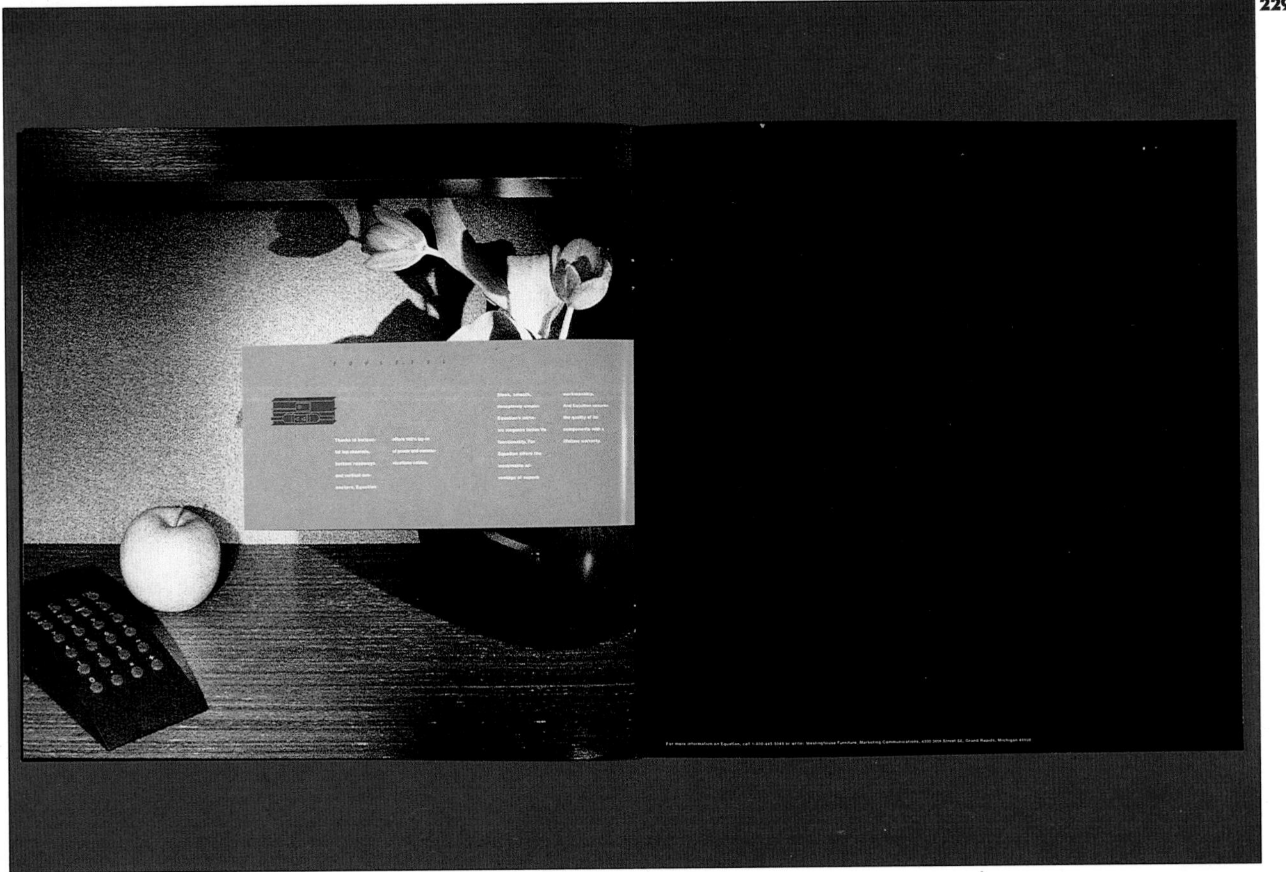

227
DESIGN FIRM: *Pentagram Design*
DESIGNER: *Michael Gericke and Peter Harrison*
HEADLINE TYPEFACE: *Delphine and Futura Extra Bold*
TEXT TYPEFACE: *Bembo*
CLIENT: *Metromedia Company*

228/229
DESIGN FIRM: *Pentagram Design*
DESIGNER: *Woody Pirtle, Colin Forbes, and Nancy Hoefig*
HEADLINE TYPEFACE: *Helvetica*
TEXT TYPEFACE: *Garamond #3*
CLIENT: *Westinghouse Furniture Systems*

230

DESIGN FIRM: *Sibley/Peteet Design*

DESIGNER: *Rex Peteet*

HEADLINE TYPEFACE: *Typo Upright*

TEXT TYPEFACE: *Typo and Bernhard Modern*

CLIENT: *James River Corp.*

231

DESIGN FIRM: *Cross Associates*

DESIGNER: *James Cross, Joseph Jacquez, and Paul Belza*

HEADLINE TYPEFACE: *Univers*

TEXT TYPEFACE: *Univers and Extended Times*

CLIENT: *Simpson Paper Company*

230

231

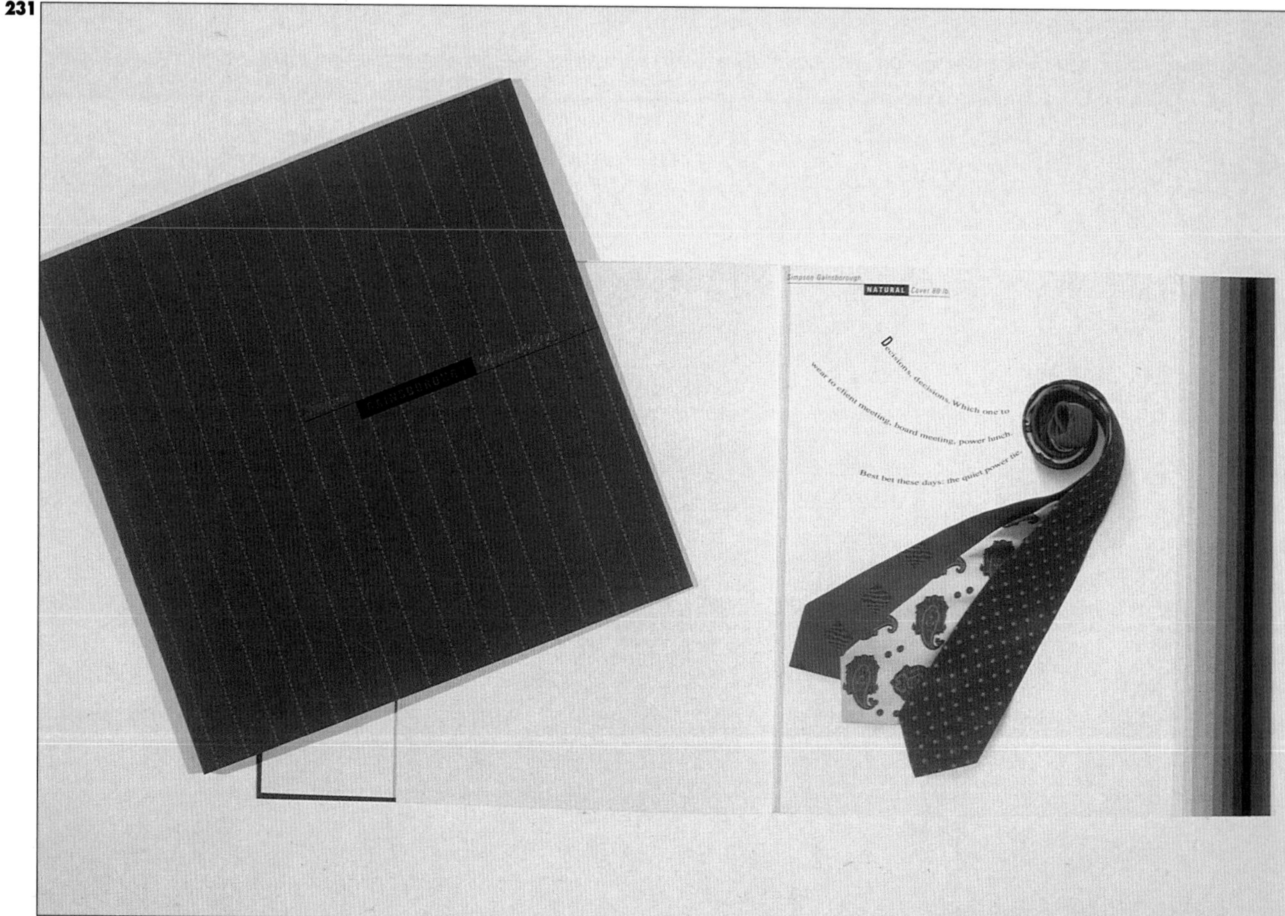

232

232
DESIGN FIRM: *Corning Corporate Design*
DESIGNER: *Frederick Murrel, William Lucas, and Douglas Harp*
HEADLINE TYPEFACE: *Sabon Roman*
TEXT TYPEFACE: *Univers 47 and 67*
CLIENT: *Corning, Inc.*

233

233
DESIGN FIRM: *Sibley/Peteet Design*
DESIGNER: *Don Sibley*
HEADLINE TYPEFACE: *Corvinus Skyline*
TEXT TYPEFACE: *Futura Bold*
CLIENT: *Weyerhaeuser Paper*

234

235

234/235
DESIGN FIRM: *Pentagram Design*
DESIGNER: *Woody Pirtle*
HEADLINE TYPEFACE: *Goudy and Futura Condensed*
TEXT TYPEFACE: *Bodoni*
CLIENT: *Champion International*

236

237

236
DESIGN FIRM: *Altman & Manley*
DESIGNER: *Steven Guarnaccia and Brent Crokton*
LETTERER: *Steven Guarnaccia*
TEXT TYPEFACE: *Copperplate*
CLIENT: *Physicians*

237
DESIGN FIRM: *Left Coast Press*
DESIGNER: *Dorothy Yule*
HEADLINE TYPEFACE: *Various Wood Type, Script Types, and Copperplate*
TEXT TYPEFACE: *Century Schoolbook*
CLIENT: *Left Coast Press*

238

239

EVOLUTION OF A MUSEUM

July 1984	The MCA expresses interest in National Guard Armory site.
November 1985	Initial feasibility planning study confirms need for new MCA facility.
March 1986	Mrs. Beatrice C. Mayer hosts party where nine trustees commit $5 million.
April 1986	Governor Thompson appoints task force to determine future of Armory site.
January 1987	Governor's Task Force recommends development of Armory site as park with museum and sculpture garden.
April 1987	The MCA submits proposal to Governor.
December 1987	R. R. Donnelley and Sons donates Calumet Avenue building to the MCA.
May 1988	Governor grants Armory site to MCA in exchange for Donnelley building.
May 1989	Fund-raising study confirms strong support for new museum and recommends action plan.
June 1989	Jerome H. Stone accepts chairmanship of Chicago Contemporary Campaign.
August 1989	John D. and Catherine T. MacArthur Foundation awards $2 million grant.
November 1989	Trustee Phase of Chicago Contemporary Campaign is launched at dinner party hosted by Mrs. Edwin A. Bergman.
December 1989	Trustees participate in lengthy case-development discussions.
April 1990	Initial leadership gifts are pledged by trustees.
May 1990	The MCA signs lease on Armory with Illinois Department of Conservation; Donnelley building given to Illinois National Guard.
January 1991	Chicago Contemporary Campaign Trustee Phase surpasses goal.
May 1991	Major Gifts Phase of Chicago Contemporary Campaign is launched; Architect of new building is named.

[10]

A
COMPREHENSIVE
PLAN

REFERRING TO THE MCA's planned new building, a noted director of another prominent contemporary art museum said, "It is the most important piece of art you'll ever acquire. And the opportunity you have to make it a masterpiece is unprecedented." To this end, the museum staff completed a comprehensive building program document which describes the full scope of requirements ranging from gallery space needs to functional specifications of security system design. Preliminary evaluation of the overall plan to construct a 125,000-square-foot museum with a landscaped sculpture park on the two-acre Armory site places the total needed to complete the facility at $30 million.

The State of Illinois has demonstrated its support for the new museum project by entering into a 99-year lease (with extensions) on the Armory site at an annual rent of one dollar. Also, the state has given preliminary approval for the issuance of approximately $30 million of tax-exempt revenue bonds on behalf of the museum. The bonds will be issued by the Illinois Educational Facilities Authority, which assists in the financing of capital acquisition and construction projects undertaken by not-for-profit educational or cultural institutions located in Illinois. Other institutions on whose behalf the Authority has recently issued bonds include the John G. Shedd Aquarium, the Art Institute of Chicago, DePaul University, the Chicago Historical Society and Northwestern University.

« If
a CITY does
not MAINTAIN its
VITALITY,
corporations will leave.
The MUSEUM
is a prime factor
in Chicago's
VITALITY. »

Proceeds of the bond issue will be loaned to the museum to finance the costs of constructing, furnishing and equipping the new museum. Bonds will bear interest at the tax-exempt rate, which is favorable to the museum, and will be repayable by the MCA over a period of years.

Of equal importance to the challenge of constructing a major cultural edifice are the long-term considerations of staffing, programming, and daily operations once the building is complete. Through years of careful planning and professional consultation with financial advisors and programming analysts, many critical studies have been conducted by the MCA's board of trustees and administrative leaders to determine the ongoing fiscal requirements of the new museum project. These priorities have been fully considered throughout the process of structuring and establishing a goal for the fund-raising campaign to endow and operate the new museum.

A five-year operating budget has been incorporated into the planning for the campaign goal to ensure the MCA's financial stability through its inaugural years of growth in membership and revenue-generating programs. Staffing needs have been thoroughly analyzed with due emphasis on public relations and marketing staff to concentrate on building the museum's local and international patron base and promoting continual participation in the museum's programs by a great variety of Chicago area citizens. Curatorial staff, which is already exemplary, will be expanded to meet the great diversity of exhibition and programming challenges which will cement the MCA's reputation as one of the most progressive and dynamic contemporary art museums in the world.

[11]

238/239
DESIGN FIRM: *Pentagram Design*
DESIGNER: *Susan Hochbaum and Woody Pirtle*
HEADLINE TYPEFACE: *Bodoni*
TEXT TYPEFACE: *Bodoni*
CLIENT: *Museum of Contemporary Art*

240

241

240
DESIGN FIRM: *Lisa Levin Design*
DESIGNER: *Lisa Levin*
HEADLINE TYPEFACE: *Matrix Wide*
TEXT TYPEFACE: *Adobe Garamond*
CLIENT: *George Rice & Sons*

241
DESIGN FIRM: *Pentagram Design*
DESIGNER: *Neil Shakery*
TEXT TYPEFACE: *Bodoni and Franklin Gothic Bold Condensed*
CLIENT: *Mirage Hotel*

232

242
DESIGN FIRM: *Morla Design*
DESIGNER: *Jennifer Morla*
HEADLINE TYPEFACE: *Handlettering*
TEXT TYPEFACE: *Futura Ultra Bold*
CLIENT: *Levi Strauss & Co.*

243

DESIGN FIRM: *The Duffy Design Group*
DESIGNER: *Sharon Werner*
LETTERER: *Lynn Shulte and Sharon Werner*
HEADLINE TYPEFACE: *Handlettering*
TEXT TYPEFACE: *Eurostyle Bold Extended and Brush*
CLIENT: *Fox River Paper Company*

244/245
DESIGN FIRM: *Art Center Design Office*
DESIGNER: *Rebeca Mèndez and Ellie Eisner*
HEADLINE TYPEFACE: *Gill Sans Bold*
TEXT TYPEFACE: *Gill Sans*
CLIENT: *Art Center College of Design*

244

245

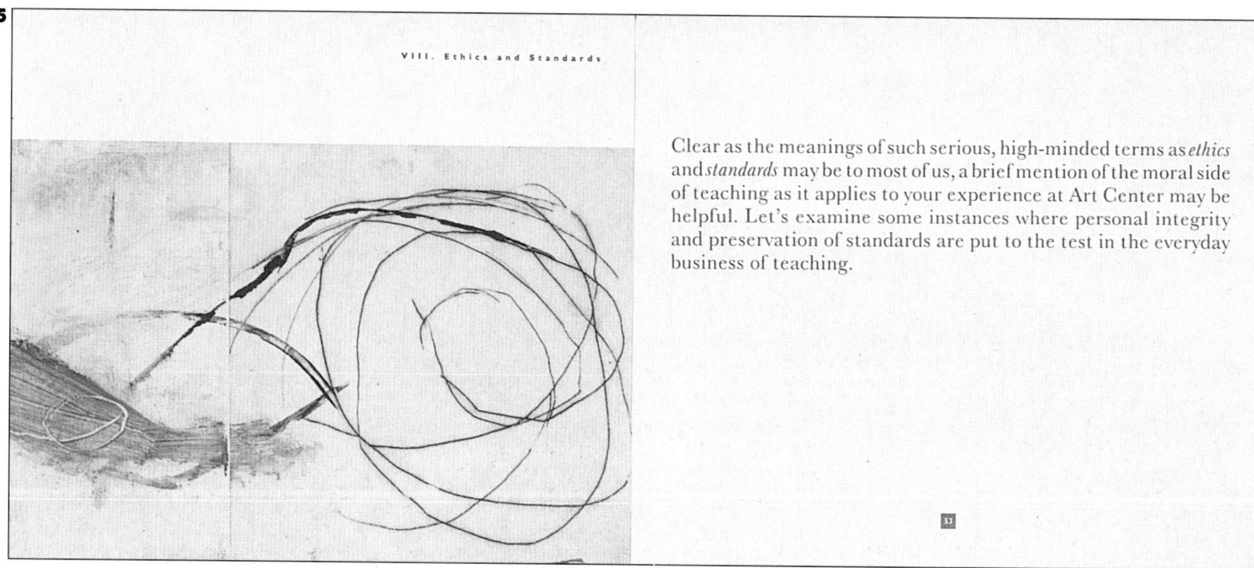

254

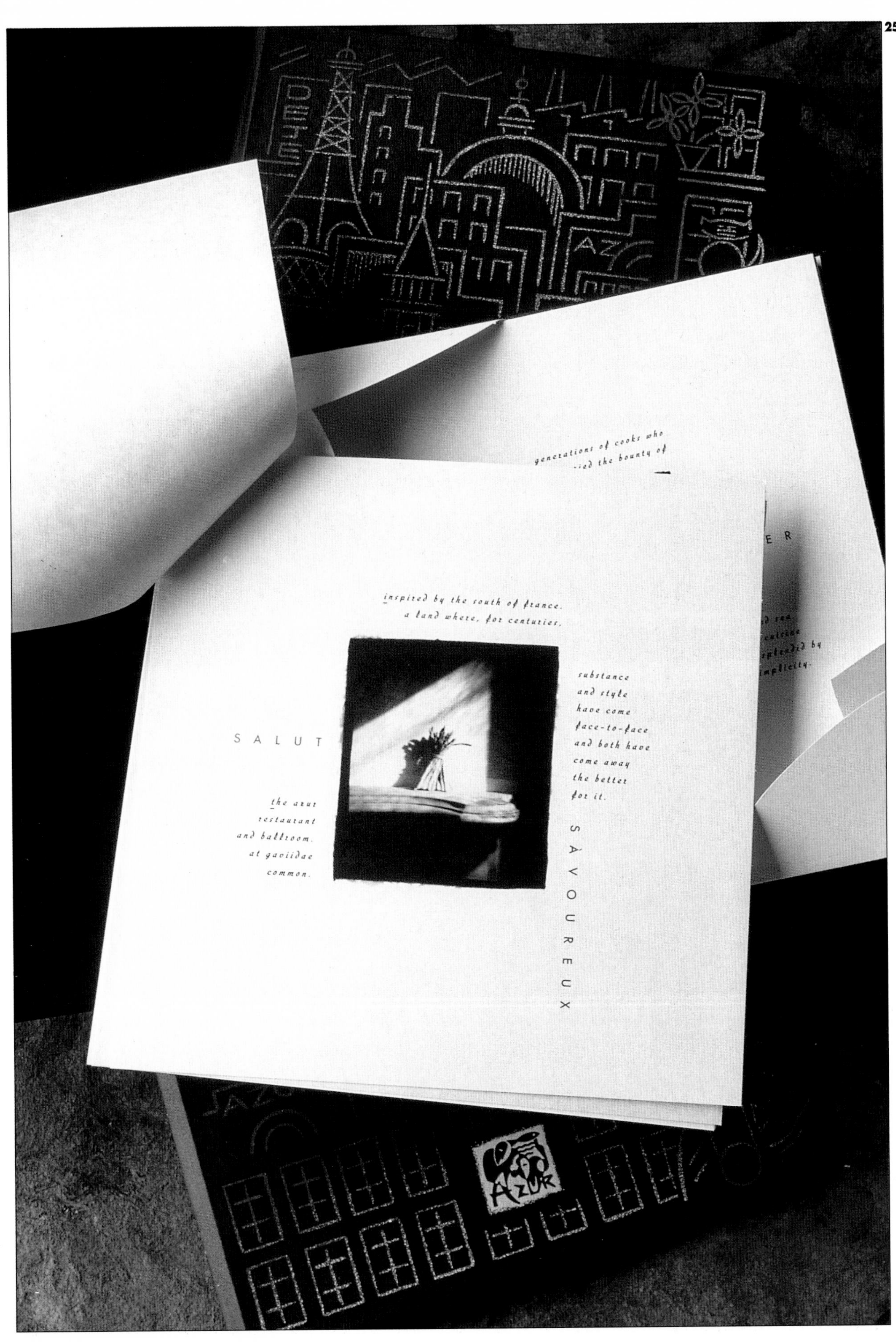

254
DESIGN FIRM: *The Duffy Design Group*
DESIGNER: *Haley Johnson*
HEADLINE TYPEFACE: *Discus*
TEXT TYPEFACE: *Spartan Medium*
CLIENT: *D'Amico & Partners*

255/256
DESIGN FIRM: *Pentagram Design*
DESIGNER: *Michael Gericke and Woody Pirtle*
HEADLINE TYPEFACE: *Bernhard*
TEXT TYPEFACE: *Helvetica Condensed*
CLIENT: *Champion International*

255

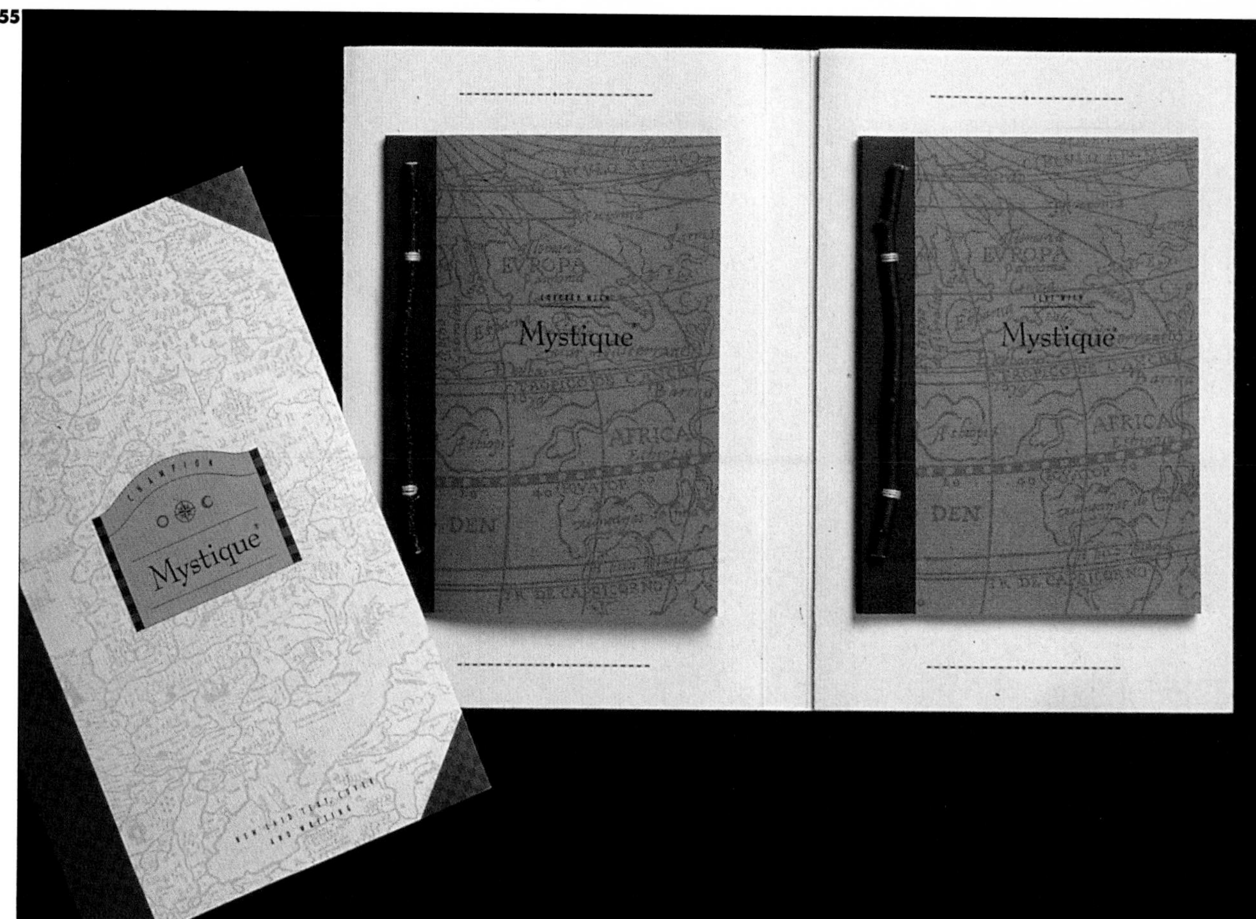

256

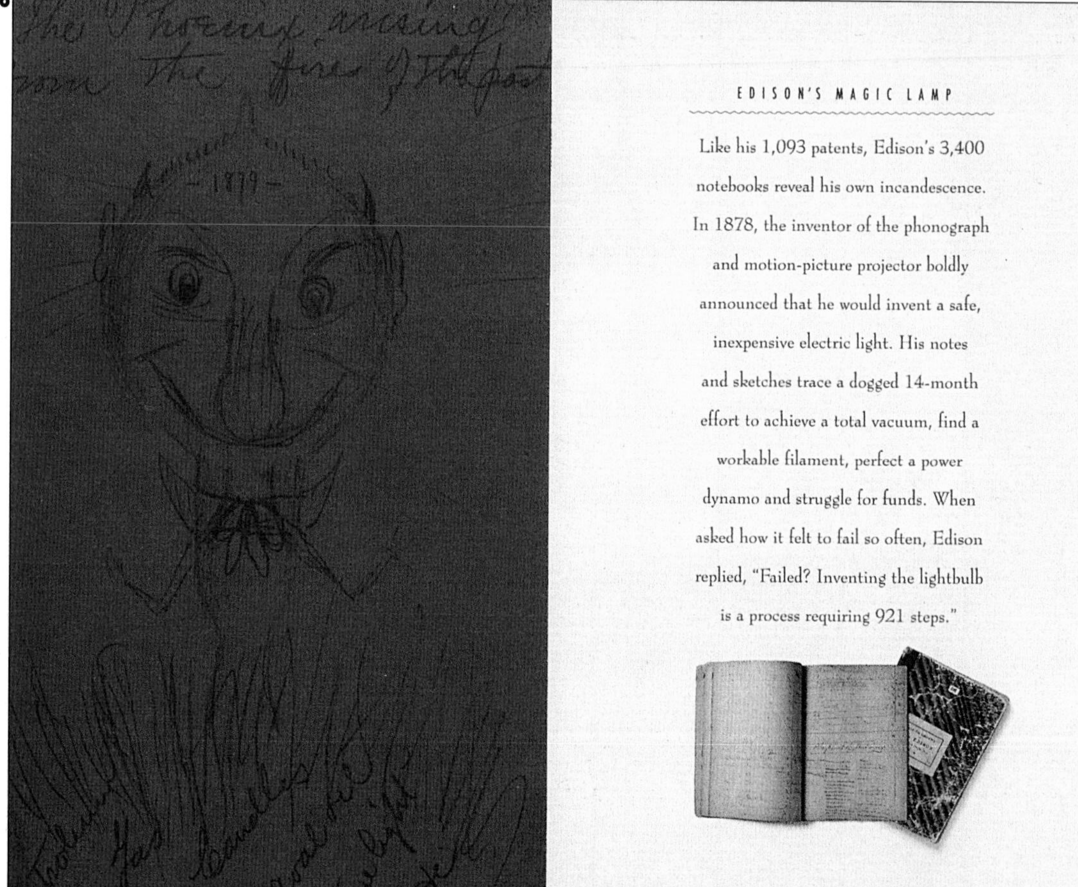

257

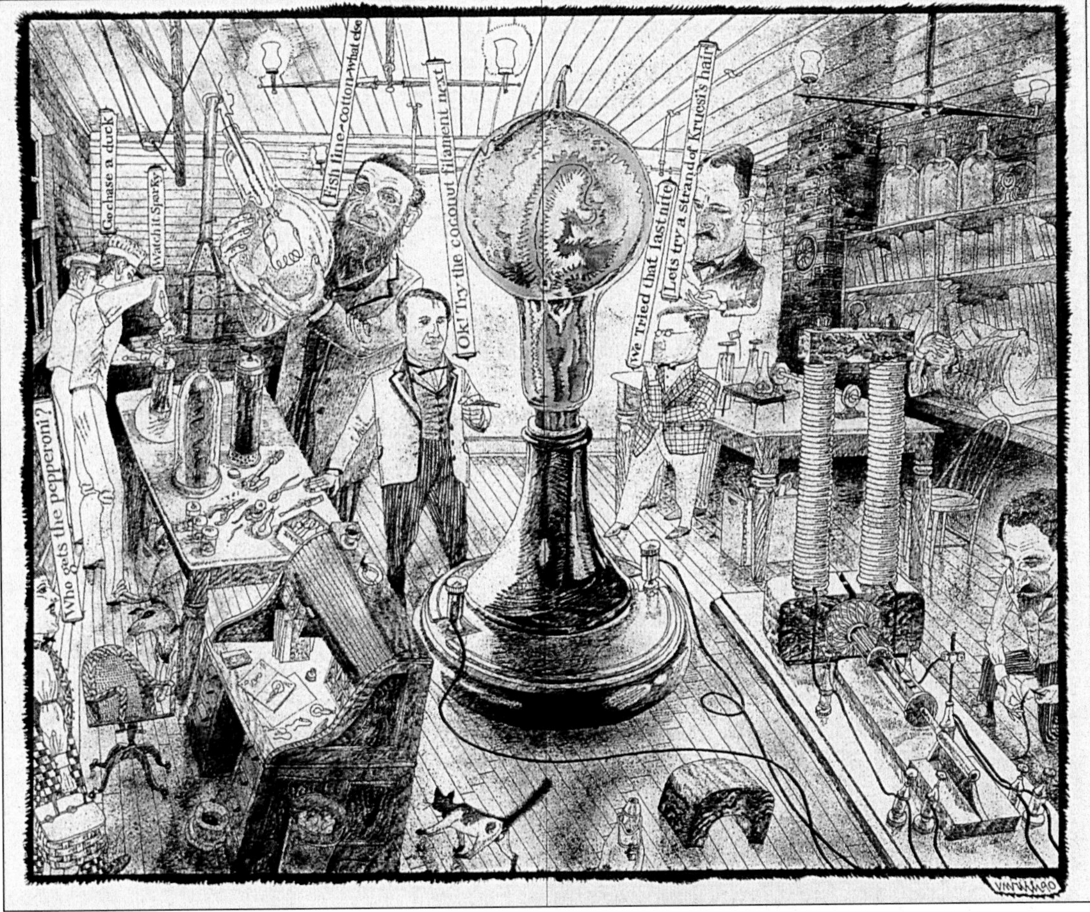

258

JAPANESE IREZUMI

In Japan, tattoo masters do not advertise. They are listed in no phone books. Their clients will not reveal their addresses. This secretive Irezumi clan, which means "insertion of ink," believe that tattoos bestow upon the body a powerful Mystique. During the Edo Period of the 18th Century, when the rising class of merchants were forbidden to adorn themselves with the fine silks and precious ornaments that noblemen wore, Irezumi rose to the level of a fine art. Even Utamaro, the great Ukiyo-e artist, designed tattoos. Sinuous in line, often richly colored, the tattoos depicted samurai, dragons, landscapes, birds and flowers. A century later, it was the ricksha coolies and fishmongers – men

who stripped down to loincloths to work – who adopted full-body tattoos as "imitation clothes." Today, an Irezumi's initiation still begins with light staccato taps, as the the master pricks a tattoo outline in black Nara ink. Under the skin, the ink turns blue. Red makes a tattoo shine, but contains deadly cadmium. It can take up to ten years to complete a full-body tattoo. Only one out of one-hundred will endure the pain – or the price. From this ordeal emerges a work of exquisite beauty, and a lifelong bond between tattoo artist and subject. Indeed, if there is no rapport, nothing can entice the master to perform his most intimate art.

257/258
DESIGN FIRM: *Pentagram Design*
DESIGNER: *Michael Gericke and Woody Pirtle*
HEADLINE TYPEFACE: *Bernhard*
TEXT TYPEFACE: *Helvetica Condensed*
CLIENT: *Champion International*

259
DESIGN FIRM: *Designframe, Inc.*
DESIGNER: *James Sebastian and Junko Mayumi*
HEADLINE TYPEFACE: *Sabon*
TEXT TYPEFACE: *Sabon*
CLIENT: *Martex/West Point Pepperell*

259

260
DESIGN FIRM: *Designframe, Inc.*
DESIGNER: *James Sebastian and Junko Mayumi*
HEADLINE TYPEFACE: *Block Gothic*
TEXT TYPEFACE: *Block Gothic*
CLIENT: *Martex/West Point Pepperell*

261

262

263

261/262/263
DESIGN FIRM: *Muller & Co.*
DESIGNER: *John Muller*
HEADLINE TYPEFACE: *Univers 39*
TEXT TYPEFACE: *Various*
CLIENT: *Strathmore Paper Co.*

264

264
DESIGN FIRM: *Studio Guarnaccia*
DESIGNER: *Steven Guarmaccia*
LETTERER: *Steven Guarnaccia*
HEADLINE TYPEFACE: *Handlettering*
CLIENT: *American Illustration*

_ _ OGRAPHIC DESIGN

is interested in your views on this series of books. Kindly fill out the form at the right (or a copy of it) and fax it to: Editor/TYPOGRAPHIC DESIGN at (201) 896-3974

ATTENTION EDITOR/TYPOGRAPHIC DESIGN

What I like best: ______________________________

____

____

____

What I like least: ______________________________

____

____

____

What can be improved: ______________________________

____

____

____

My favorite aspect: ______________________________

____

____

____

I own:

- ❑ *TYPOGRAPHIC DESIGN Volume 1 Book 1*
- ❑ *TYPOGRAPHIC DESIGN/PROMOTION Volume 1 Book 2*

I've been borrowing my colleague's book, and would like to order a copy of:

- ❑ *TYPOGRAPHIC DESIGN Volume 1 Book 1*
- ❑ *TYPOGRAPHIC DESIGN/PROMOTION Volume 1 Book 2*

❑ ***Yes, I'd like to receive future mailings regarding TYPOGRAPHIC DESIGN. I've included my address below.***

Name: ______________________________

Firm: ______________________________

Address: ______________________________

Phone: ______________ *Fax:* ______________

It is OK to publish comments: ______________________________
SIGNATURE DATE

It is Not OK to publish comments: ______________________________
SIGNATURE DATE

We look forward to reading your comments so please take a few moments to fill out the form at left and fax it to us. No cover sheet is necessary.

INDEX

DESIGN FIRMS

DESIGNERS